EAST EUROPEAN MONOGRAPHS, NO. CCXVII

For Don and our sons John, Thomas, Paul, and Mark

PARTITIONED POLAND

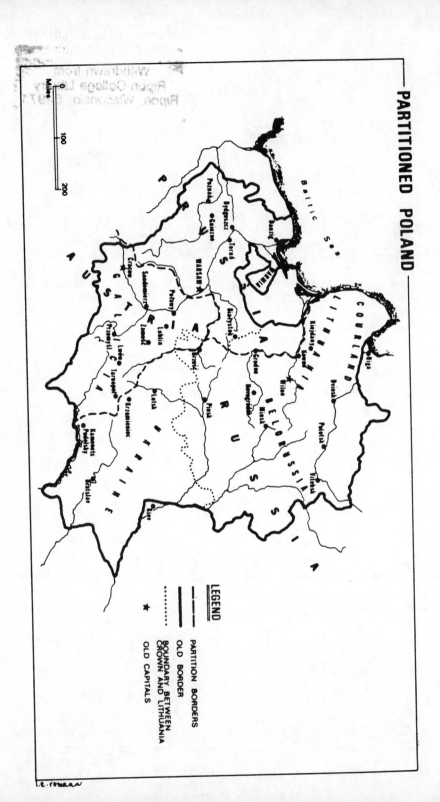

LEGEND

PARTITION BORDERS

OLD BORDER

BOUNDARY BETWEEN
CROWN AND LITHUANIA

★ OLD CAPITALS

CONTENTS

INTRODUCTION

The question of Poland's place in Europe has been of major concern for nearly two hundred years; defined in terms of Poland's relations with Russia, however, it has been of continuing significance since the tenth century.

Despite a common heritage of Slavic ethnic origins and Christian religion and culture, Russia and Poland underwent a diverse development which in turn contributed to important religious, cultural and political differences. Looking to Rome, Poland joined Latin Christendom, becoming part of the Western European cultural tradition and evolving political forms similar to those which developed in the west. In contrast, Kievan Russia, initially looking toward Byzantium, was subjected in the thirteenth century to Mongol rulers who destroyed the old state and disrupted the development of much of its indigenous and Byzantine culture. In its place two new and powerful states arose, Lithuania and Muscovite Russia, each laying claim to the Kievan lands. By the end of the fourteenth century, already in control of most of the disputed territory, Lithuania chose to enter into a dynastic union with Poland and thereby was drawn into the Roman Catholic and Western European cultural orbit of which the Polish Kingdom was a part. This dynastic union was further reinforced in the sixteenth century by the Union of Lublin which created the Polish-Lithuanian Commonwealth.

The other claimant to the Kievan lands, Muscovite Russia, once free of Mongol rule, developed its own religious, cultural, and absolutist political traditions in relative isolation from western contacts.

Throughout the sixteenth and seventeenth centuries, battles raged almost constantly between the two powerful states of Poland-Lithuania and Muscovite Russia for possession of the Kievan lands. At one point in the early seventeenth century it seemed as if Poland-Lithuania had

gained the upper hand and the son of Poland's king even acquired
the Russian throne in 1612 during a long and catastrophic interregnum
which occurred after the death of Ivan the Terrible. Nevertheless,
appearances were deceptive, and Poland's inability to maintain its hold
over the Ukraine left it vulnerable to its rival to the east. By the end
of the seventeenth century it was becoming ever more clear that as
the Polish-Lithuanian state declined in vigor, the Russian state was
experiencing a new dynamism under the leadership of Peter the Great.

Attempting to profit from the new balance of power in Eastern
Europe during the eighteenth century, Russia was torn between two
alternate policies with regard to the Polish-Lithuanian state. On the
one hand, Russia's leaders favored the idea of indirectly dominating
the Polish-Lithuanian lands by increasing their influence in the court
and thereby controlling Polish affairs; on the other hand, they also
saw the advantage of outright, if piecemeal annexations of its eastern
territories. Prodded further by similar Prussian and Austrian interests
at the expense of the declining Polish-Lithuanian state, Russian
annexationist policy recorded a major victory in 1772 when the three
powers partitioned a significant amount of the country's borderlands.
Russia's share was the largest: all of the Commonwealth's White
Russian lands and the territory to the Dvina and Dnieper rivers with
some 1,800,000 inhabitants as well as Livonia went to St. Petersburg
in what became known as the First Partition of Poland.

This policy, however, was followed by a return to the policy of
indirect control which then attempted to deal with spirited Polish
reform efforts emanating from the truncated state during the next
twenty years.

Eventually convinced of the futility of this policy and angered by
Polish resistance to foreign intervention, Catherine II of Russia (in
conjunction with the other two partitioning powers) agreed to divide
the rest of the Commonwealth. In the Second Partition of 1793 Russia
obtained most of Lithuania and the Western Ukraine with a population of over three million. A third partition in 1795 saw Russia receive
the rest of Lithuania and the Ukraine, plus the Duchy of Courland,
an area inhabited by another 1,200,000 persons.

Under Catherine, as well as under the rulers of Prussia and Austria,
Poland was treated as a terrain for exploitation, a source of raw
materials, manpower, and taxes. Fortunately for the Poles, Catherine's
son Paul dealt with the Poles in a more conciliatory manner, as did
his son Alexander I.

The youthful Alexander, particularly susceptible to liberal ideas of
constitutional government and personal freedoms, and sympathetic to

Polish dreams of national regeneration, made common cause with the Polish prince Adam Czartoryski, nephew of the last king of Poland. Alexander appointed him a member of his "Secret Committee" of favored personal advisors and minister of foreign affairs, and together they planned a restoration of the Kingdom of Poland by the emperor of Russia.

Alexander, however, was not alone in reviving the Polish Question to the particular chagrin of the other partitioning powers; even more directly Napoleon chose to bring to the attention of all Europe the plight of divided Poland. Dangling before the eyes of patriotic Poles the hope of a gloriously restored Napoleonic state, Bonaparte anticipated and received devoted support for his ambitions. Nevertheless, years of war with Russia, Napoleon's powerful and persistent competitor, convinced the French emperor of the necessity of at least a temporary compromise on a number of issues, including Poland. The result was the creation of a Polish rump state, the Duchy of Warsaw, for the most part formed out of territory taken by Prussia during the partitions. In 1809, as a reward for the Duchy's help in defeating Austria, the Duchy received Vienna's share in the third partition, including the city of Krakow.

Both Napoleon and the Poles viewed the Duchy as a step toward the achievement of their differing ambitions: Napoleon expected it to be a loyal French outpost helping to make possible his eventual victory over Russia, while the Poles hoped that the Duchy would signify an initial step toward complete restoration of their old kingdom. Russia, for its part, could not be more disturbed about the existence of the French intrusion on its very border, and saw the Duchy as a real threat, not only to its own plans for Poland, but also to its national security. In 1810, growing alarmed at Napoleon's vague talk about the possibility of Polish restoration, Alexander requested Napoleon to give his promise that this would never happen. Napoleon never granted Alexander such an assurance, a factor in the development of Franco-Russian hostilities in 1812.

Victory came relatively soon to Alexander, and in 1814 he entered Paris at the head of the Allies. Not having won any notable support from among the still pro-French Polish nobles, Alexander turned to Great Britain, Prussia and Austria for approval of his plan of Polish restoration. Clearly aware of the significance of Poland and fearful of Russian expansion, the Allies viewed suspiciously all of Alexander's liberal proposals, however. Even Czartoryski's independent overtures, particularly toward the English, failed to dispel the distrust of Russian intentions. For that reason, the Polish Question was left for resolution

at the Congress of Vienna where it proved to be one of the most bitterly
contested issues.

In the end, by grudgingly making certain concessions to Austria
and Prussia, Alexander succeeded in winning acceptance for the
establishment of his "Congress Kingdom" of Poland. Th:s Kingdom,
territorially only a remnant of the Duchy of Warsaw, consisted of
127,000 square kilometers and included about 3,300,000 inhabitants,
three-fourths of whom were Poles.[1]

Alexander had won a great diplomatic triumph; from the Russian
point of view its western border had been secured by the creation
of the vassal Polish state. Other repercussions of the agreement were
less favorable to Russia; henceforth, St. Petersburg would be regarded
with mistrust and, in time, hostility by the European powers.

There is much to suggest that what Alexander, in conjunction with
Czartoryski, had in mind for Poland was considerably different from
what the Powers feared and what radical Poles demanded. In 1815,
due to Alexander's liberal views, as well as his understanding of the
cultural differences separating his new subjects from the Russian
population, Alexander undoubtedly intended the establishment of a
truly liberal Polish constitutional state, autonomous from, though in
union with Russia. That the Poles and, for that matter, the Great
Powers, never completely believed in this arrangement, however, is
not surprising, for if it ever existed, it was only for a short time. In
1815, a dynastic union and relative cooperation united the Polish Congress Kingdom and Russia. Yet, by 1830, this promising relationship had degenerated into a state of war and with Poland's complete
defeat even the appearances of a constitutional regime in Warsaw were
erased.

The central concern of this study is precisely an attempt to explain
the reasons for the breakdown of Russo-Polish relations in the fifteen
year period. Answering this question, however, is impossible without
considering the person of the Russian Grand Duke Constantine
Pavlovich, *de facto* ruler of the Congress Kingdom, an individual who
up to the present has been neglected in historical research.

Although many views have been presented with regard to Constantine, two are most popular. The first tends to disregard Constantine
entirely, arguing that he played no significant role in determining the
course of Russo-Polish relations. Further, it maintains that the breakdown that occurred in Russo-Polish relations was due simply to the
basic difference that existed between the Russian and Polish perspectives toward the Polish Question, with the Russians favoring direct
integration and the Poles insisting upon independence. A second view

claims that Constantine's role in the Kingdom was of crucial but largely negative significance; this position asserts that Constantine's tyrannical rule in the Kingdom was the provocation for the Poles' inevitable turn to revolution. In addition to investigating the plausibility of these and other less popular views, I will try to define the character of Constantine and his actual role in Russo-Polish relations.

Chapter One of this work considers Constantine's early years in Russia and those factors which influenced his character and his future attitude toward Poland. Chapter Two takes up the question of Constantine's role in the establishment of the Congress Kingdom of Poland as Acting Commander in Chief of the Polish Army and his initial attitude toward, and behavior in, the Kingdom. Chapter Three includes a discussion of Constantine's part in the formation of the Kingdom's army, the impact of his particular philosophy of military training on his Polish troops, and finally his significance as commander in chief relative to the strengthening or weakening of the existing Russian-Polish connection. Chapter Four includes a consideration of Constantine's relationship with his brother Tsar Alexander I, the shifting nature of their views toward Poland, and the evolution of Constantine's policy of autonomy for the Kingdom. Chapter Five treats Constantine's role as *de facto* ruler of the Kingdom both in terms of domestic and foreign affairs and his attempts to win Polish support for his rule as well as his plan for the Kingdom's autonomy. Chapter Six discusses Constantine's relationship with his brother Tsar Nicholas I and the reasons for his failure to win support from both Nicholas and the Poles during the years 1825 to 1830. The Conclusion, besides considering the most commonly advanced views held on the subject of Constantine and his role in Russo-Polish relations, includes an evaluation of those aspects of Constantine's character and policy relevant to the shaping of Russo-Polish relations during the period 1815 to 1830. It also takes up the question of Constantine's significance in the history of Russo-Polish relations.

This work, an outgrowth of my doctoral research, is, almost in its entirety, based upon primary sources (government documents, personal letters and unpublished memoirs) and important secondary works reviewed during several extensive stays in Europe. Among the most important sources of information have been the Archives of the Military Commission (Zespol Akt Archiwum Komisji Rzadowej Wojny i Militarii Krolestwa Polskiego z lat 1814-1846), the Protocols of the Administrative Council of the Congress Kingdom (Protokoly Rady Administracyjnej Krolestwa Polskiego), and the records of Constantine's secret police (Policja Tajna Konstantego) all to be found in Poland. Constantine's private archives (Archiwum Wielkiego Ksiecia Konstantego) dealing with the Kingdom's domestic and foreign affairs after the year 1822 located in the Polish Library in Paris also have been very helpful.

Further, there is an abundance of printed Russian and Polish sources, including histories, memoirs, and letters, dealing with Constantine and general and specific aspects of Russo-Polish relations during the period 1815-1830. Without doubt, the most important of these is the correspondence between Constantine and Nicholas during the years 1825-1831 found in the *Sbornik Russkago Istoricheskago Obshchestva.*

Of a secondary nature, studies such as Szymon Askenazy's *Dwa stulecia* and *Lukasinski,* Wladyslaw Bortnowski's *Wielki Ksiaze Konstanty podczas Powstanie Listopadowego,* E. P. Karnovich's *Tsesarevich Konstantin Pavlovich,* N. Chechulin's "Konstantin Pavlovich" in the *Russkii Biograficheskii Slovar,* Jerzy Lojek's *Studia nad prasa i opinia publiczna w Krolestwie Polskim (1815-1830),* and Waclaw Tokarz's *Armja Krolestwa Polskiego 1815-1830* were of particular importance. In addition there is a mass of Russian and Polish periodical literature on the period, although most of this material deals only in passing with Constantine. Also included in this study is research published in this country, most of which has appeared in the *Slavic Review* and the *Polish Review.* Finally, I have tried to consider Constantine and his years in Poland by reading the works of novelists, playwrights and essayists who have written on the subject. Among such works one may include Karolina Beylin's *Tajemnice Warszawy,* Jan Czynski's *Cesarewicz Konstanty i Joanna Grudzinska czyli Jakubiny Polscy,* Waclaw Gasiorowski's *Ksiezna Lowicka,* along with several interesting dramas about the events and personalities of the November uprising. One is the play *Kordian,* by the nineteenth century Romantic author Juliusz Slowacki. Three others, *Warszawianka, Lelewel* and *Noc Listopadowa* are the works of the early twentieth century leader of the "Young Poland" movement in literature, Stanislaw Wyspianski.

Regarding Russian and Polish spellings, I have generally followed the Library of Congress transliteration system for the Russian language, while I usually have anglicized Polish names wherever possible. In that the Russians of the time followed the Julian calendar, which was twelve days behind the Gregorian system, I have tried to provide both dates in the text or have indicated that I am using the old style (o.s.) Julian schedule.

All serious research is made possible through the guidance, suggestions and cooperation of many individuals, some of whom I would like to thank personally here. I am especially appreciative to Professor Michael B. Petrovich of the History Department of the University of Wisconsin, not only for his generous efforts in directing my dissertation, the foundation for this work, but also for shaping my understanding of the character and dynamics of Russia's development through the centuries. I am grateful to Professor Stefan Kieniewicz of the University of Warsaw for his help during my stays in Poland. Encouragement and advice came from several scholarly friends, most notably Professor Frank Renkiewicz of the History Department of St. Mary's College in Orchard Lake, Michigan and Professor Emeritus M. Kamil Dziewanowski of the History Department of the University of Wisconsin—Milwaukee. May I also take this opportunity to thank the many research librarians, both in America and Europe, who helped me locate the documents I needed for this research.

Mrs. Lois Kohlmetz graciously gave of her skills in typing and retyping the text. Mr. Jan Lorys of Chicago deserves my gratitude for providing the pictures used in this book. My thanks also go to my husband Donald for his assistance, which took many forms during this research and writing effort.

Several institutions and organizations helped support my research at various times: the United States Department of State, which granted me a Fulbright Fellowship to Poland, IREX, the International Research and Exchanges Board, and the University of Wisconsin Graduate School. Without the assistance of these agencies, it is obvious that no serious scholarship requiring extensive time spent abroad can be readily performed. It is truly imperative that such commitments to the enlightenment of our people be continued and Federal support for research should remain an important element on our country's agenda.

As I was completing this introduction in May, 1986, it was hardly possible to proceed without reflecting upon the past and the current state of Russo-Polish relations. While the twentieth century and in particular the years since the First World War have witnessed profound changes in many aspects of Polish and Russian social, economic and political life, the national relations between the two peoples have remained unstable and antagonistic. And, given the aims that a series of Russian rulers have defined with reference to Poland, its one-time rival for leadership of the Slavic world, since 1945, one cannot be any more optimistic about the satisfactory resolution of this situation now than during the years of Grand Duke Constantine Pavlovich's sojourn in the Congress Kingdom, more than one hundred and fifty years ago.

Chapter 1

GRAND DUKE CONSTANTINE PAVLOVICH IN RUSSIA, 1779-1813

Grand Duke Constantine was born in 1779, a time during which his grandmother Catherine II of Russia was in the midst of formulating her ambitious "Greek Project." This project, together with the Polish Question, was to be dominant in Catherine's foreign policy, as well as in the life of Constantine Pavlovich. Originally Gregory Orlov's[1] plan for the exclusion of the Turks from Europe, the Greek Project was further developed by Potemkin,[2] who shaped it into a more grandiose one, thereby giving expression to Catherine's love of great plans of conquest, and also creating a very fitting and lofty throne for her second grandson, Constantine.

Essentially, the Greek Project envisaged the restoration of the Byzantine Empire under the rule of Constantine who, appropriately, was to bear the name of the founder of the Eastern Roman Empire. The splendor and festivities surrounding his birth can perhaps best be explained by the anticipation of his glorious destiny, which Catherine unabashedly predicted. His birth was greeted not only by poetry, balls, and fireworks, but also by the Manifesto of May 5, 1779, which broadly hinted at his Greek imperial future. A large gold commemorative medal, minted for his christening, had on one of its sides a relief of the Church of St. Sophia in Constantinople.[3]

Greeks immediately became important parts of Constantine's entourage. Among them were his nurse Elena, and his first servant and life-long friend and aide Dmitrii Kouruta. His childhood playmates were selected Greek children. All this was done so that he would become familiar with the Greek people and their language, which he continued afterwards to speak fairly well.

Unfortunately for Catherine's's dream, it was easier to make a Greek of Constantine than to achieve her plan diplomatically and militarily. During the disappointing campaigns of 1787-88 against the Turks she continued to hope, but Potemkin, growing ever more resigned to failure, instead suggested placing Constantine on the throne of Sweden, which also was at war with Russia at that time. In October, 1788, the ever optimistic Catherine replied in answer to Potemkin's suggestion: "Constantine is not to be in the North. If he cannot be in the South, then leave him where he is; Constantine is not of the same religion as the Swedes."[4] In the same vein, she wrote a year later that "Constantine is a good boy — in thirty years he will go from Sevastopol to Tsargrad. We are now crushing the Turks and when they will be broken it will be better for him."[5]

Thus, before the age of nine, Constantine had already been proposed for two thrones. Although neither ever was to be his, the powers of a king were to be Constantine's, if not in title, then certainly in fact.

Catherine continued to dream of Constantinople for Constantine until her death in 1796, yet she was forced to admit defeat with the Treaty of Iasi[6] in 1792. In her eyes, the Greek Project had failed, but in fact, efforts to realize it did make possible significant territorial gains for Russia in the Black Sea area. Also, the Russian war with the Turks brought still another offer of a throne for Constantine, this time that of Poland. In return for Catherine's approval of certain changes in the Polish constitution, King Stanislas August Poniatowski[7] offered Polish support against the Porte and suggested that Constantine be his successor as king. The conditions of Constantine's election were impossible, however: Constantine would have had to give up his rights to the Russian throne and become a Catholic. In the spring of 1792, King Stanislas August, under the threat of a Russian invasion into Poland, made a second and similar proposal. Again, after the bloody battles between the Poles and Russians in 1794, the Polish statesmen Ignace Potocki and Thaddeus Mostowski repeated the offer.[8] This offer too was rejected, although future events would again link Constantine with Poland.

Born April 27, 1779 (o.s.), Constantine Pavlovich was the second son of Paul Petrovich, heir to the Russian throne and his wife Maria Fedorovna. Catherine was extremely interested in their growing family, doted on their firstborn son, Alexander, and was particularly pleased at the coming of their second son, Constantine.

From the beginning, Catherine regarded Alexander and Constantine as state property, that is, her own property. They lived with her and from 1780 on, when Paul and his wife moved to Gatchina, their country estate near St. Petersburg, Alexander and Constantine were permitted visits from their parents only infrequently and then only by appointment. In 1786, for example, Catherine began to prepare for a trip to the Crimea and intended to take her grandsons with her. Although the parents were not informed of this by Catherine, they learned of her plan and in a respectful letter protested. They asked that the children remain in St. Petersburg or that they also would be permitted to make the trip. Catherine replied negatively to both requests and added "Your children are yours, they are ours, they are the State's."[9]

Although Catherine paid a great deal of attention to Constantine, Alexander was always her favorite. Paul, on the contrary, from the start indicated a very strong preference for Constantine. Whether this was due simply to natural reasons or an urge to differ with his mother in every possible way is not known. However, it is clear that there was very little harmony between mother and son, and that Catherine refused to allow Paul to mount the throne and deliberately tried to remove him from all affairs of government. Paul, nevertheless, was ambitious and active and to fill his empty hours, he indulged his real passions, which were the army and military life. In fact, he personally drilled his Gatchina garrison in accordance with the military regulations of Frederick II, imitating the Prussian king even to the point of suiting his troops in Prussian-style uniforms. As the years went by, Catherine hardly concealed her hostility toward Paul, and when Alexander and Constantine grew older, they, as well as the entire court, came to feel the tensions resulting from the unhappy and bitter relationship.

Just as Catherine was insensitive about Paul's and his wife's feelings concerning the removal of their children from parental care, so was the Empress unwilling to allow any interference on their part in her grandsons' education. Believing Alexander and Constantine to be the future Russian and Greek emperors, Catherine personally paid great attention to their training. Influenced by the Enlightenment, she even planned a special and very detailed system of education for them known as her "Instruction." In the process, however, she did not seem to consider whether all of her proposals could be applicable to normal human beings, much less future rulers. Worse still, she failed to consider whether those individuals chosen to apply her system had sufficient knowledge and abilities to realize in their charges the more realistic and desirable aspects of her educational program.

In her Instruction, Catherine proceeded "from the propositions that education and formation must develop only those beautiful dispositions which she found in her grandsons in high degree. . ."[10] Their education was to be based on two principles, justice and love of

4 THE IMPERFECT AUTOCRAT

neighbor. They were to develop their physical and mental health, their tendency to do good works and they were to be diligent in their studies, particularly languages.[11]

Further, although Catherine emphasized that character and intellectual development were of the greatest importance, she also insisted that the acquisition of factual knowledge was not to be neglected. In this regard, she indicated that her grandsons were to learn to read, write and do arithmetic; they were to study astronomy, geography, mathematics, history, ethics and civil law. Her concern for her grandsons extended even to the most incidental aspects of their well-being. Indeed, she decreed that there was to be plenty of fresh air, snacks, and the room temperature must be just so![12] The remarkable part of Catherine's Instruction, however, was that having observed certain character deficiencies in her grandsons, especially Constantine, she also gave advice on how to deal with them. The fact that Constantine never really succeeded in overcoming his weaknesses was thus probably not due to any unawareness or lack of interest in his character development on the part of Catherine.[13]

As infants, both Alexander and Constantine were under the care of Sophie Benckendorff, but when she died in September, 1783, Catherine decided to put them under the care of men. General Adjutant M. I. Saltykov was chosen to have chief responsibility over them. Although in certain respects not the best possible model for young boys, he was, however, vigilant and industrious and more importantly, he had the confidence of both Catherine and Paul. Yet, perhaps the main reason for his appointment was his ability to pacify and mediate between mother and son.[14]

With the naming of Saltykov to direct the education of the grand dukes also came the appointment of several other tutors. For the most part, the brothers were educated together because of the slight difference in their ages — one year and seven months. Each, however, had several tutors of his own. Constantine, for example, had as tutors Koshelev, Lamsdorf, and the Greek, Baldani. Each also had one *sous-gouverneur* and four *cavaliers de service*. Constantine's *sous-gouverneur* was Baron Osten-Sacken, former Russian minister to Denmark.

Teaching both Alexander and Constantine were Archpriest Somborskii, M. M. Muravev, Pallas, Kraft and A. P. Masson. Most important of all their tutors was the Swiss Frederic-Cesar de la Harpe. Originally LaHarpe (as he came to be known) was hired to teach the boys only French, but soon he became tutor in other subjects such as history, geography and mathematics. LaHarpe tutored them from

1783 until 1795; his influence, however, particularly on Alexander, endured much longer.[15]

During the period of his tutorship, LaHarpe was required to make reports to Saltykov about the progress of his charges. As a result, there is a running account of LaHarpe's estimate of the grand dukes' academic progress and character development.[16] Very early, it became apparent to LaHarpe, as it did to others, that Constantine and Alexander were quite different, temperamentally as well as physically. Thus, Constantine manifested a very rugged, uncouth and violent side which struck observers, particularly in contrast with the gentle and quite refined disposition of his brother. The doting Catherine worried that Constantine, already at the age of two, was so lively that he was unable to concentrate; "also that he had other defects that Alexander did not have."[17] These differences became more pronounced as the brothers matured. Nevertheless, despite them, from their earliest days Alexander and Constantine demonstrated for each other a genuine feeling and friendship.

Not only was Constantine's behavior a problem; his academic progress was also poor. It appears that, unlike Alexander, Constantine's life-long and burning interest in the military had its roots in his childhood and nothing was of greater importance or interest to him than playing with his soldiers. Studies were for him only a bore and nuisance and anyone who attempted to interfere with his chosen occupation was in for trouble.[18] Constantine's educational progress was so slow that he, perhaps in a moment of adolescent self-examination and regret, once wrote to LaHarpe that "at the age of twelve I know nothing, not even to read. To be rude, coarse, impertinent, this is to what I aspire. My knowledge and ambition were worthy of any army drummer. In a word, I will never amount to anything."[19]

LaHarpe's reports indicate that history was the main subject of instruction. In addition, LaHarpe sought to influence his pupils morally and ethically. Great stress was placed on classical and modern history, but LaHarpe also taught them some geography and geometry. Other tutors taught them English (Somborskii), physics and natural history (Kraft). Later, they were introduced to war studies and more mathematics (Masson). How well they fared in those studies is not precisely known.

In general, these years of formal education for both grand dukes proved quite inadequate, despite Catherine's lofty intentions. Academically, Alexander seemed to profit more, no doubt due to his different temperament and interests and also due to LaHarpe's great personal influence over him.

Their boyhood together came to an abrupt end when Catherine married the fifteen year old Alexander to Princess Louise of Baden, who became Grand Duchess Elizabeth. Soon after came Constantine's turn. Of all the old and important dynasties the Saxe-Saalfeld-Cobourg family pleased Catherine most. An added attraction of the family was that it included three unmarried princesses. Both Catherine and Constantine liked the youngest, Julia, best, so the matter was settled. At her baptism into the Russian Orthodox Church Julia took the name Anna Fedorovna.

In an interesting letter to her husband back at home, Anna Fedorovna's mother wrote her most flattering first impressions of Constantine: "He looks not less than twenty-three (although he is sixteen) . . . He has a wide round face; and if he was not snubbed-nosed he would be handsome. He has large blue eyes in which there is much wit and fire . . ."[20]

It appears that Constantine too was pleased with the match, for he wrote to LaHarpe on 11/22 March, 1796; "I am at present in the most happy state of life, I am promised to Princess Julia of Saxe-Cobourg. I am sorry that you have not seen her, she is a good person and I love her with all my heart . . ."[21]

Their first meeting proved to be the high point of their relationship, however, for practically from the beginning their marriage floundered and their separations grew more prolonged. There are many possible explanations for this, among them Constantine's bad temper, coarseness and his greater affection for and interest in the military.

In 1794, Constantine first began frequenting Gatchina where he and Alexander had their first real exposure to army life. Having reached an age that was considered manhood, it was time for them to progress from military theory to practice and by the end of 1794 Constantine had a small detachment of fifteen men. Although as children, Constantine was interested much more than Alexander in soldiers and war games, both soon fell under the spell of Paul's Prussian drill and both displayed a great aptitude and fondness for what has been called the "paradomania" of Paul.[22] At Gatchina, Constantine came to hold the view that a soldier was a simple machine and that "all a commander commands his subordinates to do must be fulfilled even if it were cruelty." This view, however, was not shared by Alexander, for he wrote in February, 1796, to LaHarpe that military studies had turned his brother's head and that Constantine was sometimes rough with his soldiers.[23] As much as Constantine's harshness often aggravated Alexander, their mutual interest in the army further strengthened their already close relationship. Constantine was far superior to Alexander in his military knowledge and skill, and at least in this way commanded respect and had considerable influence with Alexander.[24] In 1794, war broke out between Poland and Russia. The aftermath of this conflict was the Third Partition of Poland which resulted in a great number of Russian confiscations of Polish property, including that of the Czartoryski[25] family. Acquiescing to the request of the Austrian emperor, Catherine agreed to restore the Czartoryski property provided that the two oldest Czartoryski sons came to St. Petersburg. As a promise of Polish good behavior, the old Empress wanted to have them as "hostages" at her court. The oldest, Adam Czartoryski, was assigned as adjutant to Alexander, thus making possible an acquaintance which developed into a friendship of great importance to both of their countries. The younger Czartoryski, Constantine, was assigned as adjutant to Constantine. But as Adam Czartoryski explained:

> None of the reasons which had linked us to Alexander existed for Constantine, and his capricious and hot tempered character made impossible any other reaction than that of fear and made all closeness with him less desirable; Grand Duke Alexander asked that my brother indulge him willingly and that his confidences remain unknown to Constantine, for whom he had however fraternal feelings.[26]

As a result of this close association, Adam Czartoryski came to know both brothers very well. Despite their friendship and closeness, Czartoryski observed that they also had many differences of opinion. Among them were that "Constantine did not share his brother's liberal political opinions nor his more tolerant and forgiving attitude toward their grandmother."[27] Thus, it is easy to imagine that Constantine was not among the most grief-stricken at the news of her death on November 6, 1796 (o.s.).

After the death of Catherine and the accession of Paul, many changes took place which affected not only Alexander and Constantine but all of Russia. Paul, the new emperor and long frustrated father, could now at last have control over his sons. And Gatchina, once only his private domain, was now to become the model for all Russia. According to one observer, "a visit to Gatchina was like a visit to a foreign country, Prussia to be exact." The sudden change that took place under Paul in just a few days was scarcely credible, for

"Petersburg ceased to look like a modern town, having become much more like a German one of two or three centuries back . . ."[28]

At the forefront, immediately reflecting this change, were of course Alexander and Constantine who "appeared in their new costumes, looking like old portraits of German officers walking out of their frames."[29] This change, however, was more than just superficial, for Paul meant to reform the entire land. Despite Paul's short reign (1796-1801), he became quite popular with the masses because he, in contrast with Catherine, demonstrated real concern for their welfare. He gained a reputation as being personally economical, yet generous with his subjects, especially in the matter of pensions, and he made himself available to his people by granting frequent audiences and hearing petitions.

Although Paul was genuinely esteemed among the masses, the nobility from the beginning failed to share this feeling. Under Catherine, they had enjoyed almost perfect personal liberty, but under Paul, they were subjected to what they considered, especially in comparison, the pressure of a despotic, chimerical ruler."[30] Much of the nobility's hostility toward Paul can be explained by some of his governmental measures. In the interest of the country, for example, he imposed special taxes on their landed estates. Most of their hostility, however, was also directed against his person. Paul's early education and surroundings were hardly such to form a well-developed intellect and sound personality. And, as the years passed and the pressures of governing increased, Paul became more and more irritable, unreasonable, temperamentally unstable, suspicious and authoritarian.[31] Thus, it came to be that despite Paul's more admirable traits, such as generosity and a strong sense of justice, he acquired powerful enemies who saw him as unfit to rule.

By 1801, even relations between Paul and his sons had deteriorated, but in 1796 they were still full of promise, since at last they had been freed from the restrictions imposed by Catherine. Although all along Paul preferred Constantine to Alexander, both were drawn closely to him. Treating them as his closest friends, he showered them with gifts and honors. On his accession, he immediately increased their many allotments and named them commanders of his most important guard units, Constantine, the Izmailovsky Guards, and Alexander, the Semenovsky Guards. In May, 1797, Constantine accompanied Paul around his empire, and then in quick succession he was named Head of the First Cadet Corps, Governor Inspector of all the Cavalry (a title he chose to retain all his life), and Governor General for St. Petersburg.

When war broke out with France, Constantine asked to serve with General Suvorov who was then head of the joint Austrian-Russian army moving into Italy. In March, 1799, having received Paul's permission, Constantine, under the name of Count Romanov, left for the army's general headquarters in Verona. The following day his wife Anna Fedorovna left for her home in Saxe-Cobourg.

It seems that Constantine's sudden appearance at the front created considerable consternation and real problems. Despite his high rank, his still limited military knowledge and experience made it impossible to give him any responsible position. Yet he was eager to participate, and more than once placed himself in danger or interfered unwarrantably. Finally, Suvorov placed Constantine under his watchful eye at general headquarters. Constantine attended the general staff meetings and participated in various military exercises preparatory to battle.[32] He quickly gained the reputation of being a hard worker and a "good trooper" who willingly participated in the hardships of camp life and long marches in all kinds of weather. He also showed himself to be, in marked contrast with his earlier behavior, sympathetic to the situation of the soldiers and on several occasions paid for extra supplies for them out of his personal funds.[33] Even French prisoners were recipients of his kindness. He gave them money, visited their hospitals and in general tried to make their plight more bearable.[34]

Unfortunately, Constantine also drew attention to himself in another way. His temperamental outbursts, his angry and strange behavior at times, particularly toward Austrian officers and Italian aristocrats, provoked less complimentary comments.[35]

During his first months of service, Constantine participated in the difficult march through Italy and was present at the battle of Trebbia, at the taking of the Alexandrine Citadel and at the particularly bloody battle near Novi. After this battle, Suvorov had high praise for Constantine and wrote in his report of August 25, 1799 to Paul that Constantine must be commended "for his courage and good example which inspired the entire army to greater effort."[36]

Encouraged by his Italian victories, Suvorov decided to move into Switzerland. Here his army was soon placed in serious danger. During this time, Constantine took part in the highest military councils and several times made proposals which were accepted. Suvorov was pleased with Constantine's contribution during the Swiss campaign and again reported favorably to Paul about him.[37] Obviously pleased, Paul gave Constantine the title of "Tsesarevich" in a special *Ukaz* of October 28, 1799, noting that "in seeing with sincere satisfaction as Emperor and as father, what brave and exemplary deeds our beloved son His Highness Grand Duke Constantine performed against our enemy during the war in defense of our country and faith, we wish to grant him as reward the high title of Tsesarevich.''[38] This indeed was a most interesting and even shocking development, for the title of Tsesarevich was reserved for the eldest son as successor to the throne: by rights it should have only been granted to Alexander. At the same time Paul also gave Constantine the ''Commander's Cross of the Knights of St. John of Jerusalem'' and fifty thousand roubles. Soon after, Constantine received the ''Order of the Annunziata'' from the Sardinian king and the ''Military Order of Maria Teresa'' from the Austrian emperor.

Satisfied that Constantine had acquired some military experience and glory, Paul now felt it was time for him to return home. Constantine was greeted as a war hero on his arrival in St. Petersburg on December 29, 1799, and was honored at several balls and in a special allegorical ballet presented in the Hermitage Theater, ''The Return of Polioctete.''[39] This idyl lasted only a few days, for soon Constantine was faced with the problems created by his father's degenerating mental and emotional condition. Paul's state was such that he could be provoked by the slightest or even imagined infraction of his rules. He scrupulously studied all of his associates' behavior and was hyper-sensitive to every remark and action, particularly those of his sons. Of necessity, they spent a good deal of time with him, for aside from their personal and familial encounters, there were frequent military parades, inspections, exercises and meetings in which they all participated. More and more frequently, Paul found fault with them and soon it became apparent that the grand dukes had become deathly afraid of their father, so much so that, according to N. A. Sablukov, Head of Constantine's Horse Guards, ''they became pale and shook like an autumn leaf'' in his presence.[40] They even sought protection from others, asking the help of those who were at least for the moment in the good graces of Paul.[41] Such searching for favor, however, did not noticeably help the sons. In time, Alexander and Constantine began to lose the court's respect and popularity. This was especially true for Constantine, who did not even possess the impressive good looks or pleasant personality of Alexander.

In general, Constantine was better able to handle Paul's moods and to avoid irritating him. But even though Paul preferred him to Alexander, soon even Constantine was subject to his father's anger and suspicion. At the end of his rule Paul was just as suspicious and hostile toward Constantine as toward everyone else, and on March 11, 1801, both Alexander and Constantine were arrested and made to swear loyalty to their father.[42]

The evening of the same day, March 11, Constantine had dinner as usual with his father, mother and guests. A few hours later, at 1 a.m., Prince Platon Zubov woke Constantine with the news that his father was dead.

Despite much speculation implying Alexander's awareness of the assassination plot, if not direct participation in it, there is no solid evidence that Constantine even knew about the plot or was in any way involved. Rather, there is the considerable evidence of several eyewitnesses that Constantine was completely surprised by his father's murder and reacted with sincere sorrow and great anger. It was reported, for example, that Constantine loudly said, just before taking his oath to the new emperor, his brother Alexander, that "he would hang them all."[43]

Although Constantine was filled with hatred and thoughts of revenge, Alexander reacted quite differently. He chose to disregard what had happened and began his reign without any investigations or repressions against the guilty, thereby giving even greater impetus to rumors of his personal involvement in his father's murder. Undoubtedly, this course of action was also very politic, for much of his most powerful support came from those responsible for his father's death. Interestingly enough, the different reactions to their father's death, like many other future differences, did not disrupt the basic harmony and good feeling between Alexander and Constantine.[44] However, Constantine's bitter and violent reaction did contribute to strained relations between Constantine and many in the highest positions around Alexander, a situation which was later to have grave repercussions on Constantine's aspirations.

After Alexander's coronation Constantine retained his old posts, but in his great devotion to his brother-tsar he doubled his efforts. With the more friendly and tolerant attitude of Alexander, Constantine was now able to begin a new and freer life, one he had never enjoyed under Catherine or Paul. As usual he could devote himself wholeheartedly to the military, but now without any fears of Paul's criticism, and, for the first time, he could begin to indulge himself socially, something that Paul had never permitted.

Although toward the end of 1799, Constantine made efforts toward reconciliation with his wife Anna Fedorovna they were not successful. On his way home from the front he visited her at her parents' home in Saxe-Cobourg and persuaded her to return to St. Petersburg. She stayed until the end of 1801 and then left St. Petersburg, never to return to Russia. Constantine was a source of constant gossip, with rumors hinting at the causes of their discord, their impending divorce and the scandalous behavior of Constantine with several ladies of varied rank and nationality.[45]

It was more than rumor, however, that already by the end of 1800 Constantine was linked seriously with the Polish princess Helena Lubomirska. While on summer maneuvers in 1800, he met the then sixteen-year-old Helena and became so infatuated with her that he proposed marriage. The growth of their relationship, however, was inhibited by Constantine's marital situation and Helena's lack of enthusiasm for the already portly and temperamental Tsesarevich. Yet her indifference did not seem to deter him, for during the fall and winter of that year he showered her with letters and sent her his portrait. (Curiously enough, in it he was wearing a uniform such as was worn by Polish soldiers in the Kosciuszko Insurrection of 1794 against Russia.) In the main, his letters to her were woeful because of his separation from her and because of the terrible atmosphere in St. Petersburg during Paul's last days. However, three days after Paul's death he wrote to her: "We have a great change. My father is no longer; my adorable brother is Emperor. He is dearly beloved by all. Petersburg revives. Russia, dear fatherland breathes."[46]

Constantine's enthusiastic reaction to his brother becoming tsar was at least in part due to his belief that Alexander would approve his romantic plans, something Paul had adamantly opposed. Contrary to Constantine's expectations, Alexander also refused to give permission for a divorce and new marriage. But unlike Paul who would not even consider the matter, Alexander was able to convince Constantine of his wisdom in refusing permission. Evidently Constantine's disappointment was short-lived, because before long he was involved with not one, but two shining stars of the Russian salons, the princesses Maria and Zoneta Czerwertynski.

The years to 1805 were exciting in liberal and governmental circles, for Alexander and his "Secret Committee" made no secret of their intention to reform Russia. Not sharing his brother's political views, Constantine was not part of Alexander's circles and seemed more than content to busy himself only with military matters. However, in his own way, he too, was interested in reform. And so as Chairman of the War Commission and as Inspector of the Cavalry, he initiated a number of military reforms, mainly dealing with army size, supply and education. During this period it was noticed that Constantine had developed a rather peculiar view of an army's purpose. Henceforth, for Constantine the army was basically to be for show, not war. His experiences in Italy and Switzerland seem to have created in him a strong dislike for war, and from that time on he was most often on the side advocating appeasement to avoid military involvement. One rumor claimed that Constantine's main objection to war was based on the fact that war dirtied uniforms and spoiled the appearance of his army. Unfortunately for Constantine, this particular rumor was hard to combat, because it was well known that he almost drove his subordinates mad with details, such as perfection in dress, cleanliness and parades.[47]

When in 1805 war again broke out with France, Constantine was given command of a reserve guard unit with instructions to proceed to the front. At the decisive battle of Austerlitz, December 2, 1805, the allied Austrian and Russian armies, including Constantine's unit, were badly beaten. There was a short breathing space after the Treaty of Pressburg, but war again resumed in November, 1806. Prussia, Russia's only remaining ally, was quickly defeated at Jena, and Russia was left alone to face Napoleon. At this point Constantine tried to convince Alexander to initiate peace talks, advice that went unheeded until after the Friedland debacle of June 2, 1807, in which over ten thousand Russian soldiers were killed or wounded.[48]

Soon after, the famed Tilsit talks between Alexander and Napoleon took place, and an uneasy peace was agreed upon. Constantine accompanied Alexander to the talks and during the course of the meetings with Napoleon came to have very strong opinions about him. Although Constantine personally disliked Napoleon, he admired him greatly as a soldier and military genius.[49] Constantine was present at the ratification of the Tilsit Treaty on June 27. On that day he received from Napoleon the order of the Legion of Honor and a gold sword as a mark of Napoleon's ''attachment and esteem that I always had for you as a friend or enemy,'' and recognition for what he did for the French wounded.[50] Constantine saw Napoleon only once more, in 1808, when he accompanied Alexander to the Erfurt talks.

During the years of truce, 1807-1812, Constantine resumed his previous activities, concentrating as before on the military. In these years, Constantine personally became more and more unpopular, and was generally disliked in both military and social circles. His temper and general disposition seem not to have become moderated, and in the army he was considered to be violent, moody, overly demanding and picayune.[51]

Similarly, in non-military circles, opinion about Constantine was poor. One might take as an example the account of State Secretary

G. I. Villamov's conversation with Constantine's mother, Empress Maria Fedorovna. According to him, he was asked by the Empress whether public opinion about Constantine had changed at all. He had to reply that it had not, and continued to be unfavorable.[52]

Although politics and diplomacy continued to be of little interest to him, by 1812 the course of events had taken such a turn that even Constantine came to be concerned about the rapidly deteriorating relationship between France and Russia. However, contrary to popular opinion, Constantine believed that it was necessary to appease Napoleon and that war must be avoided at all costs. Aside from the fact that Constantine was a great admirer of Napoleon's military prowess, he believed Russia was too weak to withstand an onslaught by the French and their allies. In the hopes of achieving a better understanding with Napoleon, Constantine personally volunteered to go to France and deliver a message of conciliation.[53] He was never able to realize his plan, because already in June of 1812 Napoleon began his invasion of Russia.

Although frustrated and angry that his advice had not been followed with greater determination and speed, Constantine nevertheless had to participate in the general mobilization which followed Napoleon's attack. At first, Constantine favored a retreat even before Napoleon's rapid movement into Russia. Before long the Russians were forced to fall back as far as Smolensk. Here a war council was called and Constantine, in a very sudden change of mind, called for an immediate offensive against Napoleon. He, among all the members of the council, was most in favor of a Russian counterattack, and after a bitter debate his view prevailed.[54] Still, the council's decision was not the final word. Many, not in the council, were opposed or undecided. The tsar himself, although sympathetic to Constantine's views, was also basically unsure as to the preferable course of action.

Facing Napoleon were three Russian armies, including the First Army of the West under General Barclay de Tolly. Constantine was directly under him, in command of the Fifth Corps of Infantry which included twenty-six battalions, twenty squadrons and seven companies. General de Tolly was chosen by the war council to lead the offensive. He began an advance, but then on July 26 halted. It was known that General de Tolly had not favored an offensive, but when he halted and then began to draw back it began to appear that he was deliberately avoiding battle, despite the war council's orders. As the retreat continued, dissatisfaction began to spread throughout the army, and Constantine was at the forefront of those who made plain their disagreement with their commander. At the time the retreating army reached

Vitebsk General de Tolly asked Constantine to deliver an "extraordinarily important" message to the tsar in Moscow, thus removing his dissident voice from the front.

However, Constantine was not to be quieted and was determined to return to the front. For the time being, he was given in Moscow the task of forming a new cavalry company, but succeeded in so completely antagonizing both his superiors and subordinates that Count Rostopchin asked that the tsar remove Constantine from the city.[55] Alexander suggested to Constantine that he undertake the task of forming the militia in Nizhni-Novgorod, but Constantine was so determined to do nothing other than return to the front that Alexander finally gave him permission to do as he wanted. Constantine arrived at the front on August 6, just at the time that the French were driving the Russian army from Smolensk. According to General Zhirkevich, in anger and frustration at the humiliating scene, Constantine appealed to the people of Smolensk saying: "What are we to do friends! We are not to blame, they did not allow us to rescue you. Russian blood does not flow in him who commands, and we, although it is painful to us, must obey him. My heart, not less than yours, is being torn."[56]

Hearing of Constantine's outburst, General de Tolly immediately dismissed him from the front and ordered him to return to the tsar who was then in St. Petersburg. Upon his arrival at the capital, Constantine gave the impression of "being a man utterly lost. Particularly after the Borodino battle and the retreat from Moscow, Constantine's behavior produced such an unfavorable impression that it was considered best that he left St. Petersburg."[57]

The next two months Constantine spent at the home of his sister, Grand Duchess Ekatrina Pavlovna in Tver. But even there, he continued to express his opposition to the high command's decisions and argued with all who came his way, including the court historian Karamzin.

Constantine's "exile" was short-lived, for by October the great retreat of the French army from Moscow had begun. On their heels, the Russian army began to advance and undertook a small offensive against the rapidly collapsing Grande Armee. At last Constantine no longer had any quarrel with the high command and was permitted to rejoin the army. On January 13, 1813, Constantine, together with Alexander, crossed the Nieman River into the Duchy of Warsaw and by January 27 they were in Warsaw.

From this time on, Constantine was again permitted full participation in military affairs. He was put in command of the forty thousand allied reserves in the First Allied Army under General Schwarzenberg, and in the following months took part in a number of important battles. In three of these battles, Constantine particularly distinguished himself. For example, in August, for his contribution at the battle near Dresden, he was awarded a gold and diamond sword with the inscription "For Bravery." In October, at the Battle of Leipzig, he commanded his reserves so well that he obtained the "Order of St. Gregory, Second Class." And in the last battle near Paris, Constantine's command of his troops and brilliantly planned attacks were praised as being among the most outstanding of the entire Napoleonic Wars.

The march into Paris on March 19, 1814, was an especially triumphal one, but amid the celebrations Constantine drew attention to himself by continuing war exercises, never for a moment relaxing the rigors of army life and discipline.[58]

In June, Alexander sent Constantine back to Russia with the official news of peace. In their great enthusiasm, the merchants and nobles of the city offered to give a ball in Constantine's honor. He, however, declined their offer and asked that they instead use the money for the needs of the wounded.[59] Constantine remained in St. Petersburg only a few days; he then went to Vienna again bearing official news of peace. Here, Emperor Francis named him chief of a regiment of hussars.[60]

In September, the first sessions of the Congress of Vienna began. Constantine was joined by Alexander at that time for the convocation of the Congress. However, Constantine's stay in Vienna was very brief. His main focus of attention was now to be Warsaw, and from this time on he was able to make only very short and sporadic visits to Vienna.

Chapter II

CONSTANTINE AND THE FORMING OF THE
POLISH CONGRESS KINGDOM, 1813-1815

Within a few months after the main Russian army crossed the frontier, the entire Duchy of Warsaw came under Russian control. And, after hearing the news of Napoleon's defeats, many of the Polish aristocracy and *szlachta*[1] abandoned their pro-French orientation and became open, if not favorable to, a realistic relationship with St. Petersburg.

Nevertheless, a considerable part of the nation, including segments of the poorest *szlachta*, townspeople and army, continued to hope for Napoleon's eventual victory and were willing to carry on the struggle against Russia. The peasantry, in general, was anti-Russian and was particularly fearful that its already impoverished and precarious economic condition would be worsened by the conquering and perhaps vindictive tsar.

In an attempt to restore governmental and administrative order which had collapsed after the flight of the King of Saxony,[2] the army, and most of the pro-French administration, as well as to calm the fears of all those who were suspicious of the new regime, Alexander convoked the Provisional High Council of the Duchy of Warsaw on March 14, 1813. It was made up of five persons, the Russian Nicholas Novosiltsev, (1761-1836), Xavier Drucki-Lubecki, (1778-1846), Thomas Wawrzecki, (1753-1816), the Prussian Columb, and the Russian general Lanskoi who was president of the Council for a short time until he was replaced by Novosiltsev. In the main, the Council was composed of docile followers of the tsar who did not represent the population of the Duchy. However, the Council did restore public order and it recommenced the activities of the local administration and courts. At the same time, the administrative apparatus of the Russian occupation began to function, and soon it became clear that, despite appearances, Polish independence was a fiction and opposition to the Russian occupation resulted in repression and arrests.[3]

Already, at the end of 1812, when the defeat of Napoleon was becoming ever more certain, Adam Czartoryski[4] again began to put forward his ideas for a Polish restoration. His plan envisioned the "total restoration of Poland" (that is, to the pre-first partition borders of 1772), under the rule of the Russian tsar, who would be king of Poland. Although his plan won the support of many, including the majority of the Polish nobility, it also engendered a great deal of opposition. Both Austria and Prussia, Russia's partners in the Partitions, were opposed to any change which could threaten their Polish territories. Many landowners too, both in the Duchy and in Russia, feared change, believing that it would mean a revision in the status of the peasantry.[5]

During the years preceding Napoleon's final defeat and abdication, Alexander was hesitant to express clearly his intentions with regard to Poland. Still, it was evident that he had a very special interest in Poland's future. In a speech to his army as it approached the Polish border he said:

> And one of the great results, to which it (the war) must lead, must be the realization of the aim, equally valuable for the Empire, as it is dear to my heart — the resurrection of Poland. And you drawing near to that country. . . bring to the shores of the Vistula assurances of my respect and my good feelings for the Polish nation. Tell them that I always valued their virtue, their love of country and their faithfulness to it and to their monarch. Tell them, that I have decided to establish a Polish Kingdom and to announce myself king at the time when my divisions have driven out the enemy.[6]

In December, 1812, Alexander also said:

> Tell them that united to Russia by my person and in that of my successors, they will conserve the faith of their fathers, a separate administration and national laws based on the Constitution of the Third of May, 1791, which to them has always been so dear.[7]

Then, about a month later, apparently disturbed that he was unable to do anything at that time toward the realization of their mutual hope of reestablishing Poland, Alexander wrote to Czartoryski to explain the difficulties involved. First, he indicated that Russian opinion was so hostile to Poland, as a result of the war which caused the revival of "ancient hates," that he did not dare to announce the formation of a new Polish state with concomitant restoration of ancient Polish freedoms. Further, he expressed the fear that an untimely announcement of his intention to resurrect Poland would throw Austria and Prussia into the arms of France.[8]

Consequently, due to the delicate political situation and the still raging war, contacts between Alexander and Czartoryski were few. And, although Czartoryski by early 1813 was recognized as the semi-official representative of Poland and voiced the views of Polish statesmen of pro-Russian orientation such as Thaddeus Mostowski, Thaddeus Matuszewicz and Ignace Sobolewski, the general agreement reached by Alexander and Czartoryski could only be considered as semi-secret and unofficial.

However, a year later and after his march into Paris, Alexander hesitated no longer; he now publicly and confidently announced his plans for Poland. He openly called Czartoryski to his camp and proclaimed his intention of joining all the Polish lands under his rule. Then, in order to win support from the Poles, he took several actions which demonstrated his interest in winning their loyalty. Alexander took special interest in the five thousand Polish soldiers remaining in France and encouraged them to return home while allowing them to retain their arms and Polish and French orders. In reorganizing them, he honored them by naming his brother Constantine Acting Head of the entire Polish Corps, and he called into existence an Organizational Army Committee made up of eight Polish generals (Dabrowski, Kniaziewicz, Woyczynski, Wielhorski, Zajaczek, Sierawski, Paszkowski, and Sulkowski) under the presidency of Constantine. Alexander also agreed to assist financially the impoverished Polish army. He ordered the freeing of all Polish prisoners in Russia and asked for their release in Prussia, Sweden, Spain, and England.[9] During this time, the Polish hero, Thaddeus Kosciuszko who had fought against the Russians, was received with great honor by Alexander in Paris.

But winning Polish support for Alexander's and Czartoryski's plan was relatively easy compared with the problem of gaining approval from the European powers. As Alexander anticipated, his plans for Poland provoked great opposition; indeed "the Polish problem became the central test, even as it constituted the essential crisis of the Vienna Congress."[10] The Congress, called to restore order and stability after the great revolutionary upheavals of the previous twenty-five years, saw that the so-called Polish Question was crucial to the European balance of power and the fate of revolutionary reforms introduced in formerly French-controlled territories. Not surprisingly, numerous alternate proposals for the resolution of the Polish Question were presented.[11] But Alexander held so tenaciously to his plan that opposition turned to real hostility. This was true to such an extent that already by the end of 1814 there was talk of the coronation of Alexander as king of Poland without the Allies' approval and even of a new war, this time between the Allies. Reflecting this tension was one of Constantine's orders of the day to the Polish Army in December, 1814:

> His Majesty Alexander, your powerful protector, makes this appeal to you: Gather around your standards, arm yourselves in the defense of your fatherland and to maintain your political existence. While this august monarch prepares the happy future of your country, show yourselves ready to sustain his noble efforts with your blood. . . Others can promise you much, but only he can make it possible. His power and his virtues are his guarantees to you.[12]

The news of Constantine's proclamation made a shocking impression on European public opinion and especially on the pleasantly occupied monarchs and representatives at the Congress of Vienna. Alexander completely denied that Constantine ever made such a statement "although it was known that the proclamation was composed in the Tsar's cabinet in Vienna."[13]

Two points in particular met with great surprise and hostility. First, it was asked, by what right did Constantine proclaim Alexander protector of Poland; and second, what was the menace to Poland which justified a call to arms, since supposedly all Europe was working for the achievement of a general peace?[14]

In the end, however, the matter was smoothed over and compromise with regard to Poland was reached. In return for Allied approval for the establishment of a Polish Kingdom under his rule, Alexander gave grudging agreement for a division of those Polish territories not to be included in his Kingdom to Austria and Prussia. Still, despite his desire to assure for his new Kingdom the largest possible amount of territory, Alexander was unwilling to permit a reunion of the new Polish Kingdom with those Polish territories taken by Russia during the partitions. This was probably because he thought that many in Russia would view such a decision as a border revision at the Empire's expense.[15]

In preparation for the final settlement, a number of newly established commissions began the work of determining the exact size of the population and the extent and value of the various Polish territories. Before this was completed, however, Napoleon returned to France and the Hundred Days began.

After watching the Allies arbitrarily decide their fate, one not really to their liking, many Poles quickly and quite desperately turned again to Napoleon with the hope that he would realize their dreams of a real and complete Polish revival. Aware of this, the Allies deemed it imperative to conclude immediately the division of the Polish territories and determine the form of the new Kingdom of Poland. Therefore on July 9, 1815, the fate of post-Napoleonic Poland was settled by the concluding acts of the Congress of Vienna, which supposedly made the agreement subject to international sanctions.[16]

By this agreement, the Duchy of Warsaw was partitioned among Prussia, Austria and Russia. Prussia obtained the provinces of Poznan (Posen) and Bydgoszcz, (Bromberg) together with the towns of Torun (Thorn) and Gdansk (Danzig). To Austria, went the districts of Tarnopol and Podgorze. Because the city of Krakow continued to be disputed, it was decided to make it a "free city" under the jurisdiction of the three powers, with its own constitution. What remained of the Duchy of Warsaw was to become the "Congress Kingdom" in "perpetual union" with Russia by the tsar, who took for himself the title King of Poland. The Congress Kingdom was to be composed of eight provinces (voivodships); Krakow (excluding the city), Sandomierz, Lublin, Kalisz, Plock, Mazovia, Podlasie and Augustow. The total population included 3,200,000 people with 127,000 square kilometers of territory.[17]

At the time of this agreement, Alexander indicated that he reserved for himself the right to "internally expand" the Kingdom, thus giving birth to hopes on the part of the Polish *szlachta* of eventual incorporation of the former Polish provinces held by Russia into the new Congress Kingdom.

During the course of the Congress of Vienna, England had been concerned that the new Polish Kingdom be granted a constitution and its representatives advised that this constitution be harmonious with Polish laws and customs with Polish the official language. Thus, as a result of English pressure, Polish appeals, and for that matter, even his own personal sympathy for constitutional government, Alexander agreed to grant the Kingdom its own constitution, administration and permission that Polish be the official language. At the same time, as corollaries to the Vienna settlement, the Austrian and Prussian governments promised their Polish subjects such institutions as would "assure the preservation of their nationality." All three powers granted a general amnesty. Lastly, in the entire area which was formerly the Polish-Lithuanian Commonwealth, free trade, navigation and contacts between the populations were also guaranteed by Russia, Austria and Prussia.[18]

Because Alexander himself was not completely satisfied with the final settlement, it was not difficult for him to understand the Poles' dissatisfaction. Yet, he very much wanted them to know that he had done everything possible to achieve a total restoration of Poland in the old boundaries. In his first statement to the Poles after the Vienna settlement he said:

> In taking the title of King of Poland I wanted to fulfill the desires of the nation. The Kingdom of Poland will be joined with the Russian Empire through its own constitution on which I wish to base the happiness of the country.

> If the great aim of general peace does not permit that all Poles be joined under one scepter, at least I made all efforts to sweeten the difficulties of such partition and to obtain for all peaceful recognition of their nationality.[19]

Despite Alexander's altruistic explanation for his concern for Poland, it was clear to those at the Congress of Vienna, as well as to the Poles, that his motivations might not be so lofty. Rather, they feared that Alexander was motivated by more selfish and chauvinistic considerations, and that if they did not check Alexander in Poland they would incur "the danger of substituting for French domination the domination of Russia. It thus came about that the statesmen, who at the Congress of Vienna planned the new European system, were less concerned with the danger of French militarism than with the menace of Russian expansion toward the West."[20] Moreover, despite protestations on the part of Russia, Prussia and Austria that each had received less than its due, the real loser at the Congress was Poland. For again Poland was subjected to what might be considered a fourth partition, but a partition of greater significance than the previous three.

Now, for the first time, a partition of Poland received the approbation of a congress of European nations and even though the borders agreed upon were to remain fixed for over a hundred years, the international sanctions and provisions for limited self-government guaranteed by the signatories of the Congress soon became a dead letter.[21]

But however disappointed the Poles were with what they believed to be the fourth partition of their country, and however disappointed Alexander was with what he considered only a compromise settlement, these sentiments were more than matched by the anger and frustration of many Russians. Obviously, they favored any territorial expansion of Russia, regardless of the guise; yet they were totally skeptical of Alexander's hope for a Polish Kingdom under his rule and were completely unsympathetic toward Polish aspirations for independence. Fearful that the establishment of the Polish Kingdom could only lead to Polish demands for independence and a return of all Polish territory, they opposed all projects for even a limited Polish revival, much less an autonomous, constitutional kingdom.

In the forefront of the opposition were the prominent tsarist statesmen Charles Pozzo di Borgo, Charles Nesselrode and John Capo d'Istria. The Russian court historian, Nicholas Karamzin, as well as the major Russian figures already executing Alexander's policy in Poland, among them Lanskoi, Novosiltsev and Constantine, were also opposed to Alexander's creation.[22]

Pozzo di Borgo, for example, contended that the union of two roles, that of constitutional monarch with that of autocrat, was impossible. Further, more importantly and perhaps more difficult, Polish interests would have to be subordinated to Russian interests.[23]

Agreeing with Pozzo di Borgo was Alexander's secretary of state, Nesselrode, who, in a special memorial, expressed his opposition to any plan of rebuilding of Poland for the reasons that Russia would gain neither "strength, peace, nor influence" and that "Poland dreams about full independence" would not be satisfied.[24]

Still another reason suggested for Russian opposition to an autonomous Polish Kingdom was that

the Russian governing classes were jealous of the Poles (who they rightly regarded as being more intelligent than themselves) and did not like the idea of liberal institutions being accorded to Poland which it would be disturbing, dangerous and premature to accord to Russia herself.[25]

Indicative of some Russians' alarm at Alexander's pro-Polish tendencies was the fact that they organized a secret organization called the "Russian Knights" to combat this dangerous tendency.[26]

As an alternative to Alexander's plan for Poland, Karamzin called for a return to Catherine's policy of direct annexation. Although changing his opinion later, in 1814 Constantine shared Karamzin's view. Perhaps under the influence of a "court cabal," elements of the bureaucracy, or the so-called "governmental-army party," which was without doubt a large part of the most influential and informed segment of Russian public opinion, Constantine favored a total incorporation of the newly acquired Polish territories into the Russian Empire as new provinces on the model of earlier acquired Polish territories.[27] According to one authority, when there was talk of an autonomous Polish kingdom, and particularly when mention was made of this kingdom having its own constitution and army, Constantine went mad with anger.[28] Yet, despite Constantine's difference of opinion with Alexander over Poland, Constantine conscientiously tried to serve his brother. For example, Constantine, as newly appointed Acting Head of the Polish Corps, tried to echo his brother's pro-Polish sentiments. In the beginning, despite his own feelings, Constantine seemed to have some success in this difficult undertaking.

From the time of his appointment, Constantine demonstrated great interest in the Corps and heaped lavish praise on it. Both he and Alexander attended the Corps' reviews and celebrations and made a favorable impression on the Corps. One occasion, a dinner given by General Krasinski, was particularly notable; both Alexander and Constantine evoked a tremendously enthusiastic response from the Corps, Alexander with his words, "I have taken upon myself the sacred and solemn obligation to work for your happiness,"[29] and Constantine with his impetuous toast to the "brave Polish nation."[30]

Poles in Warsaw similarly responded with enthusiasm to reports of Alexander's and Constantine's expressions of interest and good feeling toward the Poles in Paris. They regarded Alexander's decision to permit the reorganization of the Polish Army as at least one positive sign for the future of Poland. However, the Russian reaction to such news was drastically different. According to Niemcewicz, who was having dinner with Novosiltsev and Governor General Lanskoi at the time they received a letter from Alexander informing them of his plans for the Polish Army, it was difficult to describe their anger. But not only were they angry, they considered the idea of a new Polish Army as "stupidity" and complained about the "madness of the Emperor."[31]

Constantine, as Alexander's most important personal representative, was the recipient of the Poles' enthusiasm. This grew following the issuing of his Order of the Day of May 27, 1814, in which he announced Alexander's permission for the return of the body of Prince Joseph Poniatowski[32] to Poland. Indicative of Constantine's personal popularity and the popularity of Alexander's policy was the fact that, even before Constantine arrived in Warsaw, his namesday, June 2, was celebrated there. Polish officers expressed their good wishes to Prince Lobanov-Rostovski and to Lanskoi; there was a special presentation in Constantine's honor at the Great Theater and homes and public buidings were decorated. His namesday was similarly celebrated in the provinces. There was also a great deal of interest in Constantine's personal activities. His travels between Paris, Berlin, St. Petersburg and Vienna were noted in the Polish press, and his arrival in Warsaw was impatiently awaited. When Constantine finally arrived in Warsaw on October 26, 1814, he was warmly and festively greeted.[33]

Some time earlier, the newly organized Polish Corps had returned to Warsaw under the leadership of Generals Dabrowski and Krasinski. Now that Constantine too had arrived in Warsaw, the Corps' executive committee, the War Committee, could begin its work. Constantine, as its president, called the first meeting on October 27. At this time, as was the case from the beginning, the Polish generals on the committee considered their work only preliminary, since the fate of Poland and the Polish Army were still to be decided at the Vienna Congress. At this time, Constantine accepted their position.[34]

Constantine threw himself energetically into his new work, but not much was accomplished, because within just a few weeks he was again called to Vienna. He remained until the latter part of November and then, upon his return to Warsaw, made a most disturbing request of the War Committee. Even though at this time he had no further specific information about the status of Poland, he asked for an immediate and full reorganization of the army and the promise of the committee's total commitment to Alexander in case of war.[35]

The committee responded to Constantine's request in three letters. Although expressing loyalty and gratitude to Alexander, the committee refused an immediate reorganization of the army for the reasons that the Polish Army had not yet been officially freed from its oath to the King of Saxony and more importantly, because the Polish Army could not regularly exist and reorganize until the Polish state had been constitutionally re-established. At best, they said, the committee could support confederation, and that, only if there was an actual threat of war.[36]

Constantine's reaction to their letters was both harsh and demanding. In his letter of December 3 to the committee, he assured it that favorable results were to be expected in Vienna, and he called upon the committee to begin immediately its work of reorganization. Indeed, the deliberations of the Congress might be long and there was a possibility of a rupture among the Allies. Suggesting that their slowness and unwillingness to reorganize was hampering the Emperor's efforts on their behalf, Constantine finally asked what their reaction would be if someone else would offer them what Alexander was promising.[37]

Constantine's response revealed considerable disparity in views among not only the generals in the committee, but also in the ranks of the Army. At this time many Polish soldiers expressed their opposition to the formation of a Polish Army created to serve Russian interests and, in letters to their generals Zajaczek and Dabrowski, they declared that "although we are in his [Alexander's]' power, only the fatherland has the right to our blood. If [Alexander] guarantees our fatherland we will die for it and our great protector . . ., otherwise [we] rather remain prisoners. . ."[38]

Reflecting the difference of opinion among the members of the committee was the report of December 4, sent in answer to Constantine's demands. A minority of the committee including Generals Kniaziewicz, Woyczynski and its secretary, Paszkowski, held the opinion that the committee did not possess the necessary authority to reorganize the Army fully. The majority, Generals Sulkowski, Wielhorski, Sierawski, Dabrowski and Zajaczek, declared their trust in Alexander and agreed to support Alexander's and Constantine's request for reorganization.[39] Soon after the minority resigned, and in their place Prince Genroyc was named to the committee.[40]

Constantine now had a free hand to make ready the Army in case of need, and soon three brigade divisions of infantry, two divisions of cavalry, two regiments of guards, and a corps of artillery and engineering were formed. All together, about twenty thousand Poles were placed under arms. At the same time forts were repaired and the general staff, the quartermaster corps, and the military tribunal were organized. Thus, despite initial tensions Constantine brought the Poles over to his brother's point of view and began the reconstruction of a Polish army which would support Russia. Whatever bad feeling Constantine generated at this time among the Poles because of crudely put demands or lapses into temperamental behavior notwithstanding, nothing was permitted to mar the hopes created by Alexander's promises; besides, it was expected that Constantine would not remain long in the position of chief of the Polish Army.

In June, 1815, Alexander himself finally came to Warsaw and, amid great celebrations, triumphantly proclaimed the Kingdom of Poland. At this time Alexander also named those chosen to make up the Provisional Government of the Kingdom. With the exception of Czartoryski, who replaced the Prussian Columb, they were the same officials who made up the Provisional High Council set up in March, 1813. The major responsibilities of the Provisional Government, as delegated by Alexander, included organizing the ministries and supervising the writing of the Kingdom's constitution.

Even before the end of the Vienna Congress, Alexander had approved Czartoryski's constitutional draft, and now the Provisional Government was to supervise its eleboration in final form. Largely due to the initiative of Czartoryski, the government made considerable progress with regard to the constitution in every area but one, the military. Here, a problem arose because earlier it had been decided to separate military matters from civilian ones, and Constantine and the War Committee had been given control over these. Yet, from the beginning of their dealings, it became apparent that civilian and military matters were so closely bound together that cooperation was imperative, especially when considering the question of finances. The government was very concerned with the Kingdom's precarious financial situation and was determined to cut expenses to the very lowest level possible. Constantine, on the other hand, was concerned with making available to his Army as much money as possible. The majority of the government, including the Russians Lanskoi and Novosiltsev, agreed that it was necessary to put military affairs under the Provisional Government by forming a ministry of war, which, like every other ministry, would be responsible to the government. Open to the idea of a compromise with Constantine, the Provisional Government indicated its willingness to give special consideration to the financial needs of the Army if Constantine would accept the formation of a regular ministry of war. But Constantine emphatically rejected this offer, and soon the dispute over the creation of the War Ministry and its finances became overshadowed by a larger problem, that of Constantine himself.

Actually, at this time, the government had still not yet felt the total financial pressure of Constantine's demands because a great deal of the money for the Army was still coming from St. Petersburg in the form of a loan. Nevertheless, it was clear that eventually the burden would have to be assumed, and hence the government's determination to have a say in army spending. In the course of the discussions Constantine showed himself to be intractable, and the government began

to see the difficulty of its predicament, given Constantine's position
and personality. Because Alexander ordered the reorganization of the
Polish Army prior to and independent of the government, and because
Alexander had named Constantine Acting Head of that Army, Constantine's position of authority in military matters *vis-a-vis* the government was unassailable. Further, by virtue of the fact that he, as brother
of the tsar, was so highly placed, the government found it nearly
impossible to reject his demands or even disagree. To make matters
worse, Constantine, feeling the frustrations of opposition, as well as
the belief that Alexander's plan with regard to Poland now had Allied
support, made little effort to control his temperamental outbrusts,
further alienating many, both civilians and military with his erratic
and arbitrary behavior.[41]

Already in July, 1815, Czartoryski felt compelled to inform Alexander of the situation. He wrote that Constantine stood in the way
of realizing their mutual wishes and

> that all would go well if one circumstance did not disturb the new order.
> That is the separate power of the army, with which the government cannot
> fight. . . He nourishes hatred for the country which is growing in an alarm-
> ing manner and has no respect for either the army or the population. . .
> He mocks the constitution, scoffs at laws and regulations, and after words
> comes deeds. He does not even observe his own military rules and wants
> to rule the army with a truncheon. Many officers are talking about resigning
> from the Army, desertion is increasing. All are gaining the impression
> that a 'plan' exists to destroy and frustrate the goodness of the Emperor.[42]

In another letter, seconded by Novosiltsev, Czartoryski claimed that
"no enemy could harm the Kingdom more," and that "if it was
necessary that Constantine remain in the Kingdom let him be no more
than its head, but not administrtor and judge as well."[43] But
Czartoryski and Novosiltsev were not alone in this plea, many in the
Kingdom, Poles and Russians alike, hoped for at least this, if not actual
recall.

It was rumored that Alexander would soon be coming to Warsaw,
but in the meantime the government continued to find it impossible
to control Constantine and limit his influence beyond the Army.
Typical of Constantine's interference in civilian and judicial matters,
as well as military matters, was his concern with soldiers on unlimited
furlough. Such reserve soldiers did not fall under his jurisdiction

according to law, yet he wanted to place them there. In protest, General Joseph Chlopicki[44] resigned and many in the Army began to desert. At the same time he insisted that the civilian authorities of Warsaw, including the president of the city, report to him personally.[45] When finally in November Alexander returned to Warsaw he was sincerely and happily greeted by the population and especially by the Army and the government officials, who looked to him for relief from Constantine's interference. On November 27 Alexander proclaimed the constitution and named those who were to hold the highest positions in the new permanent government.

The new constitution or Constitutional Law was elaborated in eleven chapters and one hundred and sixty-five articles.[46] In it, the new Kingdom of Poland was designated a constitutional hereditary monarchy in "perpetual union" with Russia through the person of the King who was also Tsar of Russia. The foreign policy of the Kingdom was to be "in common with the Tsardom" and the interests of the country were to be represented in St. Petersburg by the Kingdom's secretary of state.

The constitution specified a division of power among the executive, legislative and judicial branches, but, in fact, the executive power was to become dominant as it was the power of the King. Alexander, as King, reserved for himself full executive power and considerable authority in the legislative sphere. He alone could initiate legislation and had an absolute veto over the resolutions of the *Sejm,* the Kingdom's bicameral legislature. He had the right to call and dissolve it, and he could, without the participation of the *Sejm,* add to the constitution and decide those matters not specifically designated to the *Sejm.* To the King belonged the right of nominating all the highest officials, senators, marshals, marshals of the local or lesser *Sejms* and communes, bishops and higher clerics. The courts handed down their decisions, in the name of the king, and he had the right of pardon.

Decisions, statutes and orders of the King, however, had to be countersigned by the proper minister. In light of the fact that the King would only infrequently be in Warsaw, he was to appoint a governor general with wide powers to draft laws and decide matters under the prerogative of the king. A Council of State (*Rada Stanu*) was established and governmental functions were to be fulfilled by the Administrative Council (*Rada Administracyjna*) composed of the heads of the ministries under the presidency of the King or the governor general. There were to be five ministries: a ministry of religious affairs and public enlightenment, a ministry of justice, a ministry of interior and police, a ministry of revenue and treasury, and a ministry of war.

The *Sejm* was to be made up of a Senate and a Chamber of Deputies. Senators were named for life, while deputies were elected by "lesser *Sejms*" and local communes. Seventy-seven of the total 132 representatives were of the *szlachta*, the remaining fifty-five were not of the *szlachta*. Rules governing elections to the "lesser *Sejms*" and communes were such that the *szlachta* chose its representatives at the "lesser *Sejms*" and the rest of the citizenry at the meetings of the communes. The right to vote was based on property and education.[47] The *Sejm* was to gather every two years for thirty days. It could deliberate only on matters specifically designated by the constitution. Such matters included civil and criminal law, administrative law, and if the King desired, it could also take up questions dealing with the size of the budget, the level of taxation, and the number to be conscripted into the army.

Twenty-four articles in a section titled General Guarantees, dealt with the rights of the citizen such as the right to use Polish as the official language, freedom of religious beliefs, and freedom of the press. It was specified that only Poles or naturalized citizens could hold governmental positions.

Articles 9, 10, 153-156 entrusted the defense of the country to its own armed forces, which were to consist of an active army and a militia (which was never organized), that never were to be used outside of Europe.

In some ways, the constitution of the Kingdom was more liberal than the previous constitution of the Duchy of Warsaw and was nearly the most liberal constitution in existence in Europe. For example, in France only eighty thousand persons had the right to vote, while in the Polish Kingdom, with a considerably smaller population, there were around a hundred thousand enfranchised voters. Still, the constitution was so structured as to represent the interests of the higher classes. It was, not surprisingly, accepted enthusiastically by the *szlachta* who also believed that the Kingdom would soon come to include the former lands held by Poland in the east.

Their enthusiasm, however, was ill-founded; for the prospects of maintaining the limited autonomy of their Kingdom and expanding it were practically nil. The new constitutional Polish state of three million had become bound with a semi-feudal, absolutist Russia of forty-five million people. In this union, the preponderance of power was to be on the side of Russia and the Russian ruling circles. Thus, from the beginning, the Kingdom was subject to the influence and pressures of the Russian Empire, and in every sphere the possibility of greater Russian influence was openly established. Consequently, the constitution was violated almost from the time of its promulgation.[48] Setting the precedent was Alexander himself, who chose as commissar of the Council of State his trusted confidant, the Russian Novosiltsev, despite the constitutional ban prohibiting foreigners from the Kingdom's governmental service. Other high officials appointed by Alexander included Ignace Sobolewski as secretary of state, Thaddeus Matuszewicz as minister of the treasury, Thaddeus Mostowski as minister of the interior, Stanislas Potocki (1752-1821) as minister of culture and religion, Thomas Wawrzecki as minister of justice, and Michael Wielhorski (1759-1817) as minister of war.

Despite a general disappointment that most of the appointed officials were hold-overs from the Provisional Government, the greatest disillusionment regarding Alexander's selections concerned his failure to name Thaddeus Kosciuszko Chief of the Polish Army. Instead, Constantine was confirmed in that position permanently, and, to make matters even worse, Alexander, in naming him commander in chief of the Polish Army, specifically granted him complete control over "all that belonged to the military."[49] The difficulties of harmonizing such a wide and vague grant of power with the provisions of the constitution would soon become apparent.

It is not completely clear why Alexander decided to retain the rather unpopular Constantine as Chief of the Army, rather than nominate the Polish hero, Kosciuszko, given the Tsar's publicly expressed sentiments about the Kingdom and Kosciuszko himself. Perhaps Alexander wanted to keep Constantine away from St. Petersburg because of the bad impression he had created and the enemies he had made there. Also, perhaps Alexander thought that Constantine, as a possible heir to the throne, might profit from a stay in Poland to become accustomed to the idea of constitutional rule, something which at least at that time Alexander had in mind for Russia.[50] There is also the possibility that Alexander "considered his brother's presence there would make the existence of the Polish state more palatable to the Russians."[51]

As disappointing as Constantine's appointment was, this was not to be the end of the Poles' frustrations. Although at this time Alexander did not name his governor general, no one doubted that Czartoryski would be chosen for this high office. And so, when Joseph Zajaczek (1753-1826), was named governor general in 1815 even the most moderate and pro-Russian elements among the *szlachta* were shocked. Zajaczek, a one time French-style Jacobin and Napoleonic officer, became in his later years reactionary and extremely ambitious. At the time of his appointment he was somewhat physically infirm and was reputed to be of weak character, a likely prospect for nothing more than a rubber stamp.[52]

That Czartoryski was not appointed governor general indicated a growing estrangement between Alexander and Czartoryski. Indeed, as Czartoryski declined in Alexander's favor, Constantine and Novosiltsev seemed to gain. Perhaps this occurred because Alexander, having decided to keep Constantine in Poland and realizing that collaboration between Constantine and Czartoryski was impossible, had decided to place his confidence in Poles who could cooperate with his brother. Czartoryski, as a senator and member of the Administrative Council, at first continued to participate in affairs of state, but before long stopped attending Council meetings in protest of Constantine's and Novosiltsev's actions and began to devote himself only to social, cultural and educational matters as curator of the University of Wilno. Nevertheless, during the years 1816-1821, he felt it his duty to protest, and in a number of his letters to Alexander there are denunciations of Constantine's arbitrary acts and cruel behavior, as well as examples of failures of the government subject to him.[53]

The concession that Alexander made to Czartoryski (and, ironically, to the Provisional Government and Novosiltsev as well) was his decision to incorporate in the statutes of the constitution their pleas for the establishment of a responsible ministry of war on equal footing with the other ministries. However, it also seems that in order to mitigate Constantine's anger at this decision, Alexander also gave Constantine the power completely to control the army as well as to name the minister of war. No one, not even Constantine, anticipated difficulties so soon resulting from such an imprecise delimitation of power. Yet trouble did occur, despite the fact that Constantine took the greatest care in choosing a minister of war.

His choice was Michael Wielhorski, a veteran officer and a member of the War Commission of which Constantine was president. At that time Constantine came to know him quite well and was impressed by Wielhorski's strong sense of order and discipline. Wielhorski was considered to be of medium intelligence, honest and patriotic, although his health was poor. For Constantine's purposes, he seemed not a bad choice; yet, because Constantine underestimated Wielhorski's sense of patriotism and responsibility, a conflict between the two developed only a few days after Wielhorski's appointment.

Each felt justified in holding and fighting for his point of view because each could point to a different but conflicting decree of Alexander's. Immediately after Wielhorski's selection, the Administrative Council requested from him, as minister of war and member of the Council, a report as to the organization of his ministry. The same day, in a written order, Constantine forbade Wielhorski to present any such report or make any statements at the Council meetings on matters dealing with the army without prior permission and instructions from headquarters because "the organization of the War Ministry belongs to him alone as commander in chief and that his own project for such organization will be sent by him directly to the Tsar and King in Petersburg and that [he would] not permit the minister to present any other project to the administration."[54]

For Constantine the matter was simple, as he stated in a letter to Zajaczek. Alexander had given him complete control over the Army, and, more importantly, had expressed "that military authority was a branch absolutely separate, distinct and independent from all other administrative branches of the government;" consequently, he alone had control over military matters and the Administrative Council's obligation was to deal directly with him.[55]

The situation for Wielhorski, on the contrary, proved to be a real dilemma, and in good faith he wrote to Constantine hoping for an answer. In explaining his problem to Constantine he wrote:

In three weeks I am to present the Council with a plan for the organization of the War Commission... and on the other hand I am informed that you forbid that such a project be presented and passed by the Administrative Council.

Chapter IV of the constitution, Article Seventy-Six states the execution of the laws is entrusted to the various branches of the public administration, among them the War Ministry. They form an integral part of the government; that is, the governor general in the Administrative Council has the right to order ministries and its presiding minister does not have the right to refuse obedience. On the other hand, because you have written instructions, it appears that I am unable to act against your will. As a result, I find myself in a most painful position for a public official because I do not know where my highest authority is. You, because of your high dignity, for you are in a very high position, are unable to understand to what danger you expose your subordinates. The constitution after all is sacred and was given to us by a monarch so well loved and adored by his new subjects, and so must have meaning and must be respected. Every Pole sees in it relief from an unhappy past and the promise of future success and general happiness. Transgressing it would be considered in the eyes of all as a real and unforgiveable crime for which a punishment is expressly stated in Article Eighty-Two of the constitution.[56]

In other words, any representative would accuse me of violating the constitution and could call me before the Highest Court which, in only considering the constitution, could not accept as my explanation an order from you. Such then would be my reward for thirty years of service and a blameless reputation won at the cost of my blood. . .

I dare to appeal to the justice of Your Highness. Deign to help me out of the dilemma in which I have found myself.

The only way out would be if Your Highness would give me a document of orders with regard to the following points: 1) Must I hold explicitly to the articles of the constitution or to the organic laws derived from it? 2) Are the minister and the Ministry of War an integral part of the government and subject to its orders or do they form a separate branch dependent upon Your Highness? 3) What are the bounds of my power, that is, what are the areas about which I can decide and give an opinion in the Administrative Council without further instructions?[57]

This letter to Constantine was ignored and Wielhorski was simply informed impersonally (by Constantine's Order of the Day of January 11, 1816) that he was to conform to those instructions already sent to him, that is, "the principle that the Ministry of War is completely separate from the government and that its presiding minister is only the representative of general headquarters in its dealings with the Administrative Council."[58] Evidently Constantine assumed that Wielhorski, as a good soldier used to obedience, would accept his view and the matter would be closed. But he was mistaken; for the next day after receiving Constantine's Order of the Day, Wielhorski proposed a project dealing with the organization and inspection of the Army that had come directly from Army headquarters. At the same time he announced to the Council that this project issued from Constantine and not the Ministry of War and therefore, he as minister considered this plan unconstitutional and refused to sign it.

Czartoryski, who at this time still participated in the meetings of the Administrative Council, joined Wielhorski in denouncing this project and told Zajaczek and all the ministers present that, "this is the first step, the first test in the attempt to violate the constitution, if it succeeds, subsequently article after article will be violated, the constitution will lose all its meaning, its entire strength and will be a dead letter. Thus during this first attempt, the first step, although with proper respect, there must be opposition."[59] During the course of this meeting, Zajaczek was summoned by Constantine and in a short while returned greatly upset and confused, evidently as a result of Constantine's great anger. Zajaczek now refused to hear any further resolutions saying, "Enough of this anarchy. . . it betrayed us, we must once and for all learn to obey and fulfill orders. What is a law, what is this country. Nothing. What has this country done for me? I faithfully execute orders and if a project is presented that the Grand Duke wants, I sign it and confirm it." In this fashion the session ended.[60]

The same day Constantine left for St. Petersburg. Among other things, while there he intended to obtain the authority from Alexander to remove Wielhorski from his position. His intention was clear because in departing, he did not entrust his command to Wielhorski but in his absence placed the Army under Zajaczek. Wielhorski had little hope that Constantine would describe the situation in a light favorable to him and so wrote to Alexander directly. In describing the significance of the matter in terms of the future development of the country, Wielhorski explained how Constantine was attempting to upset the constitutional system. He argued that despite the need for cooperation between the civilian and military branches, Constantine hindered such cooperation. Further, not only did Constantine lack knowledge of the country and its customs, he refused to listen to any advice from the ministers and acted against the best interests of the country. Finally, he pleaded with Alexander to delimit precisely the spheres of power between the commander in chief of the Army and the minister of war. He stated that if this was not accomplished, "there is no need for a minister but a secretary in the commander in chief's office would do, and then the constitution will only be a fiction, a child's toy which everyone could change and violate according to his fancy."[61]

Wielhorski's letter seems to have made some impression, for Alexander asked Wielhorski to stay on in the position, despite his difficulties in working with Constantine. Yet, because he did not wish to antagonize Constantine, he did not withdraw Constantine's unlimited grant of power with regard to the military. And so it was only a matter of time before trouble would again erupt, and it did as early as March and April, 1816. At the time, again out of frustration Wielhorski began to express his desire to resign; he said he felt he must protest in some way Constantine's excessive interference in ministry affairs and his army policies, which were driving a number of Polish soldiers to desertion and a few to suicide. The final straw, which provoked Wielhorski's letter of resignation of April 20, was Constantine's order that the government and not the army pay for some forage that Alexander had already specified should be paid out of army funds.

In his letter of resignation to Alexander, Wielhorski very precisely explained his reasons for resigning; he claimed that

The Grand Duke follows the first ideas that come into his head and gives out arbitrary orders, not bothering about whether they can be executed or if they are compatible or incompatible with the public interest. Perhaps I am upset too easily, but I admit that I am fearful that in departing from the constitution and [following] only the will of the Grand Duke, who a thousand times has repeated that he does not understand either constitutionalism or liberalism and [that] the only obligation he recognizes is blind obedience or higher commands — one must be ready to sink into oblivion from where enemies will salvage our existence only so that we become a Russian province.[62]

This letter was intercepted by Constantine on its way to St. Petersburg and then returned to Wielhorski. It was sent again, this time secretly to the Kingdom's Secretary of State, Ignace Sobolewski, who was serving in St. Petersburg.[63] Sobolewski speedily presented it to Alexander, and seeing the impossibility of the situation, Alexander granted Wielhorski's request for resignation in mid-May.[64] The significance of Alexander's action was enormous; by supporting Constantine he not only permitted the loss of a man dedicated to the welfare of the Kingdom and the inviolability of the constitution, but he also made it clear that Constantine was unquestioned head of the military with supra-constitutional powers. With this incident, it was already clear to some, particularly Constantine, that Alexander had granted him extraordinary power in the Kingdom; it was only a question of how and in which way he would choose to apply it.

The first and most immediate matter was to avoid any further mistake in the appointment of a minister of war. Chosen was General Maurice Hauke (1779-1830), Flemish by birth and a long time soldier, having served commendably under both Kosciuszko and Dabrowski. As minister, he proved to be an honest and intelligent administrator, with an appreciation for perfection in detail and discipline. Although knowing well the needs of the Army in his adopted country, he was indifferent to political matters and looked to Constantine in every matter, great or small. So this time Constantine did choose correctly; in Hauke he found a man who would behave as he desired, giving him total service and subordination.

From the Protocols of the Administrative Council it is apparent that under Hauke the functions of the War Ministry drastically changed. During Wielhorski's ministry the Administrative Council took under consideration major military matters, while under Hauke even discussion of such matters ceased.[65]

During all the years of his service, 1816-1830, Hauke was praised and rewarded by Constantine and Tsars Alexander and Nicholas, but in the eyes of his contemporaries he was regarded as little better than a traitor. He was killed during the early days of the revolution.[66]

Chapter III

THE GRAND DUKE AND THE POLISH ARMY,
1815-1820

By naming Constantine commander in chief, Alexander made him head of not one, but two armies in the Kingdom. In addition to the newly established Polish Army, Constantine was to have supreme authority over all Russian troops stationed in the Kingdom. According to the Protocols of the Administrative Council of February 6, 1816, there were, at that time, over thirty thousand Russian soldiers in the Kingdom. This number increased in 1819 when Russian troops forming part of the occupation force in France were stationed in the Kingdom.[1]

The presence of these troops in the Kingdom, however, was not meant to be only a reminder of Russian occupation. Rather, at least for Alexander, they were part of a plan to bring about a firmer union between Poland and Russia. Viewing the army as a key institution, Alexander hoped that the presence of Russian army units and their interaction with the Polish Army would lead to their peaceful integration. A united Polish-Russian Army would then become another major support for the union of the two states.[2]

A policy aimed at the integration of the two armies, nevertheless, was a dangerous one. To Alexander it might have been a plan for a mutually beneficial merger of equals; however, to others it was regarded as a means of eliminating the Polish Army and simply incorporating the Polish soldier into the Russian military system. Aware of this other point of view, Alexander made clear his continued support for the existence of the Polish Army, although he made no secret of his eventual intention of integrating the two armies.[3]

To achieve that eventual union Alexander charged Constantine with a definite policy which included three major recommendations. First, there was to be greater standardization and association in the two armies; secondly, efforts were to be made to weaken the Polish Army's relationship to the Kingdom and to tie it more closely with the person of the Tsar-King; and thirdly, the Polish Army's independence and size were to be limited.[4]

As could be expected, this policy met with considerable hostility from government and military groups. However, the only opinion that counted was that of the person who was to enact this policy. This, of course, was Constantine, yet soon he too, for largely personal reasons, came to oppose the policy, particularly the last two points.

In pursuance of the first goal, that of greater standardization, as early as November, 1815, Constantine had proclaimed in an order of the day that the "Tsar and King wishes all rules applicable in the Russian Army be applicable to the Polish Army." Concretely this meant that not only Russian military regulations, but also Russian penalties, such as corporal punishment, which up to this time was unknown in the Polish Army, were to become operative. Further, Russian models of administration and accounting, Russian arms and equipment and even Russian music were introduced into the Polish Army.[5]

In the matter of arms and equipment, standardization was rather easy to achieve. From the very beginning, the basic source of supplies for the Polish Army was Russia; industry of a military nature and arms factories were all but non-existent during the fifteen years of the Kingdom, due to a Russian ban on such manufacturing.[6] Only standardization in uniforms was more difficult to realize, due to the fact that the Kingdom's constitution provided for distinct Polish uniforms. Nevertheless, Constantine managed to evade this provision by dressing his Polish soldiers in a uniform so similar to the Russian one that in maneuvers they were practically indistinguishable.[7]

The intermingling of Russian and Polish troops, also greatly encouraged, began to take place at all levels. So many Russian soldiers were assigned to the ranks of the Polish Army that already in 1815, the first rule book of the Polish Army was published in Russian as well as the Polish language. The same was true also among the officers, for it was the practice to appoint Russian Army officers to high positions in the Polish Army. Among others, including Constantine himself, one might note General Kouruta, Constantine's chief of staff and second in command, and Generals Gendre, Lewicky, and Ross. Russian instructors were brought into train the Polish Army and if Constantine became in any way dissatisfied with a Polish officer, he was immediately replaced by a Russian one.

As a result of the first recommendation, a basis was laid for a union of the two armies; yet for a number of reasons it was never achieved. Old hard-feelings, differences in long-standing traditions, and Polish rancor over new military conditions generally separated them, despite the fact that in certain areas there was understanding and cooperation.[8] Secondly, and more importantly, Constantine himself, in time, came to stand in the way of such a union. Although not adverse to the russification of his Polish troops, he came to oppose any attempts to terminate the separate existence of the Polish Army. Reasons for this will be considered in detail later.

The second recommendation, that which had as its goal the weakening of the Polish Army's attachment to the Kingdom and the strengthening of its loyalty to the Tsar-King, was generally little emphasized during the early years of the Kingdom when Alexander was personally popular and many Poles were optimistic about the Polish tie with Russia.

However after 1825, when conditions in the Kingdom had changed radically and the much less popular Nicholas I had become tsar, this recommendation did become a matter of major concern to Constantine. By that time it had become associated with a larger question as to who possessed real authority in the Kingdom. Consequently, Constantine opposed it in the strongest possible way.

Similarly, in the matter of the third recommendation, that which aimed at limiting the independence and size of the Polish Army, Constantine at first had no objections. Because Constantine believed that the Kingdom would soon be incorporated directly into the Empire and that the Polish Army was only a temporary creation to pacify the Poles, its independence *vis-a-vis* the tsar and its size was of little concern to him, as long as all arrangements were satisfactory to Alexander. Later, when Constantine developed sharply different views about the Polish Kingdom and the role of its Army, he came to resent all restrictions placed on the Army other than those of his own making. Unfortunately, for him, however, his opposition came too late. Such was the case, for example, in the matter of the size of the Army. At first Alexander provided for the formation of a Polish Army to number around twenty-nine thousand men. Try as he would, Constantine was never able to increase the size of the Polish Army appreciably, despite the fact that there was a large pool of available men in the Kingdom. Furthermore, the militia and reserves provided for by the constitution was never organized.[9]

From its inception, Constantine took extreme interest in the Polish Army. For the first time he had a command in which he could survey

every detail if he chose, and he did so choose! He hoped to please
Alexander by producing a perfectly trained army, one that would conform in every respect to their much cherished military ideals. In this
Constantine was successful.[10] Appearances and reality, as far as the
Polish Army was concerned, were two different matters. After the
Napoleonic Wars and the introduction of mass armies and new military
forms, there had been a reaction in favor of old eighteenth-century
military ways. Many armies stagnated, and this was true of Constantine's Polish Army. Ever a strong partisan of the old Prussian military
style, harsh discipline, and fanatical paradomania, he had only hostility
for the freer military traditions of the Poles and the liberal developments of the Napoleonic period. From the start he strove to eliminate
these from the Polish Army. Constantine's hostility was particularly
directed at the officer corps, whose members he personally disliked
and believed responsible for improper sentiments within the ranks.
Such distinguished generals as Dabrowski, Chlopicki, Sierawski, and
Krasinski were forced to resign, along with several thousand lesser
officers and soldiers.[11]

Constantine had his own ideas about the military which left no room
for disagreement. For him,

> the military state, which by its honorable vocation has a right to such just
> praise, is particularly called to give an example of good order and sub-
> mission to existing laws and rules, to protect the weak and oppressed,
> to defend the inhabitant against all unjust aggression and to live peaceably
> with him, not only in the country and in time of peace, but also abroad
> in time of war...[12]

The ideals most often called to the attention of the Army were obedience and submission. These were immediately impressed upon
recruits, whom according to one of his cadet officers Ignace
Komorowski, Constantine set about turning into "a group of mario-
nettes," with a perfect exterior and the most precise of movements."
This was because he was "afraid of any mental development or association with progressive or thinking elements among them and to forestall this he overloaded them with maneuvers and drill." Because
Constantine concentrated only on the externals and the appearance
and physical needs of his Army, particularly during the early years
of his command, he gained no understanding of the psychological
makeup of his officers and men.

Constantine was determined to "impress Europe" with the perfection of his military reviews, even though this was often accomplished at the cost of the health of his soldiers. Normally, maneuvers, drills and parades took place for long hours and in all kinds of weather. According to Komorowski, "even when the temperature was eighteen below centigrade, an inaccurate thermometer was given Constantine so that he would not have to miss his beloved parades on the Saxon Square. For almost fifteen years daily parades took place there, each of which was a traumatic experience for the soldiers due to their fear of evoking Constantine's displeasure and perhaps violent reaction since he regarded them as the chief gauge of his army's worth.[13]

Also detrimental to the health of the men were the uniforms. Constantine selected the tightest fitting of uniforms, so uncomfortable that soldiers often fainted and became physically incapacitated from wearing them.[14] They had, however, the merit of looking well while worn on parade. Constantine often complained to the Poles, as he had to Russians, that he was against war because it "ruined a soldier, impaired discipline and dirtied uniforms."[15]

With Constantine order and cleanliness were almost a fetish. Uniforms, equipment, and buildings were reflections of his scrupulosity, looking almost as if they were never used. However, as much as Constantine paid minute attention to cleanliness and order, this concern was only typical of his overall concern with everything that had to do with the army. Constantine's interest and industry directed toward the Army were indeed remarkable. He himself, in contrast to his earlier years, became known as a hard working man with simple tastes. With the exception of his specially imported Cuban cigars, for which the Administrative Council was periodically billed, and his residing in several Warsaw palaces, Constantine favored the rigorous life of a soldier.[16] Every morning he awoke at 4 a.m. He usually outfitted himself in military dress and even at balls wore an *uhlan* uniform so that he could wear boots, rather than shoes, which he hated.[17]

Little interested him beyond military administration, and so he burdened himself with every matter, small and great, that concerned his Army. For example, he personally supervised the diet of the Army, often stopping in the kitchens and tasting what was near at hand. Even though vodka was included in the military rations, Constantine, who did not drink and could not stand drunkenness, became furious if he observed anyone under the influence of his rations.[18] He personally involved himself with matters as diverse as minor repairs, permissions for marriage, pensions for widows; in fact, it seems everything

that required making a decision. And, this continued for the entire
fifteen year period he was commander in chief.[19]

Major matters, such as finances, recruiting, military education, and
military justice, however, absorbed the greatest part of his time. Until
1817, the Russian treasury financed the needs of the Polish Army
and so he had no voice in determining the sums to be allotted. However, once funds were allocated, Constantine took control over the
manner in which they were to be spent in the Kingdom. In 1817 it
was learned to the Poles' dismay, that these funds, over sixty-six
million *zloty* were only a loan to the Kingdom for the expenses of
the Army and as such were added to the amount owed to Russia.
Despite this, though the Kingdom alone was required to bear the financial burden of supporting both the Polish and Russian Armies in
Poland, Constantine continued to make equally heavy demands of its
treasury. As a result, official army expenditures equalled half of the
total budget of the state. In actual fact even more was spent on the
Army. For, once Constantine had found assured support from
Zajaczek and Hauke, it was a simple matter to disregard the budget
and divert funds from civilian appropriations to the Army. Constantine continued to press for funds he considered adequate, and in the
period 1817 to 1822 the official military budget increased from 20.7
million to 30.7 million *zloty*. Only in 1822, when the Kingdom was
experiencing an extremely serious financial crisis, was the new
Minister of the Treasury, Prince Xavier Drucki-Lubecki (1778-1845)
able to check the expanding military budget and to convince Constantine that there had to be a reasonable limit to his demands.[20]

With regard to recruitment, Constantine authorized seven conscrip-
tions totaling around 38,400 men. The lists were sent to him and he
inspected them for irregularities and punished those responsible for
infractions.[21] At this time it was accepted practice that anyone wealthy
enough who did not want to serve could buy a substitute. Constantine revoked this practice, demanding that the *szlachta* serve in his
Army. Only a few categories among the populace were permitted to
have automatic exemptions, teachers, priests, and Jews, each of whom
had to pay a yearly tax of seven hundred *zloty*. Handicraft workers
and artisans, formerly automatically exempted, now were deferred
only on an individual basis.

The entire conscription procedure was extremely complicated from
the standpoint of regulations; yet it proved workable. This was due,
in the final analysis, to the fact that conscription was determined by
Constantine alone and not by local draft boards working within the
framework of conscription law. For example, in an effort to please

Constantine, local draft boards simply sent all recruits to Warsaw, including a large surplus of men, so that he could select those he wanted. Constantine also decided the exact number of recruits at a particular period and their length of service.[22]

Given his strong interest in military education, already in July, 1815, Constantine had made provisions for a school for infantry and cavalry cadets in Warsaw. He often visited this school, appointed the instructors and selected the students. He knew all the cadets by name and favored many of them, believing that they would make possible the kind of army he wanted.[23] During most of the period, the course of studies was extremely undemanding. Dissatisfaction among the cadets set in early and the commandant of the school, Paszkowski, recommended to Constantine that the cadets be occupied with serious studies and not simply drills. Constantine ignored this advice and dismissed Paszkowski. Only in 1824 did Constantine take more seriously the recommendations. At that time he permitted the introduction of foreign languages into the Cadet School. In 1828 some courses in mathematics, strategy and drawing were organized. No really basic reforms were decided upon by Constantine until November, 1830. These changes were short-lived, for the revolution broke out only a few days later.

The Cadet School provided for the education of so many officers that it would have taken an army of a hundred thousand, not an army of twenty-nine thousand, to accommodate them all. As a result, promotions were slow and became another source of dissatisfaction among the cadets.

In addition to the Cadet School in Warsaw, there were several others established later elsewhere in the country for other branches of the Army. In general, all of the schools were limited by the same restrictions. Deprived of even minimal academic opportunities, forbidden many personal and cultural contacts such as the theater and subjected to constant surveillance, the new officer corps developed serious intellectual shortcomings, with tendencies to dissipation and rebellion. The main advantages of a career as an officer at this time were the favorable material conditions and the expectation of a good pension and civilian position upon retirement, provided that one remained in Constantine's favor.[24]

As for education in the ranks, it was practically non-existent. Constantine encouraged and demanded perfection in drill and general military bearing and gave a free hand to those instructors who would achieve it. From the performance of the infantry, cavalry and artillery in the Russo-Polish War of 1830-31, it was clear that Polish instructors like Trebicki of the artillery, Turno of the cavalry and Hauke of the artillery did even more; they actually turned out good soldiers. But when efforts were made to expand military training beyond a few narrow areas, Constantine accused his more progressive officers of frivolity, or worse still, Jacobinism.[25]

As already noted, military discipline and particularly its enforcement were of primary concern to Constantine. To this end, he established a secret military police and scrupulously controlled military courts and punishments.

Along with the Army, Constantine's other major interest was the secret police. In his secret military police, a separate branch of the regular secret police, Constantine's two major interests merged. His agents came from every rank in the army and at their head was the Chief of the Cavalry, Alexander Rozniecki. Constantine was by nature extremely curious and so the main task of the secret military police was to inform him about everything that went on in the army. His information was so thorough and so rapidly received that often Constantine knew what was happening in a particular company or regiment sooner than its own officers. The only shortcoming of the system was that in time some of Constantine's spies came to be paid by various army companies not to inform. Consequently, only at the beginning were the police able to gather much information from freely speaking soldiers. Afterward, as the soldiers became more closemouthed, the police were not able to gather more than general information about the management of companies, the quality of discipline and so on.[26]

Nevertheless, Constantine obtained considerable information on the ideas and performance of his Army and particularly his officer corps through spying activities. But the price was high; the very existence and general effectiveness of the secret police had a demoralizing effect on the entire Army, and an atmosphere of suspicion and hostility, particularly toward Constantine, was created.[27]

Constantine's interest and powers were also to be felt in the military courts. The military code adopted by the Duchy of Warsaw's army had been an extremely severe one and was badly in need of revision. Although the severity of this code was somewhat mitigated after 1815, Constantine opposed and prevented any planned, fundamental reform. As was becoming apparent with other laws of the kingdom, Constantine also disregarded military law. Most disturbing, however, was that Constantine refused to allow the courts to act impartially. For him, the courts were to be an expression of his will, and whenever a higher authority accused someone, his judgement was that the accused had to be guilty. The role of the courts, therefore, was not to decide innocence or guilt, but rather to legalize a penalty. In the majority of cases, Constantine actually considered the release of an accused prisoner as a personal affront. He did not hesitate to put direct pressure on the courts and in a number of court cases Constantine's interference was notorious.[28]

Justice of this sort, unregulated by law, to say the least, was often based on Constantine's mood of the day. As Wielhorski reported in 1816, "it was practically a rule that when the Grand Duke was in a bad mood he punished violently and ruthlessly the smallest mistake, but on the next day when he was in a good mood, he closed his eyes to the biggest."

To make matters worse, Constantine was a perfectionist. His displeasure at even the slightest infraction, such as a missing button on a uniform, could result in a very severe, if not brutal punishment. Corporal punishment was the most frequent form of punishment, often inflicted even on officers. Group punishments, due to infractions by a few, were common, and included such punishments as standing for long periods in freezing weather. Officers were punished for the errors or misbehavior of their subordinates and, depending upon Constantine's mood, subordinates might decide their officer's penalty. Aside from corporal punishment, imprisonment at hard labor was the usual penalty. However, Constantine was not adverse to the infliction of unusual punishments such as the forced feeding of salted herring which caused an unrelieved thirst.[29] Constantine was known to dislike the death penalty; usually he commuted death sentences to long periods of hard labor and semi- starvation in chains.[30] As a result of such harsh and often arbitrary punishments, as well as the general rigor of life and poor medical care in Constantine's army, there were many premature retirements, desertions, cases of mental illness, crippling and a high death rate.

The most extreme and a rather frequent form of protest for the regular soldier was desertion, and during the entire period it was a particularly alarming problem for Constantine.[31] For officers, the one honorable protest was suicide, and in the first four years at least forty-nine such acts were reported to have occurred. Although the situation by 1825 had somewhat improved, suicides continued to be frequent.[32]

As the brother of Alexander, Constantine was received at the beginning with considerable enthusiasm in the Kingdom. But, within a few months, as already noted, resentment and hostility toward him had developed to such an extent that many Poles, including Czartoryski, were pleading for his recall. Nowhere was this feeling more intense

than in the Army, which particularly felt the effects of his personality and power. It is true that Constantine was less disliked by the
ordinary soldier than by the officer corps, and during certain periods
he was even slightly popular among them because of his preferential
treatment toward them. Following his father's methods of binding
the regular soldiers to him and not to their officers, Constantine did
not hesitate to humiliate officers before their subordinates, penalize
them with greater severity, and give them generally less attention as
a group than he gave to the ordinary soldiers.[33]

As for the officers, particularly during the early years, there was
no ambivalence in their feelings. They hated Constantine personally
as a temperamental and arbitrary tyrant who had a mania for out-
moded military and disciplinary forms. Those who could escape his
service did so. The rest either smoldered or learned to accept his ways.

This was made easier after 1819 for several reasons, and for at least
a few years afterward a relatively comfortable truce and some degree
of cooperation began to exist between Constantine and the Army.
First, by 1819, the composition of the Army, particularly the officer
class had largely changed. Most of the older, rebellious officers with
their Napoleonic traditions and dreams of a total Polish restoration
had left the Army, to be replaced by a new somewhat more pliable
corps of officers trained by Constantine. It appears that prior to 1819
Constantine hated the freer Polish and Napoleonic military traditions
even more than the constitution and once they were eliminated from
his Army he could allow himself the luxury of a more benevolent
attitude toward his Polish subordinates.

Secondly, after 1819 Constantine's general attitude and behavior
toward the Poles changed. As he showed himself to be less brutal,
arbitrary and provocative, opposition to Constantine in the Army considerably diminished. Even during the best of times, of course, there
was dissatisfaction; but it was at a controllable level and largely due
to usual military problems such as slow promotion, boredom and low
pay.

Thus, although Constantine's initial years as commander in chief
of the Polish Army were replete with serious tensions and hostilities
which left behind a residue of ill-will toward him, by 1819 conditions, in fact, had begun to change. Had not the rising tide of liberalism
and revolution again shaken Europe toward the later part of the 1820's
and had it not drawn into its sweep many idealistic Polish officers,
the improved working relationship established between Constantine
and his Army after 1819 might well have continued beyond 1830.
As it was, many Polish officers, although only vaguely dissatisfied,

nevertheless, could not feel any great loyalty to their Russian commander in chief, who despite his conciliatory efforts and even gradual polonization, could not compete with the hopeless dream of unfettered and complete Polish independence.

Chapter IV

CONSTANTINE, ALEXANDER I AND THE CONGRESS KINGDOM, 1820-1822

Despite their affection for one another, and Constantine's tremendous loyalty to Alexander, their views differed on many matters. One concerned the question of Poland. While over the course of the years their views did change, they still never agreed on the question. Still, in the end they reached a compromise that was mutually acceptable.

In 1815, Alexander regarded the establishment of a constitutional Polish Kingdom as at least the partial fulfillment of his dream for Poland. Even though at this time, because of Russian opposition,[1] he was unable to join together the former Polish territories, the so-called Eastern Provinces incorporated into the Russian Empire with the Kingdom, he nevertheless gave hope and promises to the Poles that this would soon be accomplished.[2] Given Alexander's amazingly pro-Polish policy, which even admitted the restoration of territory to the Poles largely inhabited by Byelorussians and Ukrainians, it is difficult to imagine why Alexander placed Constantine in power in the Kingdom, while excluding Czartoryski who originated and shared his dream of a united, constitutionally governed Poland. Moreover, Alexander knew well that Constantine was unpopular in the Kingdom,[3] and that he opposed the Kingdom's very existence, yet he still gave Constantine free rein in Poland.[4] This *carte blanche*, given in 1818, was only a preliminary verbal grant of power, yet it was this rather than his appointment as commander in chief of the Polish Army, which became the real basis of Constantine's position in the Kingdom.

Likewise, in 1815 Alexander appointed Novosiltsev as his personal commissioner to the Kingdom, a position not specified in the constitution yet having significant if somewhat undefined powers. Long after Novosiltsev's pseudo- liberal pose had been exposed and he had become known as a "lazy, riotous and always broke [sic] intriguer who skillfully aroused the Tsar's distrust of the Poles, of Poland and of liberalism and played upon the muddleheadedness and despotic inclinations of Constantine," Alexander permitted him to remain in power.[5]

As commissioner, Novosiltsev had entry into all areas of the government. He was permitted to participate in its administration and sent secret reports to Tsars Alexander and Nicholas; even Constantine was subject to his surveillance.[6]

Too, because Novosiltsev shared Constantine's conservative outlook, he was eventually appointed to several important posts related to the cultural and educational repression of the Poles. The Grand Duke successively named him president of the Committee for the Reorganization of Education in the Kingdom (1821), overseer of censorship (1822), and curator of the Wilno educational district (1824).

However, during the entire fifteen year period Constantine and Novosiltsev were required to work together, no friendship developed between them. At first it was simply a matter of personal antipathy; later they came to oppose one another because of differing policies toward the Kingdom. Novosiltsev had always hated the idea of a separate Polish Kingdom and strove to magnify even the slightest shortcoming or opposition on the part of the Poles in the eyes of Alexander. Constantine, on the other hand, in time came to support a form of Polish autonomy and tried to defend the Poles before the Tsar against Novosiltsev's exaggerated charges. In turn, he was also forced to defend himself against Novosiltsev.[7] But during the early years, when Constantine and Novosiltsev still shared the same view on Poland, Novosiltsev had a free hand to undermine the position of the most competent Polish officials and, in collaboration with Constantine, saw to it that most of the higher positions were filled with ineffective personnel more to his liking.[8] And, as the Poles increasingly came to feel the force of his immense power and provocative behavior, he, even more than Constantine, came to symbolize reactionary tsarist terror and anti-Polish persecution portrayed so often in Polish Romantic literature, e.g. Adam Mickiewicz's *Dziady*.

Alexander caused great disappointment by his appointments in the Kingdom; yet few, if any, believed that he lacked commitment to the policy of continued Polish autonomy and eventual reunion of formerly Polish territories. Still, by 1822, this had happened; Alexander had come to doubt the value of his Polish policy and was willing to accept another solution for what had become for him a troublesome problem. Yet as Alexander's views on Poland were drastically changing,

Constantine, the same Constantine who could never fathom Alexander's liberal ideas on Poland and never really bothered to get along with the Poles, came to favor a continuation of the Polish Kingdom.

Two questions, therefore, arise; first, why did Alexander become disenchanted with his Polish policy; and secondly, why did Constantine reverse his position and become an advocate of the Kingdom's separate existence? In looking for the reasons for Alexander's disenchantment, two stand out. They were connected with, first, a political crisis in the Kingdom, and second an economic crisis. Both, in a very real sense, were provoked by Alexander; yet the fact that they developed were reason enough for the Tsar to lessen and finally end his commitment to the Kingdom.

The first problem originated because the already well developed and growing liberal and national feeling of the Poles, together with the nascent organizations representing such views, were subjected to a policy of repression, which in turn fostered opposition to Alexander and his policies and ultimately led to a political crisis. Paradoxically enough, it was Alexander himself who was largely to blame for the explosion of this liberal and patriotic feeling among the Poles, a sentiment he later came to despise. For years, the Tsar had sought to persuade others that he was committed to "free institutions," constitutional government and other liberal ideas. Similarly, for years, Alexander, in messages to the *Sejm*, in public speeches and private conversations had championed the cause of a free, united Poland and encouraged the Poles to seek the realization of the freedoms of which he so often spoke.[9] Not surprisingly, the Poles had come to expect not only the fulfillment of the promises of the constitution, e.g. promises of personal freedom, freedom of speech and the press, ministerial responsiblity, but they also believed that the shortcomings of the system, as well as troublesome individuals, such as Constantine and Novosiltsev, would be eliminated. In general, there was great hope that the Kingdom would be a truly liberal, constitutional one, and this hope all centered in Alexander, both the Russians' and the Poles' "Angel."

Alexander's change of heart with regard to liberalism, in fact, did not occur overnight. It proceeded over a period of several years and was particularly manifest in Poland. As he retreated from his earlier liberal views, Alexander increasingly paid greater attention to the urgings of Constantine and Novosiltsev to limit the Poles. As they began to impose their repressive measures against the Poles, the first signs of Polish opposition appeared. Still, at the time of the first meeting of the *Sejm* in 1818, despite a lack of harmony on issues such as the very severe penal code and the imposition of preventive censorship, a certain harmony and good feeling was seen to exist between Alexander and the Poles. The Tsar expressed his general satisfaction with the Kingdom, and again he made allusions to extending the boundaries of the Kingdom. He also hinted at this time that a constitution for Russia herself would soon be promulgated.[10]

The first sign that Alexander had been converted to an anti-liberal policy in the Kingdom came when he sanctioned the imposition of censorship on periodical literature in July, 1819.[11] Soon after, he permitted the violation of other constitutionally guaranteed freedoms. This included greater restrictions on freedom of the press (now all literature was subject to censorship), limitations on freedom of association, and the establishment of at least three separate organizations of secret police. One of these was responsible to the Russian Ministry of the Interior, the second to Novosiltsev, and the third to Constantine. Each had its own agents and they strove not only to spy on and control the population; but, interestingly enough, reported on one another as well.[12]

Polish opposition to the violation of their constitutional freedoms took several forms, one of which was the development of a real parliamentary opposition to the reactionary measures sanctioned by Alexander in the *Sejm*. Another was the growth of secret societies.

Parliamentary opposition first appeared at the meetings of the second *Sejm*, held in 1820. This opposition generally represented the interests of the upper agricultural and business groups and in time developed a new political and social ideological basis for its views. It had grown more and more alarmed at the increased repressiveness of the regime and began to call for the defense of the constitution. Since many representatives of this opposition came from the province of Kalisz, they became known as the "Kalisz Party."

The organizers and leaders of this part of the parliamentary opposition were the brothers Vincent and Bonaventure Niemojowski, with Vincent evolving into the group's theoretician. Influenced by French parliamentary liberals, Vincent Niemojowski based the party's perspective mainly on the ideas of Benjamin Constant. Specifically, the Kalisz Party called for the defense of the existing constitutional monarchical system of the Kingdom and for the preservation of personal freedoms. There was no thought of breaking the Kingdom's tie with Russia.

The atmosphere of the *Sejm* of 1820 was much different from that of 1818. With the session dominated by the Kalisz Party, Alexander became furious with the course of events. On leaving Warsaw, he ordered Constantine to take stronger repressive measures.[13] Soon after, the elections of the Niemojowski brothers to the Kalisz "lesser *Sejm*" were invalidated and the Kalisz "lesser *Sejm*" was itself abolished. Thereafter, the *Sejm*, though constitutionally required to gather every two years, did not meet until 1825.

When the *Sejm* was finally permitted to convene in 1825, an "additional article" to the consitution was announced. Henceforth, meetings of the *Sejm* were to be closed to the public and elected *Sejm* members known to represent anti-government views were not allowed to attend the meetings. As a result, opposition in the *Sejm* was extinguished and every government project was accepted.[14]

In addition to the appearance of the Kalisz Party, there was other parliamentary opposition of various political shades such as that of Jan Olrych Szaniecki. But none were able to influence tsarist policy. They did, however, represent a change in the thinking of the majority of the conservative *szlachta* and provided a voice of criticism against the reactionary regime supported by the Tsar. Perhaps the main lesson of the failure of the Kalisz Party in its shaping of Polish revolutionary thinking was to show the futility of legal parliamentary opposition.[15]

Constantine's reaction and attitude toward the Kalisz Party is of special interest in showing the growing difficulty of his position in Poland. He met several times with the Niemojowski brothers and tried to convince them of the futility of their course. Although there was no doubt that Constantine had not the slightest sympathy for their liberal ideas,[16] he nevertheless wanted to prevent them from coming to the attention of Alexander. When this proved impossible, Constantine, interestingly enough, attempted to defend the Poles from charges of "liberal corruption" by creating the impression that all opposition was concentrated in the Kalisz Party, while the rest, the greatest majority, of "the noble Poles," as he put it, remained loyal and grateful to Alexander.[17]

A second source of opposition to the government's repressive policy came from secret organizations. Long before 1815, liberal secret societies were popular among certain groups of educated and highly placed Poles and the same was true among Russians. One such organization was the Masons, which even included Alexander among its membership while Constantine also joined to please his brother. By 1815, however, many other secret organizations existed in the Kingdom besides the Masons. Each represented somewhat different interests, but all shared a liberal orientation on matters of education, culture, and particularly, Poland's destiny. As such, they all believed that their major task was to contribute to the maintenance of the continuity of the Polish nation, despite its partition. This was to be done by establishing and maintaining contacts between Poles in the divided provinces and undertaking educational and literary work which would help form Polish public opinion. Yet at this time, it should be noted that there were no expressions of a revolutionary nature which would call for a disruption of the union with Russian and an armed uprising.

This changed, however, in 1822. At that time, a law was promulgated by the government which forbade membership in any secret organization. This in turn, provoked the existing secret societies onto a new course and actually stimulated the formation of new groups with revolutionary aims.[18] As a rule, these secret organizations flourished most among students and army officers. Already, in 1817, only a year after the University of Warsaw was established, a secret organization of students had been formed there.

In 1820, another and more significant student organization was founded at the University of Warsaw called the Union of Free Poles (*Zwiazek Wolnych Polakow*). It included in its membership the Polish historian, Maurice Mochnacki, and in organizational form it was similar to Masonry with various lodges including one at the School of Mining in Kielce and another at the University of Krakow. The union also made contacts with many high school students throughout the country. In order to gain adherents for its program of "fighting tyranny to restore partitioned Poland," it published and freely circulated its publication the *Dekada Polska* until Constantine ordered its suspension.[19] The *Dekada Polska* propagated the ideas of equality and freedom, gave information on European revolutionary developments, and pointed out shortcomings in the Kingdom. Given its activities, the days of the Union of Free Poles were numbered. Already at the end of 1820, the organization's contacts with high school students at Kalisz were uncovered and Constantine ordered an immediate investigation, in cooperation with the Austrian and Prussian police. The investigation quickly uncovered all the lodges and brought the arrest of all of the Union's members.[20]

Another center of student activity was at the Polish university at Wilno. Under the influence of a few liberal *szlachta* elements in Lithuania, already in 1817 a small group of students including Adam Mickiewicz,[21] and Thomas Zan,[22] founded the Society of Philomaths (*Towarzystwo Filomatow*). Although at first this secret group's aim was only mutual educational help, it soon too became interested in political problems. But by 1823, the activities of the Philomaths and all its supporting organizations were suspended, Constantine, having been informed of their existence, sent Novosiltsev to Wilno to investigate. The results of his investigation included the liquidation of the organization and the sentencing of ten of the leading Philomaths to either imprisonment or Russian exile. Mickiewicz himself was banished to Russia. In addition, a number of sympathetic professors of the university were dismissed, including the political activist and historian Joachim Lelewel. Many of the incriminated students of the secondary schools were sentenced to hard labor or ordered into the army.[23]

Aside from these and other secret student organizations, there was a number of secret organizations among groups of army officers. The most significant of such organizations was National Freemasonry (*Wolnomularstwo Narodowe*), founded by Major Valerian Lukasinski. Lukasinski was a veteran soldier, whose service went back to the Napoleonic wars. Of a liberal cast of mind already in 1809, he had joined the Masons and dreamed of a united Poland. At first encouraged by Alexander's liberalism, like many others he joined Constantine's army and hoped that through his efforts in the army he would help in the reconstruction of the country.

By 1817, Polish Masonry, with thirty-two lodges and four thousand members, was beginning to lose its character as a liberal organization and was becoming an unofficial, elite organization of the ruling groups. As late as 1815, Masonry was still approved of by Alexander, who believed that it would contribute to Russian-Polish cooperation, provided of course, that many higher Russian officers and officials would join. They did, but so did many secret agents, including a number of Constantine's men. Thereafter, a losing battle ensued between the still liberal Polish elements and the Russian conservative elements. From 1817 until the organization's abolition in 1822, the Polish movement was rent by factionalism.

Becoming disgusted with regular Masonry, Lukasinski in 1819 formed his own organization - National Freemasonry. Although similar to Masonry in terms of structure, its program was quite distinct from the ever more conservative program of the Masons of the Kingdom and those found in Russia itself.

Lukasinski's program developed in stages. Its general aim was the unification of all Polish lands, but at the beginning there was no concrete plan of action. National Freemasonry did not even deny that this could not be achieved under the scepter of Alexander. But, as repression increased, the organization began to call for full independence from Russia. Ideologically, the organization harbored two different views; one represented a liberal, though less democratic

position, and the other represented a more democratic cast and favored
the immediate total enfranchisement of the peasant. Initially, the
organization had considerable success and soon formed lodges in Warsaw, Kalisz and Poznan. But it was not long before Constantine's
secret police had learned of its existence and had informed Constantine about it. Constantine immediately ordered Lukasinski to disband
the organization. Anxious to eliminate undesirable elements which
had infiltrated the society, Lukasinski quickly complied, only to
reorganize with a more carefully selected membership and a new name
— the National Patriotic Society (*Narodowe Towarzystwo
Patriotyczne*).

Again Lukasinski's society grew quickly, particularly in the Army.
However, in 1822, during efforts to expand its membership among
the townspeople of Warsaw, it was uncovered by Constantine's police
who arrested Lukasinski and a number of others. After a long investigation lasting two years, during which time Lukasinski was imprisoned, a military trial was held that was blatantly staged by Constantine. As a result, Lukasinski was sentenced to nine years of hard labor.
He was not freed after nine years, however; for after the November
Revolution, Constantine in leaving Warsaw, took Lukasinski with him
to Russia. Altogether Lukasinski spent forty-five years in prison.[24]

Constantine personally was very much shaken by the Lukasinski
case. He, for one, never regarded Lukasinski as a patriot who had
founded a secret organization striving for Polish unification and the
protection of constitutional rights. Rather, Lukasinski, as an officer
in his Army, was nothing less than a traitor to him personally and
to the Army. To Constantine, Lukasinski's crime was serious enough
to warrant imprisonment for at least twenty years, and not nine years
as was the original sentence. According to Lukasinski, however, what
really disturbed Constantine was the possibility that the matter would
be brought to Alexander's attention. Lukasinski felt that Constantine
feared this more than anything because Constantine was convinced
that Alexander could never forgive such treachery and would turn
even more against the Kingdom. Undoubtedly, too, Constantine
believed that the entire episode would reflect unfavorably upon him
and his management of the Army. The severity of Lukasinski's treatment was one way for Constantine to protect himself from his brother's
wrath.[25]

Despite Lukasinski's arrest and imprisonment, his organization did
not collapse. However, its leadership fell to more conservative
elements headed by Colonel Severyn Krzyzanowski and its contact
with the Polish townspeople and with Russian revolutionists were

broken. Moreover, the idea of revolution for Poland was pushed into the far distant future.

In addition to Lukasinski's National Patriotic Society, there were also other secret organizations in the Army. One of the most active of these, in the Lithuanian Corps, had a membership including both Poles and Russians and was called the Comrades in Arms Association (*Stowarzyszenie Przyjaciol Wojskowych*).

As more and more reports of secret organizations came to Alexander, as parliamentary opposition grew more vocal and indignant and as public opinion turned from nearly unanimous praise of Alexander and his policies,[26] the Tsar came to believe that a real political crisis had developed in the Kingdom. In this he was of course correct. But Alexander was most mistaken in his assessment of the reasons for the crisis. It appears that Alexander never considered that he might be at least partly responsible for the state of affairs, although he himself had provoked the Poles by encouraging them in their demands for autonomy and constitutional government, while then permitting their promised freedoms to be violated by reactionary, incompetent and unsympathetic ministers. Rather, for Alexander, the Poles had become ungrateful subjects who should now be punished for their unreasonable demands by the loss of their autonomy. In a letter written in 1821, the Kingdom's Secretary of State, Sobolewski, expressed Alexander's exact views on the matter. Alexander made clear in this statement that he doubted that the Kingdom had the necessary assets of a political and civil nature to exist as an autonomous entity.[27]

The second major consideration which contributed to Alexander's disenchantment with the Poles was the chronic financial plight of the Kingdom which culminated in a real economic crisis in 1822.[28] Again, Alexander did not seem to take into account that he was largely responsible for this crisis. Although it was not his fault that the country had been impoverished by the preceding years of war, he had permitted men like Novosiltsev to interfere in the economic affairs of the Kingdom. The minister of finance originally appointed by Alexander was Thaddeus Matuszewicz. He was not at all a bad choice, and he interested himself enough in the Kingdom's financial problems to work out a plan of financial reform. But Novosiltsev without justification found Matuszewicz's plan unacceptable, and had him removed. In his place was appointed his sycophant, the incompetent Weglenski.[29] Further, although the budget was to be subject to the approval of the *Sejm*, Alexander never insisted that Constantine and Novosiltsev present it to that body. By 1820, according to the assessment of the

Treasury Commission, the Kingdom was on the verge of bankruptcy. Fortunately, during the latter months of 1821, a Pole of much financial acumen, Prince Xavier Drucki-Lubecki (1778-1846), presented himself to Alexander personally and succeeded in winning appointment as minister of finance despite Constantine's and Novosiltsev's strong objections.[30] During the succeeding years, as a result of a very sensible economic policy and an ingratiating personality, Drucki-Lubecki was not only able to maintain the confidence of Alexander, but also was able to find favor with his successor, Nicholas. Most importantly, he worked out an arrangement with Constantine, and so in this way he remained in the position of minister of finance from 1821 until 1830. Nevertheless, during the years of Drucki-Lubecki's ministry, both his plan of economic reform and his method of enacting it were subject to continuous criticism, not the least of which came from Constantine. All in all, however, Drucki-Lubecki's policy was so successful that by 1830, the treasury of the Kingdom had a surplus of thirty-four million *zloty*.[31]

Constantine and Drucki-Lubecki personally had no liking for one another. Moreover, Drucki-Lubecki further alienated the Grand Duke by restricting Constantine's military expenditures to those already appropriated in the budget. The fact that Constantine tolerated this move, and for that matter endured what he considered to be Drucki-Lubecki's high-handed manner, may indicate that the two men did share the same overriding objective, the maintenance of the Kingdom's autonomy, despite their many differences.[32]

It was thus Constantine and Drucki-Lubecki who stood in the way of the annexation of the Kingdom into the Empire and the ending of Alexander's constitutional experiment of his younger and more liberal days. Yet it still must be explained why Constantine, formerly such an opponent of Polish autonomy, came to be its chief support. It certainly was not due to any change of opinion among Russians influential with Constantine. In fact, at this time, many Russians formerly favorable to the idea of Polish autonomy now turned against it, undoubtedly following Alexander's lead.[33]

There are several reasons which may have contributed to the evolution of Constantine as the new and staunch supporter of the Kingdom's autonomy, but two stand out. They are first, Constantine's growing sense of identification with the Poles, and secondly his desire to transform the Kingdom into his own personal domain and base of power.

With the exception of a few short trips to Russia and abroad, Constantine remained and lived in Poland after 1815. During these years

he came into continual contact with the Poles and learned Polish as
well as Russian. At first, welcomed into Polish society with open arms,
he soon lost his popularity by his rather crude ways, temperamental
outbursts and ill treatment of subordinates. However, he was not
actually ostracized until he tried to introduce his mistress, Madame
Frederichs, into Polish society.[34] From that time on, Constantine felt
free to visit relatively few homes, and most of these belonged to those
officials dependent upon him, such as Governor General Zajaczek.
While at a ball at Zajaczek's Constantine met Joanna Grudzinska
(1799-1831), who became his second wife. It appears that he was
immediately taken with her and again began to try to obtain permission for a divorce from his first wife whom he had not seen for many
years.

Grudzinska was clearly attractive but was most praised by contemporaries for her goodness and intelligence. She subsequently came
to have a decisive influence over her husband and although never
intruding directly into political matters, she significantly changed his
attitude toward the Poles and helped temper his violent outbursts.[35]

There were no children resulting from their ten year marriage.
However, they raised Constantine's and his longtime mistress Madame
Frederichs' illegitimate son, Paul Alexandrovich. Despite the Imperial
Family's initial opposition to Constantine's divorce and remarriage,
it soon came to accept Grudzinska. Alexander, in his admiration,
described her "as an angel by character" and granted her on July
20, 1820, the title "Princess of Lowicz" and several large estates.[36]
The Empress Mother, Maria Fedorovna also developed an affection
for Grudzinska; she gave her many presents and left her in her will
a diamond diadem with the inscription, "for my beautiful daughter."[37]

Grudzinska was equally liked and admired by the people of Warsaw who knew her well.[38] She was particularly noted for her kindness to the poor.[39] Constantine, himself, often publicly praised her
and in a letter to La Harpe, written in 1826, he said: "To my wife
I owe my happiness and tranquility."[40]

The change that took place in Constantine became apparent very
soon after his marriage to Grudzinska. Most obvious were that his
outbursts of anger became less frequent and violent and his behavior
became less arbitrary; consequently, his relations with his subordinates
and particularly with the army improved a great deal.[41] Similarly,
his manners improved and this together with the social contacts of
Grudzinska's family made possible the opening of many Polish doors
formerly closed to him. Most importantly, due to the influence of
his wife, he came to feel so comfortable in the Polish *milieu* that he

began to consider himself a Pole, rather than a Russian. According to one report, Constantine was to have said: "In my heart I am a Pole, completely a Pole!"[42]

However, before all of this transpired, Constantine had considerable difficulty in winning permission for a divorce from his first wife so that he could marry Grudzinska. Years earlier, his request for a divorce had been denied and now again the Empress Mother and his sister, Maria Pavlovna, opposed any consideration of a divorce for fear of further scandal linked with Constantine's name. Yet, despite their opposition, in time, first Alexander and then Nicholas came to favor Constantine's request.

It was true that Grudzinska made a particularly good impression upon Alexander; nevertheless, it is clear that this was not the only consideration involved in Alexander's decision to grant permission for the marriage. Rather, Alexander saw in Constantine's request an opportunity for resolving his and Russia's great problem, the imperial succession.

The question of succession was a matter of great concern because the aging Alexander had no sons to succeed him. This made Constantine, as second son of Paul I, heir apparent to the throne. But the matter was further complicated by the fact that although there was never any doubt of Constantine's legal right to succeed Alexander, there was great concern as to whether Constantine had either the desire or the competence to rule. Already as a young man, Constantine himself had declared that he would never want to be tsar. And, when later Alexander grew older and began to speak of resigning, Constantine continued to insist that he could never rule and be tsar to his much loved and admired brother.[43]

As well known as Constantine's lack of desire to be tsar was the popular opinion that he personally was unsuited to rule the enormous Empire.[44] While still living in Russia, Constantine was never as popular as his brother Alexander; he was also never known for his intellect or self-control. He was even frequently compared by Russians with his mentally unbalanced father. Furthermore, during his years spent in Poland, he did nothing to try to improve his relations with the very Russians he had most antagonized. Instead, in his infrequent visits to St. Petersburg and Moscow, he further alienated them by criticizing the Russian government for its protection of mystical trends after 1815 and by unfavorably comparing the Russian Army with the Polish Army.[45] Perhaps it is also true that though many years had passed, Constantine never forgot the circumstances of his father's death. One Polish historian notes that he "hated the Muscovites, blamed them and

wanted revenge'' for his father's death. Unfortunately, by this attitude he incurred the hostility of not just a few individuals, but of a
whole group, "a large Moscow party which conspired against him."[46]

The first rather veiled references to a possible renunciation of Constantine's rights to the throne occurred as early as 1817. They began
to take more definite shape in 1819 after the birth of Constantine's
nephew. Nicholas' son and the future Alexander II. This birth was
especially significant because now only Nicholas had a legal successor
to himself; Alexander still had no sons and Constantine only one
illegitimate son who was thus ineligible for succession. And so from
1819, many began to expect Constantine to renounce his rights
assuming that Nicholas would be Alexander's successor. In the end,
Constantine did renounce his rights in favor of Nicholas. However,
several years of difficult and often inconclusive negotiations were
required to reach this final agreement.

The first such negotiations took place in the fall of 1819. At that
time Alexander was in Warsaw and proposed an arrangement to
Constantine. In return for granting him permission to marry
Grudzinska, Constantine was to renounce all rights to the Russian
throne for any children resulting from this new marriage. Constantine
accepted Alexander's proposition in writing and in this way Alexander
guaranteed the throne for Nicholas' son while Constantine won
approval for his marriage, which took place in May, 1820.[47]

Constantine's own right to the throne, however, remained intact
and only in several private talks between the two brothers during the
next few years was the matter finally resolved.[48] In Wilno, in May,
1822, Constantine and Alexander finally reached a written and spoken
agreement, one which remained secret, however, except to a few
persons until 1825. This agreement was based on two letters. The
first, Constantine's letter to Alexander of January 24, 1822, contained
Constantine's formal declaration of his decision to renounce all rights
of succession. In it, he said that he believed himself to have "neither
the spirit, nor the capacity, nor the necessary force to take on the
high dignity to which I was called by my birth; I beg that Your Imperial
Majesty immediately transfer this right to the one who succeeds me
immediately so as to ever assure the stability of the empire..."[49] The
second letter, that of February, 1822, was Alexander's response to
Constantine. In it he stated that

> I have read your letter with all the attention that it merits; I have not found
> anything there which should have surprised me, having always known

and appreciated the elevated sentiments of your heart; they have furnished
for me a new proof of your sincere attachment to the State and your far-
sighted concern for the conservation of its tranquility.[50]

For reasons still not clear, the fact that Constantine renounced the
throne was generally kept a secret and was not made public until after
the death of Alexander. Instead, the acts relevant to the abdication
were placed in sealed envelopes and deposited with the Senate, the
Holy Synod, the State Council and the Cathedral of the Assumption
in the Kremlin with the proviso that they not be opened except upon
the death of Alexander.

However well documented the fact of Constantine's resignation,
much less clear are the actual terms of the agreement of which the
resignation was only a part. Nevertheless, it appears that a much
broader agreement was struck between Alexander and Constantine.[51]
But it is only from subsequent developments, particularly the amaz-
ing and very visible increase in Constantine's personal power in the
Kingdom (which will be taken up in the next chapter), that it is possible to say that in return for his free renunciation of the Russian throne,
Constantine was given complete control of the Kingdom, as well as
full jurisdiction over the eastern provinces of Lithuania, White Russia
and the Ukraine.

The entire agreement in itself is a remarkable and curious one. For
not only did it result in a major decision on the part of Constantine,
it also meant a renunciation on the part of Alexander. By his willingness to give Constantine the power to rule over the Kingdom, a
rule which he knew would never be moderated by liberal political
principles, Alexander admitted that he had given up his dream of a
liberal Polish kingdom.

The reasons for Alexander's decision have already to an extent been
explored; loss of his liberal faith had permitted repression in the
Kingdom which in turn had stimulated crisis of a political and
economic nature. This then contributed to Alexander's loss of faith
in his Polish creation and his willingness to consider alternative solu-
tions for the Kingdom which now had become only a problem. But
at the same time Alexander was faced with crisis in the Kingdom,
he could anticipate crisis in Russia resulting from the undesirable succession of Constantine to the throne. Thus, in a real sense, the fact
that Constantine was amenable to Alexander's solution for the succession problem and at the same time presented a plausible alternative
policy for the Polish problem, could only have been a source of great

relief for Alexander. By virtue of their agreement, Alexander had also essentially freed himself from the burden of Poland, while placing it on Constantine. If, under Constantine, the Kingdom flourished, Alexander could at least be sure that it would be under a strong-handed, anti-liberal regime totally loyal to his person. If it failed, Alexander had at least resolved the problem of Russian succession while providing Constantine with the temporary satisfaction of having been ruler of the Kingdom and the Eastern Provinces. Thus, in a very real sense, the risk and burden was Constantine's. Why then was he willing to assume it? It appears that as Constantine increasingly began to feel excluded from Russian imperial circles, he came to view the Polish Kingdom as an alternative base. His disposition was strengthened by Grudzinska's influence and his growing identification with conservative Poles. Insecure in Russia, Constantine "increasingly came to want to bind himself to this nation (Poland) with whose help he could someday create for himself a measure of independence."[52] In sum, then, the final understanding reached by Alexander and Constantine in 1822 as to the future of the Polish and Russian states resulted in a state of affairs in which Alexander, in order to free Russia of Constantine, had given him a free hand in Poland.

But Alexander and Constantine, in that spring of 1822, were not alone in their feelings of optimism and a sense of achievement. Nicholas, too, was content, for most importantly, he had seen the throne secured for his son, if not for himself. And, time was in his favor for a solution to the Polish problem that would be more to his liking.

Finally, even many Poles could see in Constantine's independent rule some possiblity of better things for Poland. One interest, for example, that Constantine shared with the Poles from the beginning was the increase of his jurisdiction in the Eastern Provinces.[53] That the inhabitants of these provinces favored reunion with the Kingdom is clear from Count Paul Kiselev's report to Nicholas of March 29, 1835, in which he wrote: "In the years 1817- 1820 all minds in the Lithuanian and White Russian provinces aimed toward the rebuilding of an independent Poland in the old borders..."[54]

The first step in extending Constantine's jurisdiction in the Eastern Provinces was a relatively minor one; in 1817 Constantine was named Head of the Lithuanian Army Corps and the armies of the Kingdom and the Eastern Provinces were united under his authority. Then, in 1819, Constantine accepted the title of Governor of Lithuania and was granted all-inclusive powers by the Decree of July 11, 1819, and the Rescript of June 29, 1822.[55]

From this time onward, the authorities of these provinces were to refer all important matters in a normal administrative way not to the Tsar and the ministers in St. Petersburg, but to Constantine in Warsaw. Thus only after Constantine had considered a matter was it referred to the Russian Ministry of the Interior or the the Tsar.[56] That Constantine had completely come to support the Polish view of autonomy and reunion of the Eastern Provinces with the Kingdom, if only for his own reasons, is clear from his letter to Nicholas in 1826 in which he said:

> In the past few years of experience I have become convinced that it is not possible to pacify the souls of the inhabitants of these provinces, as well as the Polish Kingdom, in any other way than by reuniting into one body this part of old Poland... I am greatly convinced that it is better to have the Poles with us as good (Poles) rather than as bad Russians.[57]

Constantine, apparently, was not sufficiently persuasive, for his difficulties and differences with Nicholas were still to come. But at least for the time being, the Polish problem had been settled. Relations between Constantine and Alexander, always good, now were no longer even marred by differences of opinion over Poland. Alexander, at this time failing in health, had lost interest in many things including Poland. For this reason, he was now, more than ever, content to allow Constantine to deal with the Polish Kingdom as he chose.

Chapter V

GRAND DUKE CONSTANTINE PAVLOVICH: "VICEROY" OF THE POLISH KINGDOM, 1822-1825

At one time, during the earliest days of Constantine's stay in the Congress Kingdom, it might have been assumed that Constantine was interested in very little related to the Kingdom beyond military matters, for as he himself said, "I do not wish to interfere in civilian matters... a hundred times I shall give my life for the Monarch, but I shall not undertake something that I do not know."[1] Yet, from the beginning, Constantine did become interested in and chose to become involved in matters which extended far beyond strictly military affairs. However, this involvement could only have reached its eventual proportions thanks to Alexander's bestowal of certain powers on his brother.[2] It was out of affection and respect that Constantine always drew attention to the fact that he was only acting in his brother's name; yet these grants of power did make it possible for Constantine to become *de facto* ruler of the Polish Kingdom — this despite the establishment of a constitutional governmental system and Alexander's public guarantees of local self-government to Polish officials.

Two elements in particular were of growing concern to Constantine in his years in the Kingdom and came to determine the direction of his policies. The first of these concerned his desire to assure the maintenance and, if possible, the expansion of an autonomous Polish kingdom under his jurisdiction, while the second was an outgrowth of the essentially conservative and anti-liberal nature of his views on political, social, cultural and religious matters.

From 1815 onward, but especially after 1822, Constantine acted to consolidate his personal power and strengthen the anti-liberal orientation of the Kingdom's governmental policies in three ways. First, he made ineffectual or subservient the major constitutionally designated officials and institutions. Second, Constantine was able to generate considerable, if short-lived, support for himself and his conservative policies among many of the more influential individuals and groups in the Kingdom. Third, he succeeded in establishing parallel agencies to control the Kingdom's domestic and foreign affairs which reported to him personally.

In accordance with the Constitution of 1815, the most important officer in the Kingdom was the governor general, who was charged with representing the Tsar in Poland during the latter's lengthy absences from Warsaw. From April, 1818 until July, 1826, this position was filled by Joseph Zajaczek, who, ever jealous of his personal prestige and supercilious toward his countrymen, was both susceptible to Novosiltsev's influence and obedient to Constantine.[3]

After Zajaczek's death, the post of governor general remained unfilled and in accordance with Constantine's wishes the authority and powers of the governor general were transferred to the Administrative Council.[4] This body shared executive power with the governor general according to the constitution, and was made up of the representatives of the Ministries of War, Justice, Interior and Police, Religious Affairs and Public Enlightenment, and Revenue and Treasury. Each minister was constitutionally granted full power in his area of jurisdiction. Earliest to be eliminated was the first Minister of War, Joseph Wielhorski, who was replaced by the more malleable Maurice Hauke.

In the Ministry of Justice from 1815 to 1829 five ministers served with no single individual capable of achieving the confidence of the government. In the Ministry of Interior and Police, Thaddeus Mostowski was able to retain his position during the entire period of the Kingdom's existence, but this was largely due to his careful and continuous support of Constantine. His position was reinforced by his great knowledge of the country and his energetic activities in public works, which contributed much to the rebuilding of the country.[5] Nevertheless, his decisions were always subject to Constantine's review, and in certain instances even the most routine matters under his formal jurisdiction were decided by Constantine himself.[6]

As for the Ministry of Religious Affairs and Public Enlightenment, several years were to elapse before Constantine grew entirely dissatisfied with the original appointee. At first impressed by the competent Stanislas Potocki, (1752-1821),[7] Constantine permitted him to remain in office. But following the revolutionary events of 1820, particularly the revolt of the Semenovsky Guards, the relatively liberal-minded Potocki was replaced by the incompetent and reactionary illegitimate son of King Stanislas August Poniatowski, Stanislas

Grabowski (1780-1845), whose chief asset was that he was a member
of a pro-Constantine group of Polish nobles known as the Grzybow
party.[8]

The appointment of Drucki-Lubecki as minister of revenue and
treasury proved to be the one exception to Constantine's practice of
installing incompetent or subservient individuals to major executive
positions. Indeed, in realizing the wisdom of his policies, Constantine was forced even to include Drucki-Lubecki in the governmental
apparatus which he soon after formed to supersede the governmental
structure provided for by the constitution.

The lesser executive offices on the provincial and municipal level,
e.g., chief magistrates and precinct commissioners, were also of
interest to Constantine. He did not hesitate to fill them as he saw fit,
appointing and dismissing officials arbitrarily with little regard for
competency or qualifications.[9] Consequently, Constantine was at first
able to interfere in and then to control the executive branch of the
Kingdom's government.

The *Sejm*, however, as the constitutionally designated legislature,
proved to be more difficult to manage. Although in the end Constantine was able to convert it into something resembling a rubber stamp,
the *Sejm* did provide organized resistance to his seizure of power and
his frequent violations of the constitution.

At first Constantine was not particularly disturbed about the activities of the *Sejm* and even accepted election to it as a representative
of the Warsaw suburb of Praga.[10] However, he regarded the first deliberations of the *Sejm* in 1818 a "farce" and was amused that its very
existence should ruin "the appetites and sleep" of Russians in St.
Petersburg. Generally, as he expressed to his friend Michael Sipiagin,
Constantine made clear that in his opinion, the *Sejm* was harmless
and that "this devil is not so horrible as they paint him; let the oligarchs
in the capital know this..."[11] Nevertheless, Constantine was soon
forced to revise this opinion, for the liberal parliamentary opposition
made its presence felt and in the eyes of the government began propa-
gating "constitutional theories only calculated to produce mischief."[12]
To prevent further "mischief" Constantine undertook his successful
strategy to stifle all parliamentary opposition. By the middle 1820s
the *Sejm* was truly the "harmless" institution about which Constantine had written in 1818. Yet Constantine's concern with institutional
opposition was perhaps misplaced: while succeeding in silencing
parliamentary opposition, in the long run he helped create the conditions for the formation of radical and conspiratorial student and
military groups which eventually proved disastrous to his plans.[13]

Just as Constantine increasingly brought under his control the executive and legislative branches of the Kingdom's government, he also succeeded in making the regular court system a reflection of his will. Already very early in his drive to dominate the Army, Constantine made a sham of the independence of the military courts; in time the regular courts too were subject to Constantine's interference and personal interests with the notorious *Sejm* Tribunal deliberations of 1827-1828, the most disturbing example of his conduct. Further, the repercussions of his disregard for the constitution and the law caused sharply negative public reaction. Contemporaries claimed his actions contributed to a fast-growing "demoralization in the Kingdom" and that only "blind obedience to Constantine, rather than regard for the constitution or the law guaranteed success."[14]

During the same time Constantine was reducing the power of the legal, constitutionally-sanctioned government, he was also building support for his personal rule among various individuals and groups in the Kingdom. By 1822, Constantine was well aware that his position in Poland could be made more secure if he had the loyalty and cooperation of certain prominent and influential Poles. Of course, in this matter Alexander had been of considerable help to Constantine, for he had very early acted to lessen the authority of many of the pre-eminent families of the Kingdom, including the Czartoryskis, because of their dislike of Constantine. In their place Alexander showered his favors upon a less wealthy Polish nobility of more recent vintage, the Grzybow group, among whom Constantine soon won unqualified support. Among these families were the Sobolewskis, the Grabowskis, the Gutakowskis and the Grudzinskis,[15] from among whom Constantine had found his wife. Others joined their number as Constantine personally came to represent their hopes for their own advancement along with the maintenance of the Kingdom's separate existence. By 1825, in a surprising turn of developments, even Adam Czartoryski offered Constantine qualified support. Recognizing that Constantine was becoming in fact the Kingdom's strongest and most effectual defender against annexation into the Empire and was the strongest Russian proponent of reunion of the Eastern Provinces with the Kingdom,[16] Czartoryski found himself working with the Tsar's brother. With regard to the Eastern Provinces, each in his own sphere — Czartoryski in education, Constantine in government and in the Army — strove to maintain and strengthen their Polish character.[17] Hence the great paradox: for Czartoryski and for many other Poles, Constantine, a Russian little valuing the constitution of the Congress Kingdom, was becoming a major bulwark of Polish separatism and autonomy, such as it was, against the increasingly less sympathetic person of Alexander.

Support was generated for Constantine among the wealthy *szlachta* and higher clergy for other reasons as well. For example, Constantine won some popularity by never threatening and even appearing to share their sentiments about the Russian-Polish arrangement. Also winning their approval was his stance against all liberal, anti-clerical manifestations. In their opinion, a radical nationalism which called for a complete severance of the tie with Russia could never serve the best interests of Poland, and hence they undoubtedly heaved a great sigh of relief when Constantine quickly uncovered and liquidated radical organizations even suspected of such a goal.[18] Similarly, even though the masses at this time were hardly revolutionary in temperament and generally politically uneducated,[19] in the early 1820s there was an increase in the number of spontaneous risings manifesting severe economic discontent in both the town and countryside. Only Constantine, who had the support of his Army and police, had full power to quell such uprisings and he did so with a firm hand.[20]

Of particular concern to the Roman Catholic clergy were efforts on the part of segments of the liberal opposition to pass legislation in the *Sejm* aimed at limiting Church jurisdiction over marriage and education. Also disquieting were incidents of anti-clerical propaganda appearing in the short- lived liberal press and in *Sejm* speeches.

For example, the higher Church establishment backed Constantine in his dismissal of the liberal minister of religious affairs and public enlightenment, Stanislas Potocki, and further supported his struggle against the liberal parliamentary opposition.[21] In Potocki's place Constantine had appointed the reactionary Grabowski as well as the notorious Joseph K. Szaniawski (1764-1843)[22] as head of the committee of censorship. Thus, by encouraging the appointment of reactionary ministers and the suppression of liberal parliamentary opposition in order to prevent anti-clerical propaganda and legislation, conservative elements in the nobility and clergy worked with Constantine in support of his regime.

Finally, some Poles supported Constantine purely out of self-interest. Since Constantine personally filled many military and civilian positions not a few were anxious to gain his favor for an appointment. Others were often brought into line through fear of incurring his displeasure.[23]

Consequently, for a variety of reasons, Constantine was able to generate some support for his rule. Still, it was not enough to dominate the government, nor was it sufficient to gain a measure of support from influential Poles. More importantly, it was necessary for Constantine to establish his direct control over a governmental apparatus which would supersede the existing structures in the Kingdom. By the end of 1822 Constantine had done so by creating a Bureau of Internal Affairs and a Bureau of Foreign Affairs.[24] As their head, Constantine appointed the Russian Baron Paul Mohrenheim, who was also his personal secretary and the son-in-law of Mostowski. Too, Constantine made Drucki-Lubecki responsible to him in all economic matters and requested Novosiltsev to report directly to him in matters relating to cultural and intellectual development.[25] To the extent that these men used the information and personnel of the formal government's ministries, there was a measure of cooperation between these two governmental structures; however, it was soon clear that Constantine's personal "government" was the more significant force.

The decision to establish a Bureau of Internal Affairs came in August, 1822.[26] Beyond its considerable activity related to internal security, little is known about its operations. Constantine apparently believed that the several police systems already in operation were inadequate[27] and so ordered the formation of still another secret police system within the Bureau, one which became known as the Secret Chancellery of Grand Duke Constantine,[28] and reported to Constantine daily via Baron Mohrenheim or General Kouruta, Constantine's long time chief military aide. The first and most important occupation of this police agency was to spy on not only Tsar Alexander (and later Nicholas), but also on such officials as Novosiltsev, Rozniecki (head of the military police) and Drucki- Lubecki.[29] Second, it was to report on the activities of any suspicious individuals and organizations and to note anything that might possibly be of interest to Constantine. Due to the fact that Constantine was extremely curious and his police were anxious to satisfy such interests, the voluminous records[30] of Constantine's Secret Chancellery provide a rich source of information, opinions and conjectures on numerous subjects pertaining to the period. Included among the less momentous reports are even dutiful accounts of balls, plays, jokes and rumors.[31] Numerous secret agents, who in their efforts to report everything to Constantine, were known to harass ordinary citizens by prying into conversations and personal correspondence. These agents habitually went to coffeehouses and bars to pass their time eavesdropping upon conversations; they checked on those entering and leaving the city and on those who failed to register promptly enough a change in address. Another occupation of these agents was the opening and censoring of "suspicious personal mail."[32] Thus, in spite of constitutional guarantees of personal freedom, the population felt the pressures of a police state.[33]

The advantage of such a police system, even though it was not always terribly efficient, was obvious; Constantine was informed about development in the Kingdom. However, one serious problem did arise; because very little in fact was going on of a truly conspiratorial or revolutionary nature, the secret police tended to exaggerate incidents of unrest in the country and tended to create in the mind of Constantine a picture of perpetual and all-pervasive secret opposition.[34] This, of course, was perfectly agreeable to some, such as Novosiltsev, who were confirmed in their belief that the Poles were bent on revolution and had to be suppressed. Ironically, Constantine came to minimize even the more objective and conservative reports of conspiracy as he gradually sought to win added popularity in the Kingdom, this to his detriment in 1830. When the police then did inform him of trouble, Constantine ignored the information at the precise instant when an actual military conspiracy was brewing in the Polish capital, one which proved his undoing.

The decision to establish a Bureau of Foreign Affairs directly responsible to Constantine also occurred at the end of August, 1822.[35] Although subordinated to Baron Mohrenheim, General Robert Fenshaw, an English confidant of Constantine, seemed to have special authority in this agency.[36] Apparently reflecting Alexander's own desire to have Constantine informed about foreign policy matters, even those not directly affecting the Polish Kingdom, beginning in 1822, all Russian embassies, including the Russian Ministry of Foreign Affairs in St. Petersburg, were required to send all circular reports (these also included the embassies' correspondence with one another) and special reports to Constantine. The circular reports gave Constantine first-hand information on the international issues of the day; while the special reports related to problems of special concern to Constantine personally or the Polish Kingdom.[37] Included in the circular reports were descriptions and analyses of developments in Spain and Portugal, Greece, and United States, the state of Russo-Turkish relations and so on. Special reports included information about the Papacy (Constantine was opposed to the 1823 papal election of Cardinal Fesch), the Turkish problem, suspicious individuals (among others, General Dautancourt who supposedly was smuggling copies of *Le Constitutionnel*), revolution in France, and other subjects.[38]

Sending these reports were regular Russian diplomatic representatives, but occasionally a Russian secret agent attached to one of the embassies would also refer something of interest directly to

Constantine. Those regularly and most frequently reporting to Constantine, usually through a personal letter, besides Karl Nesselrode in St. Petersburg, were David Alopeus in Berlin, Christopher Lieven in London, Charles Pozzo di Borgo in Paris, Dimitrii Tatishchev in Vienna, Paul Gagarin in Rome, and secret agents Count de Chevegrois Schweitzer and Basil Kanikov in Dresden.

On at least one occasion, Constantine felt it necessary to disregard the usual diplomatic channels for foreign communications (which usually involved Mohrenheim at least informing St. Petersburg and then acting in relation to the proper foreign authorities) by personally contacting a head of government, e.g., Constantine carried on a lengthy correspondence with Metternich on the subject of secret organizations.[39]

At the time of the inauguration of the Kingdom it had been decreed that the Kingdom's foreign affairs were to be managed by the Russian Ministry of Foreign Affairs in St. Petersburg in conjunction with the Kingdom's Administrative Council. Yet, it was clear from the start that the Administrative Council was to have no voice, even an advisory one, in matters of the Kingdom's foreign affairs. Not surprisingly, this situation remained in force even after Alexander turned over full control of the foreign affairs of the Kingdom, as well as of the Eastern Provinces to Constantine. However, it appears, at least from some of the Protocols of the Administrative Council, that Constantine willingly enough kept the Council informed about foreign developments, and even on occasion asked for the opinion of the Council on a matter concerning the Kingdom, e.g., customs duties with Prussia.[40]

Having already hammered out a close working arrangement in 1821 with Drucki- Lubecki, the Kingdom's minister of finance, Constantine was able to maintain close supervision of the Kingdom's finances. In the area of intellectual and cultural affairs, Novosiltsev was placed in charge. Despite their personal dislike and distrust of one another, Novosiltsev dutifully reported to Constantine and generally cooperated with Constantine in the task of overseeing and regulating the intellectual and cultural life of the country. At the same time he continued to send special reports to Alexander (and later to Nicholas) about Constantine and developments in the Kingdom.[41] Two matters were of primary interest to them; that no pernicious (liberal) influences would exist either in the press or the theater and that students should be protected from exposure to "improper" literature and companions.

Together with the ultra-conservatives of Europe, Constantine and Novosiltsev shared the belief that the press and theater had an extremely important role to play in the formation of public opinion.

Moreover, they believed that if the press and theater were not controlled, they could be most dangerous to social stability.[42] Hence the
need for a thoroughgoing censorship.

Due to Constantine's and Novosiltsev's pressure on the Administrative Council, as of May 22, 1819, all newspapers and periodical
literature, "without exception," were subject to strict censorship.[43]
During the following six months, however, Constantine became
disturbed about the way censorship was being handled by the Administrative Council,[44] and in early 1820 he ordered Novosiltsev to take
active measures to improve the operation of censorship in the
Kingdom. Consequently, Novosiltsev directed the Administrative
Council to set up a censorship commission under Szaniawski "charged
with examining negligence."[45]

With the imposition of censorship, literary production was quickly
altered in character and diminished in circulation. Not surprisingly,
censorship greatly affected the content of various types of literature;
it generally became less interesting and demand dropped. Indeed,
among the forty-four literary and political weeklies and monthlies that
were begun during the fifteen years of the Kingdom, only eight
managed to survive; the failure of the other thirty-six publications
was due either to their suspension by the authorities or because of
loss of circulation, a problem connected with their censorship.[46]

Equally subject to censorship (and soon to be banned) was quite
a number of liberal foreign newspapers and periodicals. They included
*Le Constitutionnel, Le Miroir, Le Fondre, Le Courier Francais,
Allemeine Zeitung, Neckar-Zeitung*, and the *Morning Chronicle*.
Fearful that some publications were overlooked, in October, 1822,
Constantine wrote to Novosiltsev asking him to get a list from Count
V. P. Kouchubey of all the publications banned in Russia so that they
could similarly be banned in the Kingdom.[47]

Regarded as particularly dangerous were foreign publications
written in Polish and published in the zones of partitioned Poland under
Austrian and Prussian rule. Constantine personally followed this
Polish-language press and brought to Novosiltsev's attention objectionable articles. In this regard, Novosiltsev acted as an intermediary
in demanding, in Constantine's name, retractions and promises of
more careful censorship from local editors and censoring authorities.
One publication which particularly provoked Constantine was the
Krakow-based periodical *Krakus*. Constantine ordered Novosiltsev
to write to the Russian resident consul there to prevail upon the president of the Krakow Senate to take preventive action to more effec-
tively censor the journal. On March 2, 1822, Novosiltsev reported

back to Constantine that henceforth the *Krakus* and other Krakow publications would no longer incur "Constantine's displeasure."[48] Although "dangerous" foreign publications were banned in general, a few select individuals and institutions were permitted to receive them. Zajaczek, Constantine and the library of the Administrative Council, for example, received a number of subscriptions of various liberal publications. However, for fear that even these copies would fall into the wrong hands, they were carefully guarded. On one occasion, at least, the librarian of the library of the Administrative Council N. Kozuchowski incurred Constantine's anger and was arrested because he allegedly made available in an improper manner restricted materials, in this case the *Paris Moniteur*.[49]

Nevertheless, even though they were banned, a number of liberal publications continued to enjoy considerable popularity in the Kingdom. This was due to the fact that the most interesting publications were smuggled in and were circulated secretly.[50]

Books suffered a more drastic fate; during Novosiltsev's tenure, the book-selling trade was carefully limited to school books and innocuous French novels with no new books of any importance permitted to pass the ordeal of censorship.[51]

Of considerable interest to Constantine and Novosiltsev were the activities of several Warsaw theaters. Not only were play manuscripts subject to their approval, staging and costuming too had to meet their standards. Even regulations concerning proper audience behavior were set up.[52]

In addition to the press and theater, Constantine and Novosiltsev paid attention to the intellectual and cultural atmosphere among students. Working with the reactionary Stanislas Grabowski, Constantine and Novosiltsev attempted to regulate the academic life of the Kingdom and the Eastern Provinces.

Through Novosiltsev's initiative, a special Committee on Educational Reform (1821) was established to keep watch over the universities, professorial behavior and the content of lectures. Shortly afterward, a strict censorship was initiated over textbooks, which resulted in the banning of "objectionable" texts. One such work was Vincent and Kajetan Skrzetuski's study on ancient history which sympathetically described democracy in Athens. The study of history was particularly supervised in the hope of fostering proper civic attitudes, namely those inimical to liberalism and revolution. Concomitantly, tuition was raised in many schools to restrict education to the sons of the elite.[53]

Besides the supervisory activities of the Ministry of Religious Affairs and Public Enlightenment and the Committee on Educational Reform,

Constantine made use of several secret police and spy organizations to oversee student conduct. They too brought reports to him of student misbehavior, liberal sympathies and membership in secret organizations. Often, when such information was received by Constantine, he dispatched Novosiltsev to the trouble areas, which included Kalisz, Krakow and Wilno to investigate the matter and put an end to student dissidence.[54]

Scientific and cultural organizations, for example, the prestigious Organization of Friends of Knowledge, likewise felt the effects of Constantine's and Novosiltsev's oppressive surveillance. Unhappy with the progressive literary and artistic contributions of the organization, Constantine had the papers of its illustrious president Stanislas Staszic[55] confiscated and the publications of the organization burned.[56]

Thus, in these and other ways, Constantine and Novosiltsev attempted to purge the country of any and all "harmful intellectual influences." To a great extent they succeeded, but in the process they did serious damage to the intellectual and cultural life of the Kingdom which had shown so much promise in the period immediately following 1815.[57] Moreover, one cannot help but wonder how counter-productive were actions in these areas in stimulating political antagonisms to Constantine's rule.

And, although an inspection of the Kingdom's operation in the middle and late 1820s could give no other impression than one of Constantine's supremacy through his legal and extra-legal governmental structure, it still remains to be shown why this arrangement would prove to be of such short duration.

Chapter VI

NICHOLAS I AND THE EROSION OF CONSTANTINE'S POSITION, 1825-1830

The sudden death of Tsar Alexander I was more than a milestone in the history of Russia. It was also an event of calamitous significance to both the Polish Congress Kingdom and the personal fortunes of Grand Duke Constantine. In less than a decade after Alexander's death, conditions in the Polish Kingdom were so completely to change that a humiliated and exhausted Constantine would be forced to leave Warsaw permanently and the Congress Kingdom itself would be dissolved.

This chapter is concerned with the reasons for the ultimate and drastic reversal of Constantine's political fortunes by 1830. By 1825 he had established a delicately balanced policy based upon two factors, the support of the Tsar and that of the Poles. Yet Constantine's hopes for maintaining this policy after Alexander's death directly hinged on both Nicholas' and the Poles' willingness to continue to accept the *status quo*. This, however, was not to be the case, for after 1825 not only did Constantine lose Nicholas' support for his rule in the Kingdom, but Polish backing as well for the existing state of Russo-Polish relations. Thus, by 1830, because both Nicholas and many Poles favored a change, the question was no longer whether the Kingdom with Constantine as its head would continue, but when precisely the end would come.

Having by 1822 won Alexander's final approval for his Polish policy, there is no doubt that Constantine regarded his eldest and favorite brother as the main and continuing support for his Polish arrangement. Consequently, it is not surprising that Constantine tended to minimize the possibility of Alexander's abdication or early demise.[1] Obviously underestimating the possibility of Nicholas' accession to

the throne, Constantine neglected through the years to establish a
positive personal relationship with his much younger brother. Equally
important, not only did Constantine disregard Nicholas' known
negative feelings toward the Poles and the Polish Kingdom, he did
nothing to try to alter Nicholas' attitudes until it was too late.

In the years prior to 1825, Constantine and Nicholas did not develop
much more than a formal relationship. A seventeen year difference
in their ages and Constantine's almost continual absence from the
capital made difficult the establishment of close ties between the two
brothers. And, although Nicholas did regard his older brother with
the respect due his superior rank in the family and the state, and shared
with Alexander a certain admiration for Constantine's military accomplishments; nevertheless, Nicholas never felt the same devotion for
Constantine that he had for Alexander or his younger brother Grand
Duke Michael.[2] Further, as Nicholas reached manhood, other matters
began to strain even this formal relationship. Not the least of these
was the fact that neither approved of the other's wife. On the one
hand, ever hostile to close Russo-Prussian ties,[3] Constantine was
unenthusiastic about Nicholas' marriage to the daughter of King
Frederick William III and Queen Louise of Prussia. This antipathy
was deepened by Nicholas' increasing attachment to the Prussian
court, and particularly his father-in-law and brother-in-law, the future
King Frederick William IV.[4] On the other hand, Nicholas along with
the Russian and Prussian courts strongly objected to Constantine's
marriage to Joanna Grudzinska.[5] This disapproval, however, was
much less due to their negative views about the way Constantine con-
ducted his personal affairs than to the fact that in their eyes this
marriage reflected Constantine's growing ties with the Poles and his
increasingly pro-Polish sentiments. Influenced by a strong dose of
anti-Polish bias from childhood,[6] Nicholas simply could not fathom
Constantine's growing sympathy for the Poles and evidenced great
hostility to their supposed "turbulence and fanatical love of libertarian
ideas."[7]

But Constantine's and Nicholas' personal relationship and their differing views about the Poles would have been of little significance
if Nicholas had not become tsar. However, Nicholas did indeed
become tsar, and as such he opposed Constantine's Polish policy and
favored a return to Catherine's old aim — the direct incorporation
of the Russian-held Polish provinces into the Empire.

Setting the tone for Constantine's and Nicholas' relationship after
1825 was the matter of tsarist succession and its immediate aftermath.
Not only did the course of these events fail to improve relations

between the two brothers, they actually worsened them, and in subsequent years Constantine and Nicholas had many strained dealings.
Their disagreements could not then but redound unfavorably on the
position of Constantine and the Polish Kingdom.

In considering the matter of succession, which soon reached a crisis
state, it is most difficult to reconstruct the events themselves as well
as to assign responsibility because of fragmentary and sometimes conflicting evidence and reports. Yet, because both Constantine and
Nicholas blamed each other for what happened in the course of those
days, it is important to determine as far as possible the nature of the
events and two brothers' responsibility for the problems that ensued.
Adding to the complexity of the succession issue were the already
noticeable and strange arrangements made by Alexander and Constantine by 1822 regarding an eventual change in monarchs. For example,
it may be asked, why did Alexander choose to keep the succession
agreements secret, and why was Nicholas, if he truly was designated
successor, never given an opportunity to gain experience in government and administration as preparation for his future position?[8]

Although neither Constantine nor Nicholas cast any blame on
Alexander for what happened in December, 1825, it is clear that
Alexander's mysterious and improvident action prepared the way in
a real sense for what followed. Some have sought to explain
Alexander's course of action,[9] yet none seem to justify satisfactorily
the ambivalent position in which he left his two brothers, as well as
two nations, thanks to his failure to proclaim openly his successor.

The news of Alexander's death reached Constantine in Warsaw on
December 7, and Nicholas in St. Petersburg on December 9. Both
the reaction in Warsaw and St. Petersburg was one of confusion and
uncertainty. Each brother, in the absence of clear directives, followed
his own convictions which in the end laid open the way for the
Decembrist Revolt and left both filled with bitter, if veiled, feelings
against the other.

Indicative of the great difference of opinion about the manner in
which Constantine and Nicholas acted during the crisis is the fact that
some contend that only Constantine acted decisively and unequivocally, while others insist that it was Nicholas who behaved in the most
calm and consistent manner.[10] Yet, in surveying those critical days
and the numerous reports of both brothers' behavior, it appears
reasonably certain that neither could later completely escape criticism
for his actions.

Upon the receipt of a letter bearing the news of Alexander's death
and addressed to Constantine I, Constantine immediately wrote two

letters, one to his mother and one to Nicholas. In each was a reminder of Alexander's Imperial Rescript containing permission for Constantine to renounce the throne and designation of Nicholas as lawful successor to Alexander.[11] These letters and other papers relating to succession were then entrusted to Grand Duke Michael who was to deliver them to Nicholas.[12] Once in St. Petersburg, neither letter proved to have any effect on the course of events there.

Yet, while Constantine reaffirmed his decision never to accept the throne, curiously enough, he did not proclaim Nicholas tsar, nor demand an oath of loyalty from either the Kingdom's or Eastern Provinces' officials and troops.[13] In Warsaw, rumors throughout December assumed it to be certain that Constantine was to succeed as emperor, and that soon a deputation from the Russian Senate would be inviting the new sovereign to the capital.[14]

Upon receiving news of Alexander's death in St Petersburg, Nicholas and the chief governmental officials were faced with a problem when they sought to follow Alexander's wishes and order the opening of the packets of letters deposited by Alexander before his death with the Senate, the Holy Synod, the State Council, and the Cathedral of the Dormition in Moscow. A dispute immediately developed for Prince Dimitrii Lobanov-Rostovskii, Minister of Justice and Procurator of the Senate, refused to permit the opening of the packet arguing "the dead no longer have a last will and testament."[15] Nor was the packet opened at the Senate. At this time a leading role was played by the Military Governor of St. Petersburg, Count Nicholas Miloradovich, who ignored the existence of the packet entirely, declared himself unequivocally for the accession of Constantine, and used his considerable influence over Nicholas to have him immediately take an oath of loyalty to Constantine. Soon after, following Nicholas' example, similar oaths of loyalty were taken by the St. Petersburg garrison and city officials!

At a meeting of the State Council, however, another course of action was being followed. Prince Alexander Golitsin, undoubtedly not without an understanding with Nicholas, ordered the packet to be opened. For the time being, however, its revelation brought no results; for the packet deposited at the Cathedral of the Dormition remained sealed and the authorities of the city of Moscow garrison, following St. Petersburg, took their oath of loyalty to Constantine.[16]

Only one person at this time could perhaps have influenced Nicholas to take a firmer course of action and assert his own rights to the throne; this was the Dowager Empress who knew of Alexander's arrangements. Out of a desire to spare her suffering over Alexander's illness and death, she was not consulted.[17]

Only on December 15, did Grand Duke Michael arrive in St Petersburg with Constantine's letters reaffirming his decision not to accept the throne. Greatly disturbed by this and fearful that the nation would never accept such "family arrangements," Nicholas immediately sent a courier to Constantine telling him that the capital had already taken an oath to him and imploring him to reverse his decision. Soon after, Grand Duke Michael was also dispatched back to Constantine with a strong personal appeal from Nicholas.[18]

Just as in Warsaw, where it was generally accepted that Constantine was the new tsar, so in St. Petersburg early signs also indicated Constantine's accession. Already as early as December 22, stores were selling pictures of Tsar Constantine I.[19]

At the same time Nicholas' representatives were rushing to Warsaw, Constantine received the news that the packet opened at the State Council included the letter exposing his compromising request to renounce the throne. Included in this letter were the words: "Not finding in myself the genius, the talents, nor the force necessary to be elevated to the Sovereign dignity to which I would have the right by my birth..."[20] This breach of family secrecy was said to have so disturbed Constantine that he fell "into a fit of madness, and in the presence of several terrified witnesses, Kouruta, Fenshaw, Colonel Turno, and Adjutant Ladislas Branicki, threatened 'with froth on his lips' that the Polish Army and the Lithuanian Corps would be mobilized immediately in defense of his rights against Nicholas.'"[21]

Shortly after, Constantine received Nicholas' last desperate appeal:

It is in prostration at your feet, as brother and subject, that I implore your pardon, your blessing, dear, dear Constantine; decide my fate, command your faithful subject and count on his perfect obedience. Great God, what can I do? You have my oath, I am your subject, I can only submit and obey you. I shall do so because it is my duty... But have pity on an unhappy man whose only consolation is in the conviction that he did his duty and made others do theirs...[22]

Personally mollified by this letter and apparently recalling those considerations which made him amenable to the idea of renouncing the throne in the first place, Constantine replied forcefully:

You aide-de-camp, my dear Nicholas, has just given me your letter. I have read it with the most vivid chagrin. My decision, sanctified by him who was my benefactor and my sovereign, is irrevocable. I am not able to accept your proposal to hasten my departure for St Petersburg[23] and I warn you that I shall leave Warsaw only to retire to some greater distance, if everything is not arranged following the will of our deceased Emperor.[24]

Nevertheless, Constantine's humiliation was repeated within a few weeks because a number of European newspapers learned of Constantine's letter of resignation and published it. Yet at this time Constantine put his situation in a different perspective — that of a much greater loss than one of mere pride. In a letter to his friend the Marquis Dekluber, Constantine expressed the following sentiments about the significance of Alexander's death and his resignation:

...this cruel loss deprives me of an adored master, of a benefactor, of a brother, and I dare say it, of a friend to whose service all my life has been consecrated; with him all is finished for me on this earth...

I was content, happy, satisfied by him, henceforth I must remain there where he had placed me and not aspire to anything more...

All the gazettes and newspapers have judged otherwise and have heaped on my account many absurdities one more ridiculous than the other and which does not merit the effort of being refuted...

They have not had the happiness of having a master, such as I have had, and have not served him; if they had had this happiness they would have thought certainly like me and acted and reasoned the same.[25]

On December 24, Nicholas received Constantine's final and very brief refusal in St. Petersburg. That same day he received a report from General Ivan Dibich from Taganrog informing him of a conspiracy among the officers of the Southern Army and the guards. Finally now, realizing that there was no time to lose, Nicholas ordered the preparation of an edict announcing his succession, which appeared that very day.[26]

When Nicholas later viewed those three weeks of interregnum and terrible uncertainty in retrospect, it is clear that he believed himself not only to be entirely blameless, but also to be the real martyr in the cause of national stability. The following sentiments expressed

by Nicholas in his *Memoirs* make apparent the basis of his antagonism
to Constantine over the matter of succession. In these *Memoirs*
Nicholas asked:

> Which of the two made the greater sacrifice — he who repudiated the
> heritage from his father, his pretext being incapacity...and retained a posi-
> tion according to his own desires — or the one who, with no preparation
> for a dignity to which he had no right in the nature of things, the one
> who had always been kept ignorant of his brother's will, and then sud-
> denly, under the most terrible conditions, had to sacrifice all that was dear
> to him, in order to submit to another's will? Even today, after ten years,
> I venture to think that my sacrifice was much the greater.[27]

Nicholas designated December 26 as the day on which the new oath
of loyalty to him was to be administered. Although ordering the oath
to be given as soon as possible to forestall trouble, Nicholas took no
further precautions. For example, he did not order the arrest of those
named in Dibich's report. Despite the short notice, that day the conspirators decided to refuse the oath to Nicholas and to proclaim the
revolution.

The conspirators, known collectively as the Decembrists,[28] were
for the most part military men, who, despite prestigious family
background and age in common with Nicholas, came to profess different views about the proper course for Russia's future. Largely
influenced by liberal Freemasonry and prolonged stays abroad during
the Napoleonic and post-Napoleonic period, they came to espouse
the brothers Alexander and Michael Muravev, their democratic ideas,
among others. As early as 1816, a small band of young men, including
Prince Serge Trubetskoii, the brothers Serge and Matthew Muravev-
Apostol, the brothers Alexander and Michael Muravev, their second
cousin Nikita Muravev, and Paul Pestel, set about to form a secret
society which became known as the Union of Salvation.[29] Relatively
soon the group experienced dissension and it was dissolved, to be
superseded by the Union of Public Good.[30] By 1822 this organization too was dissolved, but out of its membership two new organizations, the Northern Society[31] and the Southern Society,[32] evolved
which became the forces behind the Decembrist Revolution.

The Southern Society proved much more effective; one of its most
striking accomplishments was the connection it established with the
revitalized Polish Patriotic Society.

Many, including Constantine, had believed the Polish Patriotic Society had come to an end with the arrest and imprisonment of Major Lukasinski. In actuality, the organization continued, somewhat altered, under the leadership of Severyn Krzyzanowski. Although vaguely aware of each other's existence, contacts did not take place until 1822, when the Southern Society approached the Polish Patriotic Society.[33] The Southern Society was particularly anxious for an alliance so that it could be certain of the neutrality, if not the elimination of the Polish forces represented by Grand Duke Constantine with his kingdom's army and his Lithuanian Corps. At the beginning, the Polish Patriotic Society was somewhat hesitant to enter into negotiations with the Russian organization in the hope that Alexander might still keep his promises. But by 1824, after losing faith in Alexander and observing the attachment to liberal beliefs among many Russian officers stationed in Constantine's army, the Polish Society became more receptive to the idea of any alliance which might aid its cause, even if that aid came from a Russian organization.

As a result of preliminary meetings held between Serge Muravev-Apostol and Michael Bestuzhev-Riumin with Count Chodkiewicz, the two groups reached an agreement in the spring of 1824 in Kiev. In it, the Southern Society promised to recognize the independence of a future Poland and the cession of the Polish provinces held by Russia; the boundary question, however, was not settled. Each organization was to maintain its separateness and the Polish Society pledged itself to assist in the event of a revolution only if given two weeks notice. The Poles also promised to detain Constantine and to disarm the Lithuanian Corps.[34]

The following year in January, 1825, Pestel and others of the Southern Society again met with the Poles, Anthony Jablonowski and S. Grodecki at Kiev. This time, as previously, only partial agreements were reached. Again Pestel in the name of the Southern Society confirmed Polish independence but left the boundary question open. The Poles, however, promised more with regard to Constantine, agreeing to arrest him and do with him whatever the Russian revolutionaries would do with Alexander, even if that meant execution. It was further agreed that the Russian society was to play the leading role in the revolution, while the Polish society was to establish contacts with secret societies in Western Europe. Yet, despite these arrangements, the long-accumulated national animosity between the two Slavic peoples and fear of betrayal[35] prevented complete agreement between the two conspiratorial groups. And, despite their realization of the need for common action, there was difficulty in overcoming differences in aims and programs. In general, the Polish Patriotic Society placed the national question before the social one, and its limited republican and democratic views were more in harmony with the Northern Society (with which it had no contact) than with the Southern Society. Consequently, the more radically inclined Poles were forced to make personal contacts with individual Russian radicals outside the bounds of the agreement reached by the two groups. For example, the friendly relationship between Adam Mickiewicz and some St. Petersburg and Odessa Decembrists is well known.[36]

Uncertain of the future, the two groups agreed to meet again in 1826. Of course this projected meeting never took place.

Characterizing the revolution from the beginning was confusion as to the proper course of action and doubt as to its likely success. The chief leaders of the revolution in St. Petersburg, Trubetskoii, Ryleev, and Nicholas and Alexander Bestuzhev finally decided to move when they learned Nicholas had been informed of the secret organizations' aims.[37] The Northern Society decided to begin the revolt by refusing to take the oath of loyalty to Nicholas on the pretext that it had already been pledged to Constantine. The sincerity of this position was immediately in doubt, for it was clear that given the Decembrists' views, they could only be opposed to both Nicholas and Constantine as tsar.[38] For them, Nicholas was considered the less acceptable; however, Constantine was hardly an improvement. Yet, because the Decembrists realized that for several reasons, most important of which was the fact that simple soldiers could hardly be expected to support revolutionary action in the name of a political program,[39] they adopted the slogan "Constantine and Constitution,"[40] which then became the catchwords of the revolution.

In pretending to support Constantine, the Decembrists made one of their few judicious moves, because, in fact, Constantine's image had improved somewhat during his long absence from the capital. His eccentricities were largely forgotten, while it was well known that his Polish Army was better equipped and paid than the Russian Army. In the Polish Army, furthermore, the term of service for privates was eight years, instead of twenty-five as in the Russian Army. Then too, Constantine was regarded as a liberal, for it was said he favored the abolition of serfdom. Finally, according to Colonel Alexander Bulatov, Trubetskoii's aide, many hoped that Constantine, if tsar, would abolish the hated military colonies.[41] The fact that Constantine was regarded as progressive, if not liberal, given his military and governmental policies in the Kingdom and the Eastern Provinces, is indicative of the extent of misinformation about Constantine in military circles and even among the Decembrists. Certainly, Constantine's views were known to others. For example, Prince Metternich of Austria favored Constantine's rather than Nicholas' accession for exactly the opposite reasons of the liberals, namely because Constantine shared his anti-constitutional views and because he "hated the English, scorned the French, and Prussia he considered as infected with revolutionary spirit." Furthermore, he expected that Constantine could be counted upon to maintain friendly relations with conservative Austria.[42]

December 26, the day planned for the revolt, began ominously. Though only a few of the expected regiments had been won over to the revolt, it was learned that not only had the State Council and Senate already taken the oath to Nicholas, but that Grand Duke Michael also had arrived in St. Petersburg in a show of support, thereby exposing as false the rumor that both he and Constantine had been arrested by Nicholas.

Although by afternoon the number of insurgents had risen to three thousand soldiers and thirty officers, it was clear that Nicholas had only to take decisive action to end the revolution. Fearing bloodshed, Nicholas did make several overtures to the insurgents, but toward evening, he ordered a quick liquidation of the rebel forces by artillery fire. In the process, some seventy to eighty were killed, including some civilians.

Reportedly horrified by the events of the day, Nicholas commented about his first day as tsar, "What a happy beginning of a reign."[43] He also wrote to Constantine that same evening the following, "Dear, dear Constantine, your will is done, I am emperor but at what a price, great God, at the price of the blood of my subjects.'[44] Only after receipt of this letter did Constantine finally order the Kingdom's and Eastern Provinces' army and administration to take the oath of loyalty to Nicholas. And this not until January 2, 1826.[45]

Later developments in the South were equally unsuccessful. Very early General Dibich succeeded in arresting most of the leaders of the Southern Society including Pestel. Also, although the Polish Patriotic Society did not officially oppose the revolt, its Ukranian branch refused support, thereby limiting Polish participation to rather few Poles.[46]

The aftermath of the uprising brought a large number of arrests and a legal process lasting several years. Conducting the investigation into the revolution was a special committee of investigation under Nicholas' direct jurisdiction. The Tsar personally interrogated many of the suspects, an indication of his reaction to the revolt and his desire to punish the guilty. According to one writer, Nicholas "would stop at nothing to get them..."[47]

Within a short time most of the arrested Decembrists freely gave humiliating confessions and promises of repentance. Almost six hundred persons were investigated and one hundred twenty-one were put on trial. The final sentences included the death penalty for five and deportation to Siberia at hard labor for the rest.

The Decembrist Revolution without doubt had far reaching repercussions upon Russia but this was also true for Poland. Before investigations in Russia clearly pointed to connections between the Southern Society and organizations with Polish membership, Constantine could write to Nicholas with complete satisfaction that "here in Warsaw peace reigns. All are amazed and shocked at the terrible St. Petersburg developments."[48] Throughout January, 1826, in accordance with Nicholas' wishes, Constantine publicized the particulars of the revolts in St. Petersburg and the South in several orders of the day to the Polish Army and by having translations of Russian newspaper accounts placed in the Polish press.[49] At the same time he continued to reiterate to Nicholas that, as far as the Poles were concerned, only "loyalty and honor could motivate them."[50]

Even when the confessions of Pestel and Bestuzhev-Riumin to Nicholas and the Investigation Committee left no room for any doubt as to Polish connections with the Decembrists,[51] Constantine continued to insist that such slander against the Poles could only be the result of intrigues,[52] and claimed that "the compromised are trying to drag in the Poles, but not having any proof against them, just put forth accusations."[53] Nevertheless, convinced of Polish involvement, Nicholas desired an immediate investigation in Warsaw.[54] Constantine tried to resist his brother's request by insisting again that any accusations against the Poles could only be fabrications, as proved by the fact that all secret activities on the part of the Polish Patriotic Society, according to Constantine, had come to an end with the earlier imprisonment of Lukasinski.[55]

By February, however, Constantine could no longer resist Nicholas' demands for an investigation in the Kingdom, and so on February 20, a committee in Warsaw made up of five Poles and five Russians under the chairmanship of the president of the Senate, Stanislas Zamoyski, was appointed to "investigate the involvement and the activities of secret societies in the Polish Kingdom, also their connection with similar organizations in Russia."[56]

That same day arrests began and soon Krzyzanowski and many of his associates in the Patriotic Society were imprisoned in the Carmelite prison. Nicholas ordered that it be learned from them whether "the Poles in their discussions with the Decembrists had agreed to a republican system and whether Constantine was to be killed."[57]

Hoping to lessen Nicholas' growing anger toward the Poles, Constantine tried to offer some explanation for their involvement. He even went so far as offering some justification for Polish dissatisfaction; after all, Alexander had made many promises to the Poles, some of which had not been kept. Further, if the Poles were engaged in questionable activities, they should at least be judged impartially.[58] In a letter to his friend Opochinin, Constantine expressed this attitude toward the accused Poles: "in good faith could you reproach them? Put yourself in their place and suppose that Russia had been partitioned as was Poland, what would you have done and thought yourself?"[59]

The committee carried on its work for almost a year; in the process many civil rights were violated and torture was applied in the hope of obtaining confessions.[60] To speed things along, Novosiltsev suggested that Russian criminal procedure be applied to the Polish accused; this, however, was opposed successfully by Drucki-Lubecki who argued for the application of Polish constitutional procedures.[61]

Only on December 22, 1826 and January 3, 1827 did the committee finally put before Constantine the detailed reports containing information about all secret organizations existing in the Kingdom and a list of all the individuals involved and their activities. The committee divided all the accused into seven categories; the first category being reserved for those accused of the most serious offense — collaboration with secret Russian organizations. Nine members of the Polish Patriotic Society were placed in this first category, and they, together with others in lesser categories were required to stand trial. Not all those accused by the committee, however, were to be tried in the Kingdom; Poles born in Russia were sent there for trial by the Russian Senate and the Court of the Third Section.[62]

At the same time the committee was carrying on its investigation, Constantine ordered a quiet surveillance into the internal affairs of his Army; he also ordered that all in the Army again be required to indicate in writing whether or not they belonged to any secret organization.[63]

Another problem for Constantine, which unexpectedly presented itself, was jurisdictional: before which court in the Kingdom were the accused to be tried? Several months passed before this matter was resolved, again because Constantine and Nicholas disagreed. In Nicholas' opinion, the accused should have been tried on the basis of legal principles used in St. Petersburg and before a criminal court.[64] Constantine opposed this, saying that such procedures could not be followed "without breaking all the principles of the constitution."[65] Instead, he favored placing the accused before a military court, thereby making possible the imposition of a few heavy sentences to placate the Tsar without the whole matter coming to the public's attention.[66] The Administrative Council, making a last-ditch effort in support of the constitution, insisted that the matter be placed before a *Sejm* tribunal consisting of members of the Kingdom's Senate. This view was supported widely in the Kingdom[67] and soon Constantine too came out in favor of this position, insisting that on the basis of Article 152 of the constitution, a *Sejm* tribunal would be the only correct solution.[68] In the end, Nicholas agreed to the calling of the *Sejm* Tribunal, which then opened April 18, 1827. All the senators of the Kingdom took part with Peter Bielinski as president. Having the right to observe the proceedings was a special commission of the St. Petersburg Senate.[69]

Although there was enormous popular interest in the proceedings of the Tribunal, it proceeded slowly for over a year. Only on May 22, 1828 was sentence passed on the accused, and that very contrary to Constantine's and Nicholas' expectations.[70] Nicholas' rage, however, was much greater than Constantine's displeasure. Although Constantine ranted and threatened, saying that the Senate was just as culpable as the accused, that the Senate was stupid and imbecilic, that he would put the president of the *Sejm* Tribunal on trial,[71] and although Constantine had the deliberations of the senators closed to the public and refused to allow any uncensored reports of the proceedings to be published,[72] in the end, Constantine accepted the Tribunal's verdict, contenting himself with forbidding the publication of the sentences and interning all the senators in the capital for a time.[73]

For Nicholas, however, as he wrote to Constantine, "the affair is not finished — we will wait for the end." For him the Poles were now "unfortunates, they have saved the offenders, but for this they have lost their fatherland."[74]

The outcome of the *Sejm* Tribunal's deliberations to which Constantine and Nicholas so much objected included the decision that none of the accused were guilty of treason. The only charge upheld was that of belonging to a secret organization for which Krzyzanowski and several others were sentenced to three years imprisonment or less. After considering several plans as an alternative to acceptance of these objectionable verdicts,[75] Nicholas ordered the Tribunal's findings sent to the St. Petersburg Senate and the Third Section. Finally, in 1829,

Nicholas grudgingly decided to accept the decision of the Polish tribunal, with one exception. The major offender, Krzyzanowski, was considered outside the jurisdiction of the Kingdom's court because he was born in the Ukraine, hence he was now subject to retrial in Russia. His second sentence, like that of all Poles tried by the Russian criminal court was much harsher, hard labor in Siberia, where, after ten years he died.[76]

The issue of the Decembrist Revolt also struck Constantine personally. As early as January, 1826 Nicholas informed him[77] that one of his favorite Russian officers, Adjutant Michael Lunin, was involved in the Decembrist conspiracy. Deeply shocked and upset,[78] Constantine personally investigated the matter and learned that, although Lunin had indeed belonged to the Union of Public Good and then the Southern Society through which he had contacts with the Polish Patriotic Society, Lunin had had no further contacts with the conspirators since the time of his transfer to Constantine's Lithuanian Corps. Consequently, he could have played no part in the Decembrist Revolution. This discovery made Constantine his strong defender, but to no avail. Nicholas' will prevailed and Constantine, despite his bitter disappointment, was forced to accept Lunin's sentence, twenty years of hard labor in Siberia.[79]

After the discovery of conspiratorial elements, regardless of how few, Nicholas was determined to have established a more thorough and Russian-operated surveillance system in the Kingdom and proposed to Constantine the advantages of allowing Russian gendarmes of the Third Section to operate in the Kingdom. Viewing this as an intrusion upon his management of the Kingdom's affairs, Constantine vehemently opposed this suggestion. In the face of Constantine's determined opposition, Nicholas withdrew his suggestion and permitted Constantine to continue his personal direction of all police and surveillance operations in the Kingdom.[80]

As far as Nicholas was concerned, the question of Polish involvement in the Decembrist Revolution had a most unsatisfactory outcome, but strong action against the Poles in 1828 and 1829 was impossible, because Nicholas was faced with far more pressing problems posed by the Russo-Turkish war.[81]

Reversing Alexander's policy of non-interference in the struggle between the Greeks and the Turks, Nicholas in conjunction with Britain and France entered into a conflict with the Ottoman Empire. But before tension in the Balkans turned into open warfare, Nicholas consulted Constantine as to the course of action to be followed by Russia. As early as March 4, 1826, Nicholas ordered the Russian Minister of

Foreign Affairs, Count Charles Nesselrode, to send all documents about the Greek Question to Constantine. In that same letter of March 4, Nicholas also indicated his determination to occupy the Danubian Principalities.[82] Constantine replied immediately, hesitating not in the least to tell Nicholas that in his opinion Nicholas' decision to enter the Principalities was a mistake and could only be regarded by others as a hostile act. Further, if Nicholas had in mind the achievement of an increase in commerce and the frightening of the Turks by such a step, he doubted that the desired results would ensue as a result of such action. In Constantine's opinion, Russia's chances were poor because the Turks were fanatics and would persevere in the face of difficult odds. Finally, Constantine rather sarcastically reminded his brother that the poor state of Russia's finances was well known and that it was doubtful that Russia would find money for the war.[83] In this exchange of letters it is clear how differently the two brothers regarded the question of Russian involvement in the Balkans, and more generally, how much they disagreed about the use of military power itself. Later, when Constantine tried to soften his strong stand against Nicholas' views by expressing sentiments in favor of Nicholas' achievement of his aims, he still continued to hope that "the war could be avoided."[84] Yet, when Nicholas found himself temporarily in military difficulties and asked Constantine to send Polish troops to help against the Turks, Constantine quite categorically refused.[85] In the end, Constantine was still forced to send Nicholas a handful of Poles because the Tsar made such an issue of the matter. In Nicholas' opinion, at least a token Polish force was essential to symbolize their supposed solidarity with the Russians in the conflict.[86]

Still another issue which embittered personal relations between Constantine and Nicholas and deepened Nicholas' aversion to the Polish Kingdom was the matter of his coronation as tsar of Russia and then as king of Poland.

In August, 1826, Nicholas journeyed to Moscow for his coronation as tsar. Although it was obviously proper and time was sufficient, Constantine was neither informed nor invited to this important ceremony.[87] Aware of this development, Drucki-Lubecki, then in St. Petersburg just before his departure for Warsaw, quite boldly reminded Nicholas that "it is absolutely necessary that Constantine come to Moscow for the coronation, it is necessary that he, who gave up the throne...put it on your head in the sight of Russia and Europe." In reply, Nicholas said, "it is unfeasible and improbable."[88] Drucki-Lubecki then had the courage to disagree with Nicholas and to say "it will be done."[89]

Upon his return to Warsaw Drucki-Lubecki tried to convince Constantine of the importance of attending his brother's coronation, despite the obvious slight. To Nicholas' discomfort, not only did Constantine appear for the coronation, but also was received in Moscow with considerable enthusiasm.[90] Rumors were spread noting Constantine's alleged virtues and mentioning the willingness of the powerful General Ermolov to support him should he wish to regain the crown! This enchantment with Constantine quickly subsided when, according to Benckendorff, the Grand Duke once again compromised himself by his behavior at the ceremonies.[91]

Once Nicholas had been crowned in Moscow it was expected that he would be leaving soon for Warsaw for his coronation as king of Poland. Yet, Nicholas was not crowned until 1829. This delay had two explanations. For one, Nicholas never believed that it was necessary that he be crowned in Warsaw, for, in his opinion, "the ceremony at Warsaw is not a coronation but a repetition of the crowning at Moscow for the benefit of the Poles."[92] When Nicholas finally did accede to Constantine's and the Poles' wishes, he did it merely as a conciliatory gesture after the years of tension over the trial of Polish "Decembrists."[93]

Secondly, Nicholas did not wish to follow Polish forms for the coronation ceremony even though for years Constantine tried to persuade Nicholas of their importance. From 1826 to as late as April, 1829, Nicholas and Constantine discussed the matter in a series of letters. In surely the most direct manner, Constantine made his case in April, 1829 when he asserted:

> a second crowning is different from the first where you received supremacy... Here you have inherited other rights, for the Kingdom of Poland is not incorporated but reunited to the Empire, it is the same dynasty which is called to reign in the two states, but this does not make them less distinct...[94]

Further, Constantine advocated that the Russian crown not be used in the coronation and stressed the importance of the proper religious ceremony and the wearing of the Polish uniform and insignia.

Once having decided to make what he thought were great concessions to the Poles, Nicholas successfully played the role of Polish king at his coronation ceremony. In fact, he made such a favorable impression in the Polish capital[95] that he overshadowed the jealous

Constantine, who was reputed to be in bad humor during the entire time of his brother's visit.[96]

Although it is possible to learn much of Nicholas' thinking about the Congress Kingdom from his views toward Polish involvement in the Decembrist Revolt and toward his coronation in Warsaw, nowhere does his attitude appear more clearly than in the question of the Eastern Provinces. This issue not only added to the already strained relations between the two brothers but accurately forecast what Nicholas had in mind for the Poles and their kingdom.

By virtue of his inheritance of the Polish throne as a constitutional monarch from Alexander, Nicholas was required to recognize, superficially at least, the special position of the Kingdom *vis-a-vis* the Empire. This was due in part at least to the fact that especially during the first years of Nicholas' rule Constantine proved a staunch, though not always successful defender of the Poles' point of view. Moreover, Russia's international position was so precarious due to the war with the Ottoman Empire that Nicholas realized that the time was inopportune to make changes in the Polish *status quo*.[97] Yet, it is clear that from the beginning of his reign Nicholas was dissatisfied with the Polish arrangement, and as one observer noted, "everytime His Majesty has spoken to me about the Kingdom of Poland, I have been left with the impression that this politically created state displeased and impeded him."[98] Nicholas was careful to hide his true feelings before Constantine and the Poles, and only in 1835 after the dissolution of the Kingdom asserted: "On the whole I am satisfied that things have arrived at that point at which I am only Emperor of Russia; it is in that character that you belong to me."[99]

Although at first Nicholas was unable to reverse Alexander's arrangement in the Kingdom, he did block successfully all attempts to reunite the Eastern Provinces to the Polish Kingdom and worked to undermine the Polish character of these provinces in spite of Constantine's efforts. Constantine clearly made known to Nicholas that he believed that the provinces should be joined to the Kingdom,[100] but Nicholas did not hesitate to inform Constantine that his irrevocable position was that

> Lithuania is a Russian province, it cannot be given back to Poland because that would strike at the integrity of the Empire...I would cease to be a Russian in my own eyes were I to believe it possible to separate Lithuania from Russia proper..., I cannot permit any possibility, as long as I live, that these ideas of rejoining Lithuania to Poland should be encouraged...[101]

Further, in an attempt to reverse Constantine's successful reaffirmation of Polish influence in the provinces, Nicholas ordered a large group of Russian officers and soldiers to be attached to the Lithuanian Corps and began appointing Russians to many administrative positions in the provinces.[102] These and other measures proved particularly offensive to Constantine; not only did they lessen Polish influence there, but, in acting without consulting Constantine, Nicholas undermined Constantine's special position in the provinces that Alexander had granted him much earlier. Over the issue of the Eastern Provinces, then, relations between Constantine and Nicholas became so difficult that a mutual friend, F. Opochinin, was forced to intervene. Although his mediation did lead to at least a superficial reconciliation, Constantine had clearly lost the argument.[103] Henceforth, Constantine's special prerogatives in the provinces were directly subject to Nicholas' will, and Constantine had to satisfy himself with his status in the Kingdom.[104] How long that status would remain inviolable was now open to question.

As weak as both Constantine's and the Kingdom's status had become with regard to Nicholas after 1825, it cannot be said that Constantine and the Kingdom had any more to hope for from the side of the Poles. Indeed, in the course of the five years after Nicholas' accession, many Poles became increasingly dissatisfied with the existing state of Russo-Polish relations and also looked for a change in the *status quo*. While in the early years of the Kingdom, most influential Polish leaders, including Adam Czartoryski, accepted the Russian connection, after 1826 many Poles among them Czartoryski, came to envision and believe possible a wholly different future for their country. There were two reasons for this. First, there occurred a general attitudinal shift among the young elite away from eighteenth century cosmopolitanism, so compatible with the reality of Russian power, to a romanticism which stressed patriotism and a call to action, particularly that most glorious form of action, revolution. Secondly, several issues arose which so inflamed Polish romantic and revolutionary feelings that it seemed to some that there was no alternative to a complete break with Russia, even if that meant the expulsion of Constantine. Little known, of course, to most Poles was Constantine's role as the Kingdom's advocate in trying to win the Tsar's agreement on those issues of greatest concern to the Poles. To the extent that he failed, Constantine shared Nicholas' unpopularity and was regarded simply as part of a Russian system that had to be abolished.

Romanticism as a literary perspective swept over Poland just as it swept most of Europe. Finding its most powerful expression in the works of Adam Mickiewicz and the historian Joachim Lelewel, the Polish younger generation saw in romanticism more than just a literary

expression, however. Indeed, they understood romanticism as
embodying a patriotic call to restore the old republic within its old
frontiers.[105] The absence of opportunities to form legal political
organizations in which romantic ideas could be discussed openly,
criticized and modified through debate was especially harmful and
contributed to growing political tensions in the Kingdom after 1825.
Still, these conditions alone would not have given rise to the events
of November, 1830; rather it was a specific series of issues and events
which spurred romantically idealistic youth to such dissatisfaction that
revolution could become a reality.

The first issues which shook the Kingdom after Nicholas' accession, embarrassed Constantine, and marked a turning point in Russo-
Polish relations were the repercussions of the Decembrist Revolt in
the Kingdom and Nicholas' decision to have Krzyzanowski retried
in Russia. Although at the beginning of 1826 press censorship severely
restricted what the Poles knew about the Decembrists, by July the
volume of available information had grown considerably because the
Russian government decided to allow Warsaw newspapers to publish
reports of the Russian Committee of Investigation. This permission
was granted for a very specific reason. Having discovered Polish
involvement in the conspiracy, the Russian government decided to
make known and exaggerate the extent of Polish involvement so as
to completely discredit the participants of the conspiracy, discourage
other would-be conspirators, and win sympathy for Russia's position.
The revelations, however, had an impact upon public opinion in the
Kingdom dramatically different from what had been expected.[106]
While the Polish Patriotic Society, and others for that matter,
possessed at best only vague ideas about revolution in the name of
national independence, the fact that the Committee of Investigation
imputed such goals to these organizations actually raised their prestige
among the citizenry.[107] It was even suggested that all was not to be
found in the report and that while some conspirators had been cap-
tured, others were still free to continue their revolutionary work,
including two officers who had served under Constantine, Generals
Albrecht and Gendre.[108] In the wake of such reports, some Poles for
the first time "began to consider a program of regaining independence
and breaking the union with Russia, which was an important factor
in shifting opinions towards the idea of revolution."[109]

The most damaging event undermining Russian-Polish relations did
not occur, however, until 1829 when Krzyzanowski was turned over
to the Russian criminal court for retrial. According to the reasoning
of the *Sejm* Tribunal, Krzyzanowski's activities could not be

considered technically high treason because the Congress Kingdom and the Russian Empire were two distinct political entities. Yet, when Nicholas appeared to wish a Russian court conviction for treason, "the Poles protested that not only was it an injustice to try Krzyzanowski for an offense committed outside the Kingdom, but that the very autonomy of the Kingdom was threatened... An affront was given to national feelings."[110]

In the course of events, even Czartoryski, the best known and most steadfast advocate of Russian-Polish cooperation, by his participation in the *Sejm* Tribunal's judgment gave the impression that his commitment to that policy had diminished.[111] Further, by 1829, Czartoryski had joined others including Ludwig Koscielski, Leonard Chodzko and Theodore Morawski, in informing the Western press of details of the trial and conditions in the Kingdom. This in turn generated, by 1829, the rise of a real anti-Russian and oppositional voice abroad, which not only created knowledge of and sympathy for the Poles and in the process exaggerated the amount of foreign support they could expect if they rebelled, but also caused Constantine considerable pain. Ever oversensitive to the foreign press, yet anxious to minimize its importance in Nicholas' eyes, Constantine wrote to his brother:

> I am not complaining, because that would be beneath my dignity, but it is unfortunate and truly painful to see, how such articles could be written by Poles, who always, but especially in recent years, have been so showered by good deeds and favors from your hands... Nevertheless, everything here has been ideally quiet.[112]

As interested as Constantine was in minimizing foreign reports to Nicholas, he was most concerned about what the Tsar thought about the state of Polish opinion itself. In this regard, Constantine informed Nicholas again that:

> The public spirit is good and against the Senate and it is only effete young men and some young rascals who are patriots; a healthy group and above all the bourgeoisie of the capital are animated by the best spirit, blaming loudly all that has been done.[113]

A month later, as if to make certain that Nicholas understood, Constantine again wrote that "the opinion of the Senate is not universally shared."[114]

Yet, despite Constantine's efforts to lessen the importance of the Senate's decision and the amount of public support for it, it appears that there was indeed widespread popular support for the patriotic stand of the *Sejm* Tribunal.[115] Eventually, though Nicholas became better informed of the true state of Polish feeling and did issue his ill-timed and badly-worded manifesto confirming the verdict of the Senate, it was much too late for conciliatory gestures in the face of rising anti-tsarist sentiment.

Further disturbing Polish opinion against the Russo-Polish connection were the repercussions of the Russo-Turkish War in the Kingdom. Most specifically, the Poles were interested in the growing hostility generated between Russia and Austria as a result of the Tsar's involvement in the Balkans. War seemed imminent and was predicted by many highly placed Russians, including Nicholas himself.[116] For that reason increased attention was paid to Polish opinion in the Kingdom and in Galicia (the formerly Polish province held by Austria) so as to determine popular loyalties in the event of a clash.[117]

The Poles, in contrast, did not fear a Russian war with Austria, but thought that it could redound to the Kingdom's advantage. Believing that the Austrian government took a friendly interest in the fate of the Poles and imagining that Austrian foreign policy included the creation of an independent Polish state reunited with Galicia, the Poles rapidly became receptive to Austrian overtures.[118] As early as 1827, Constantine had become concerned about Austrian propaganda in the Kingdom reminding the Poles about Alexander's unkept promises and the need for a new political order in the country.[119] In Constantine's opinion, this propaganda "could become a source of considerable disorder in this part of Europe" since "these forces are difficult to suppress in this century because the efforts of many minds are aimed at the emancipation of peoples and national independence." Still another possible trump card in the Austrian court's possession was the Prince of Reichstadt, the son of Napoleon Bonaparte, whom the Poles so much admired.[120] From 1827 through 1829, rumors circulated widely about the imminence of a new Polish Kingdom under Napoleon II as "King of Galicia."[121] These rumors were strengthened by the Prince's frequent contacts with Poles and by the enthusiastic manner in which Poles of all social classes greeted the proposition.[122]

That the Russo-Turkish War ended without a Russo-Austrian war disappointed many Poles; they, however, were grateful for Austrian interest in their plight and continued to hope that the Russo-Turkish peace would be brief.[123] Most important, these events demonstrated that Polish public opinion was open to new political orientations and even to a break with Russia. Thus, in the years 1825 to 1830 Constantine's position had become irreparably undermined; neither the Poles nor Nicholas any longer favored the continuation of the *status quo*. Through the years Constantine was not unaware of changing attitudes; still, not until the closing days of 1830 did it become clear to him that these changes meant the end of the Congress Kingdom.

Chapter VII

THE COMING OF THE NOVEMBER REVOLUTION:
THE END OF ASPIRATIONS,
1830-1831

The early days of 1830 seemed to presage a year of tranquility, yet such a beginning was to be misleading. The year brought not the hoped for peace and stability in Europe, but revolution and war. The Polish Kingdom, too, reflecting ties with a Europe increasingly convulsed by nationalistic and liberal sentiments, along with is own internal troubles, was also brought to revolution and war in 1830, which ended more tragically than in other parts of Europe.

A number of issues had already created considerable discontent in the Kingdom, but only one small conspiratorial organization was in existence by 1830 which favored revolutionary action. This organization was made up, for the most part, of young cadets from Constantine's military schools, together with a handful of equally youthful intellectuals and writers, who banded together under the leadership of Peter Wysocki. Formed in late 1828, Wysocki's organization found unusually enthusiastic support from among the young cadets, not only for the usual patriotic reasons, but also interestingly enough, because of the military conditions completely determined by Constantine. Constantine's military style and discipline though lightened after 1820, continued to prove unpopular among the young officers; yet, this was not the major cause of dissatisfaction. What proved most objectionable was the fact that Constantine did not permit the Polish Army to take part in the Russo-Turkish War. Discontent reached a new high in 1829 when it appeared more and more certain that their career aspirations would come to nothing and that they were doomed to a life of boring military routine in a purposeless army.[1] In their frustration, they then joined with young writers, stifled by Constantine's censorship, to plan a revolution despite the fact their romantic ideas lacked support from public officials, contained no defined political program nor clear set of strategies. On several occasions in 1829 and 1830 Wysocki and his group tried to stage a coup, but their efforts were ill-timed and nothing happened. At this time, however, especially during the months from July to November, developments of such a disturbing nature did occur that the ranks of Wysocki's secret organization were soon joined by elements of the population hitherto moderately loyal or politically passive.

Three easily distinguished developments provided the impetus for what was to become a full scale uprising in November. They were: first, a deterioration of the Kingdom's economic situation affecting all groups, but particularly the urban poor; second, the international situation and the Polish reaction toward it; and third, Constantine's provocative investigation into conspiratorial activity in the capital.

Economic difficulties had been chronic throughout the history of the Kingdom, yet, through the 1820s, the Kingdom's economy under the management of Drucki-Lubecki had experienced a widely felt general improvement. Signs of regression began to appear in 1830, particularly during late summer and fall as a result of a poor harvest and diminishing trade opportunities. That this was no mere cyclical fluctuation was indicated by two of Drucki-Lubecki's letters, written on October 28 and November 6, to the Kingdom's Secretary of State, Stefan Grabowski, in which he expressed great concern over the economic situation and his fear of its likely political repercussions.[2] By late fall the population had felt price increases on basic items, such as bread, meat and vodka coupled with a sharp rise in unemployment.[3] Particularly hard hit were the craftsmen, workers and soldiers of Warsaw, who received no salary adjustments to compensate for the increase in prices. Consequently, economic grievances played an important part in the politicization of the capital's lower classes and lower ranks of the army, elements in the population which previously had been passive.

The second immediate cause of the insurrection was the international situation, particularly revolutionary developments in France and Belgium, and their impact in the Kingdom. Constantine carefully followed events in France, sensed the seriousness of the political situation and feared its possible consequences for his domain. Nevertheless, in assessing the mood of the Kingdom, in late July, Constantine could still write that all was well.[4] His mood, however, quickly changed with the news of the Paris Revolution. According to General Krukowiecki, one of Constantine's close aides, Constantine was so disturbed that he could not be calmed, reportedly asserting:

Paris had a horrible revolution… The king acted stupidly, all lost their
heads, ministers and generals were not able to appreciate the power which
they had in (their) hands, and the mobs, excuse me, the nation triumphed.[5]

Further, Constantine angrily added that the Royalists would have
done better "if they had come out with their whole army and bombed
all those hooligans out of the city…'' From that August 8, Constantine more than ever censored publications appearing in the Kingdom,
yet he was frank enough with Nicholas to inform him that he could
do nothing to prevent foreign reports from being smuggled in from
Poznan.[6]

Within a few days Constantine apparently calmed himself sufficiently to leave Warsaw for a short holiday. At this time he again wrote
Nicholas assuring him that "all was calm." The fact that Constantine doubled surveillance in the Kingdom by his secret police may
have contributed to his peace of mind.[7]

Upon his return in September, satisfied with conditions in the
Kingdom, Constantine confidently promulgated the order that nothing
should interfere with the freedom of the press to publish full information about all foreign developments, provided that the newspapers did
not embellish the reports with their own commentaries. This surprising decision Constantine justified to Nicholas by saying that it "would
prevent false interpretations."[8] The significance of this decision was
immense: henceforth seven daily newspapers in Warsaw began giving full reports on revolutionary events first in France and then
Belgium, later increased by reports of riots and uprisings in other
European countries including Spain, Portugal, England and Ireland.
Polish readers avidly followed these accounts and soon public opinion
reflected the view that the whole of Europe was undergoing
revolution.[9]

As serious as the Poles' ultimate reaction to these developments
was for Constantine, more immediately troubling was Nicholas'
response. Given his political preference for the *status quo* and his
fear of French revolutionary expansionism, Nicholas expected to win
support for his plan calling for a partial mobilization involving Russia,
Austria and Prussia, along with a call-up of Constantine's Polish
Army.

Well aware of growing Polish pro-revolutionary feeling and fearful for his army, Constantine did not hesitate to inform Nicholas of
the inadvisability of a mobilization of the Poles. He used the argument that it was not to Russia's best interests to mobilize in the face

of Austrian and Prussian passivity about which he was informed. Constantine also tried to frighten his brother with the vision of another St. Petersburg revolution. Because Nicholas seemed so concerned about the state of Polish public opinion, Constantine used one last argument: that "it would be misleading to think that if the Sovereign violated the constitution he could continue to demand faithfulness from the population."[10] On a personal note, Constantine categorically rejected Nicholas' offer that he take command of the new army, indicating his awareness that the position had only been offered to him as a bribe. Earlier General Dibich had been offered the same office.[11] Then, as if to make sure that mobilization of the Polish Army would be impossible, Constantine released many from the ranks who had already completed their terms of service.[12]

In the face of Constantine's opposition, but more significantly Austria's and Prussia's, Nicholas began to resign himself to non-intervention. This resolve lasted only a short time; in September the Belgian Revolution broke out and again mobilization became the issue of the day. According to Nicholas' new plan, the Kingdom was to play a greater role than ever. The Russian interventionist army was to concentrate in the Kingdom, to join up first with Polish units and later with additional forces from Austria and Prussia. This time, knowing well his brother's view, Nicholas circumvented Constantine. Instead of even informing the Grand Duke of his intentions, Nicholas requested Secretary of State Grabowski to give Drucki-Lubecki his order to prepare sufficient funds from the Kingdom's budget to make possible the mobilization of the army and to pay for provisions for the Russian contingents.[13]

As inspiring as the July Revolution was for the Poles, the Belgian Revolution proved even more so, since the Poles saw in the Belgian situation one analogous to their own.[14] With the news of the Belgian victory, joy was unrestrained in Warsaw among all elements of the population. Spontaneous demonstrations, signs and slogans all gave evidence of support for events abroad and a determination to follow a more revolutionary path. Students particularly left their mark on the city through their political graffiti. Constantine personally felt the sting of their wit: one day posted on his Belvedere palace was the sign "From the beginning of the New Year — For Rent."[15] More importantly, impressed by the Belgians' demonstration of how armed masses could defeat regular troops, politicized groups among the capital's lower classes became convinced that they could do the same.[16]

Most interested and encouraged by events was of course Wysocki's organization. Rumors predicting Polish participation in the interventionist army horrified the conspirators and they found quick support for their views from among the cadets and civilian groups.[17] At this time, a second lieutenant, Joseph Zaliwski, became prominent in the organization and began forcefully advocating early revolution. Wysocki had already postponed the outbreak of the revolution several times in 1830 and Zaliwski feared that sooner or later Constantine would uncover the organization and arrest the conspirators.

On November 19 and 20 the Warsaw newspapers announced the mobilization of the Russian and Polish armies; with this announcement it began to appear that armed intervention against France and Belgium was imminent. This drove the conspiring army officers and their civilian allies even closer to revolution.[18]

The third immediate cause of the revolution was the arrest by Constantine's secret police of several conspirators. In early November, the police had discovered information that conclusively implicated several army officers and students. This disclosure proved very disturbing to Constantine, for all police information involving the Army at this time also went directly to Nicholas.[19] But both Novosiltsev and Czartoryski proposed a way out for Constantine in arguing that the conspiracy only included students influenced by Lelewel and that they were merely "expressing youthful lack of balance" and hence no serious problem.[20] Constantine accepted this theory, which exonerated his Army. In contrast, Drucki-Lubecki considered the information of conspiracy to be much more serious and acting without Constantine's knowledge, he urged the speedy occupation of the Kingdom by Russian troops.[21]

Aware that his brother had learned of the results of the investigation via police reports, Constantine wrote to Nicholas about the matter, but only in the most general terms. The Tsar's reply was contradictory. On the one hand he gave Constantine *carte blanche* power to deal with the problem as he saw fit; on the other he suggested that Constantine should place the accused before a military court without further consideration of either the Polish constitution or St. Petersburg.[22]

Rejecting the second suggestion, Constantine called together the main representatives of the Polish aristocracy, including Czartoryski, and told them it was in their mutual interest to help keep the peace. He admitted some of his past errors and even predicted a reconciliation with the one-time leaders of the Kalisz party, the Niemojowski brothers.[23] In return the Poles promised to try to influence the young people to be reasonable.[24] Constantine also decided to continue the investigation while, in a gesture of questionable wisdom, he lessened military and police surveillance in the capital and reduced his personal guard at the Belvedere to three men.[25] While Constantine openly exhibited his confidence in the state of affairs in the Kingdom, others, including Novosiltsev and Szaniawski left Warsaw on various pretexts.[26]

Realizing that a number of their colleagues had just been arrested, and feeling the effects of more strict surveillance by the new director of the Cadet School,[27] the conspirators chose the evening of November 29 for the revolt. Their decision was arrived at in a haphazard way, with no real plan and without informing any prominent sympathetic Poles: only the time for the rising was set definitely.

On the night of the 29th the prearranged signal (the burning of a brewery) was bungled and the fire was put out before most of the conspirators saw it. Consequently, only fourteen showed up to attack Constantine's palace, making possible his easy escape, although General Gendre, who was mistaken for Constantine, was killed. According to Schmidt, the Prussian consul who found him wandering about on the evening of the attack, Constantine was in a state of nervous fright and the following conversation ensued between them:

> All is lost! Let us run away, Let us run away together! Yes Sir, all is now lost; but your Imperial Highness could have appeared at the head of the troops if you had harangued the soldiers. Ah, my dear Schmidt, no one could resist the soldiers that I have formed, if they had followed me. Let us not talk any longer, Sir, it is a fact of the present, but we still have the future. What measures will your Imperial Highness take? Nothing for the moment, I will think about it tomorrow.[28]

If Constantine apparently had had enough for one night, the revolutionaries, though disappointed with the failure of the attack on the Belvedere, moved aggressively to secure more support. In this too they failed, with one crucial exception. After unsuccessfully attacking the Russian cavalry barracks, Polish troops, stationed near Lazienki Park, refused their invitation to join the revolt. In retreat, Wysocki and his men then moved into the heart of the city's working class districts and there finally found real support for the first time. The working population *en masse* spontaneously joined the insurrection, and by storming the Arsenal was able to insure armaments for thirty thousand insurgents. By dawn of November 30, the revolutionaries held most of the city even though they were without the support of the groups that they had most counted upon, Constantine's Polish troops and the city officials. In fact, it was only thanks to the backing Constantine received from most of his Polish troops that he was able to maintain possession of the southern part of Warsaw. Now that the city was an armed camp, the question was what action the Polish officials and Constantine would now take.

By midnight of the 29th, Drucki-Lubecki learned that the insurgents had not yet organized and as yet demonstrated no intention of creating a new government. On his own initiative, he decided to establish a ruling body consisting of members of the Administrative Council (including Czartoryski) to determine a course of action against the revolt. Clearly the most pressing matter was to reach an understanding with Constantine, and after some difficulties in locating him, a delegation was sent. At a brief meeting, Constantine unequivocally stated that he personally would take no steps to restore order in the city or to suppress the revolution. That task, he said, was up to "the Poles themselves."[29] According to Leon Dembowski, a contemporary memoirist, Constantine elaborated by saying:

> I am far from wishing to commit the same fault which my cousin from Orange has committed. To fight in the streets, is exposing myself to spilling the blood of the brave... It is up to you, Sirs, to employ those measures which you judge efficacious to tranquilize this struggle.[30]

Amazingly, Constantine had placed the burden of responsibility on Drucki-Lubecki, Czartoryski, and their newly formed council to find their own way out of the crisis. Their first decision was to invite new members to join the council, including the highly regarded writer Julian Niemcewicz and the popular General Joseph Chlopicki, who had gained some fame over his long-standing disagreement with Constantine. The inclusion of these individuals, and particularly Chlopicki, was believed to give the council some added authority.

Deciding to follow an anti-revolutionary policy and clearly hoping not to offend Nicholas, the council tried to restore order in the capital. To begin with, General Chlopicki was appointed commander in chief by the council to put down Wysocki's uprising, which he considered "pure folly." Second, the council sent orders to regiments in the provinces to come to Warsaw. Many of these troops believed the call was in support rather than against the revolution, and were more than willing to heed it, even though Constantine had also sent orders for these same troops to join him just outside the city. In the end, many troops chose sides according to their own inclinations, with a good number immediately going over to the revolutionaries.[31] Thus, within a short time a new danger developed. The council now was not only faced with an insurgent city, but with the appearance of a number of Polish soldiers who had been won over to the side of the revolution and who were anxious to launch an attack on Constantine's remaining troops so as to provoke a war with Russia.[32] Concerted action with Constantine had been imperative but was rendered increasingly difficult by the fact that, after November 30, the council was forced by popular demands to include in its ranks radicals who were committed to leading the Kingdom to a total break with Russia.

On December 2, Drucki-Lubecki, Czartoryski and two new radical delegates, Lelewel and Ostrowski, went to Wierzbno to meet with Constantine. Drucki-Lubecki initiated the discussion by attempting to describe to Constantine the difficulties of the council, most specifically its lack of military strength to put down the revolution and its own inability to prevent more radical persons from entering its ranks. They further explained that the revolution was a natural and popular reaction against violation of the constitution. This last premise Constantine refused to accept, claiming that in his opinion, it could only be the work of hooligans, and that the population and the Army, given all those who flocked to his support, could obviously not be in support of the revolution. Not reaching an agreement on any of the issues before them, Drucki-Lubecki and Czartoryski tried next to assure Constantine that at least for the time being the council remained committed to a restoration of the King's power and hoped to avoid Nicholas' anger. Accepting their assurances, Constantine willingly promised his continued neutrality, and agreed not to attack Warsaw without giving at least twenty-four hours notice. He also agreed not to summon his Lithuanian Corps to the capital. Not satisfied with this arrangement, the more radical members in the council pressed Constantine to intercede on behalf of the Poles with Nicholas for the protection of constitutional rights and the reunion of the Eastern Provinces. In this matter, too, Constantine acquiesced.[33]

On December 3, the previous day's understanding were undone by new more radical developments in Warsaw, including the dissolution of the council whose members had just succeeded in reaching agreement with Constantine. In its place a new more radical Provisional Government of the Kingdom of Poland was established. That same day, Constantine issued a proclamation permitting his Polish troops to leave his command[34] and announced that he would withdraw with his Russian troops beyond the Polish border. Perhaps Constantine's decision reflected his loss of hope, given the new circumstances. He might also have thought that his decision to withdraw all Russian influences might diminish revolutionary feeling and provide an opportunity for the Poles to resolve their crisis on their own.[35]

The question as to what action Constantine could or should have taken to prevent the spread of the revolution is of considerable interest and has been answered in several ways. Two conflicting views are the following: first, that Constantine could have done nothing; and secondly, that Constantine could have put down the revolution, but chose not to do so. The first view contends that Constantine greatly misunderstood the nature of the Polish revolutionary movement and as a result, he underestimated the situation so completely that his defensive measures were utterly insufficient to quash the revolt.[36] Others support this view by claiming that Constantine was either so incompetent or in such a disoriented state of mind during the crucial night that he was unable to make necessary plans to suppress the revolution.[37] Another opinion of a Marxian theoretical character contends that even if Constantine had been capable of effective action and had used all his available troops, it would have been impossible for him to put down the revolution because the workers had thrown their support against him.[38]

A second and more popular view holds that Constantine could have crushed the revolution, especially during its earliest stages, but that he chose not to do so.[39] The reasons which various authors have given for his action are diverse: some contend that it was because Constantine felt that he should not interfere in a matter which he considered to be purely of Polish concern.[40] In this connection, Constantine could have believed that any intrusion with Russian troops was a violation of the Kingdom's autonomy and even an act of war; besides, there seemed to have been an understanding dating back to Alexander that Russian troops were not to become involved in internal Polish problems.[41] Another explanation offered, and a most probable one, is that Constantine refused to interfere because of his fondness for the Poles, his fear of bloodshed and his historic unwillingness to use his troops for actual fighting.[42]

Constantine himself seemed to have had no doubt about his ability to suppress the revolt. In an interview with the *Sejm* deputy Wolicki, he made clear that:

Had I wished you would all have been annihilated at the very beginning... Fundamentally, I am a better Pole than you all, Gentlemen... I have spoken your language for so long that it is now difficult for me to speak Russian. I have proved my sympathy with you by forbidding the imperial troops to fire on you.[43]

Still another reason why Constantine may have refused to take action was because by 1830 he had developed a rather defeatist attitude toward the possibility of maintaining both the *status quo* in the Kingdom and his own position within it.[44] It was known that Nicholas viewed the autonomous status of the Kingdom quite negatively; it was also no secret that Nicholas was striving to reduce Constantine's power in Poland and the Eastern Provinces. On several occasions in 1830 alone, Constantine complained to Nicholas of the difficulty of his position and attempts on the part of some to force his retirement. Constantine also made plain that he knew Nicholas was permitting intrusions on his prerogatives.[45] Similarly, Constantine's deteriorating health, amply documented in letters to friends and relatives, as well as by his frequent trips to European health spas, could well indicate that he was becoming resigned to retirement.[46]

In considering Constantine's actions, some Poles contended that he should have been allowed the option of actually supporting the revolution. One general, Ignace Pradzynski, for example, suggested appealing to Constantine's pro-Polish sympathies as well as his sense of mistreatment by Nicholas, by asking him not only to issue a manifesto calling for the reunion of the Eastern Provinces to the Kingdom, the reunion of the Lithuanian Army Corps to the Kingdom's army, and the formation of a new government under Czartoryski, (points which he had already supported) but also to join the revolution.[47]

Upon learning of Constantine's resolve to return to Russia, General Chlopicki offered Constantine supplies to facilitate the journey for himself and his Russian troops.[48] Constantine's and his troops' passage was further eased by the generally non-belligerent attitudes of the local population in the eastern parts of the Kingdom. During the march, Constantine and his wife stayed at several estates and, thanks to several recorded conversations with the local *szlachta*, it is possible to learn of Constantine's attitude toward recent developments. Particularly hurt by the attack on the Belvedere, which, in his opinion, was an attack on his life, Constantine nevertheless did not disavow his affection for the Poles. In fact, he pledged once more to try to forget what had happened and indicated his willingness to present the Polish point of view to his brother.[49] Along the way, many seemed convinced that Constantine was committed to reconciliation above all else.[50]

Because of the distance between St. Petersburg and Warsaw, it was not until December 7 that Nicholas was able to learn what had transpired. Upon receiving the news of the revolution, he ordered a partial mobilization, but only on December 17 did he issue a manifesto to the Poles condemning the insurrection and ordering the Polish corps commander to the city of Plock; in this manifesto the Tsar actually promised pardon to all those who returned to their duties. At the end of December a Polish delegation representing the Provisional Government arrived in St. Petersburg and placed before the Tsar promises of loyalty and requests for reunion of the Eastern Provinces, along with greater guarantees of constitutional freedoms and finally a general amnesty. From the outset, Nicholas made clear that he would grant no constitutional concessions, a stance which stiffened the Poles' hostility still more. In the newly formed Warsaw *Sejm* the cry was heard: "We are finished with Nicholas."[51] The break was now in sight: on January 23, 1831, Nicholas was dethroned as King of Poland by the Provisional Government.

For his part, in many letters to Nicholas from the border, Constantine sought to keep his promise to mediate between the Tsar and the Poles. From the beginning, however, he saw the hopelessness of the task, as Nicholas said: "You judge who must lose in the struggle, Russia or Poland, since one side must lose."[52] Nevertheless, Constantine continued presenting the Polish point of view and implored Nicholas to opt for a policy of "generosity of soul" rather than "force."[53] On another occasion Constantine begged Nicholas to be "magnanimous" to the Poles,[54] and again another time he reminded the Tsar that "moderation and generosity were the best policy."[55] Constantine's pleas, however, were in vain for by the end of January General Dibich with the Russian Army had begun to move westward; on February 5, his forces crossed the Lithuanian-Polish frontier. Permitted to accompany Dibich on the campaign, Constantine was present at the first important engagement of the Russo-Polish War, the battle of Grochow. From a Russian point of view it was here that Constantine completely compromised himself by betraying his pro-Polish sympathies. During the course of the battle he noticed that many of the Polish soldiers were his own trainees and he openly cheered them, exclaiming "Good, good, children, Polish soldiers are the best in the world."[56] Tempering his enthusiasm in a letter to Nicholas, Constantine still could write about their performance that "the Poles, i.e., the regulars, fight marvelously well and if the numbers were equal, it would have been quite a different thing."[57] Even more damaging to Constantine was that at least some blamed him for the Russian failure to defeat the Poles decisively at Grochow. According to certain observers, at the crucial moment in the battle, the Russian advance was halted because Constantine intervened and forced Dibich to order a cease fire.[58]

How Nicholas accepted these reports is unclear; what is certain, however, is that within days of the battle, Constantine was asked to leave headquarters. Soon after, not mincing his words, Nicholas wrote Constantine that he had been "retired, so as not to be hurt."[59] As if to prevent even the slightest misunderstanding, the following month Constantine received "an expressed invitation to suspend a return to the army."[60]

By June, Constantine was completely demoralized by his complete inactivity, and in several letters asked Nicholas to permit him to return to the army in whatever capacity Nicholas would consider proper.[61] Receiving nothing but polite evasions to his request, Constantine was forced to accept the truth of his position; he no longer was to play any role in the affairs of either the Empire or the Kingdom. Not hiding his feelings, Constantine wrote: "I am cut to the heart, I did not think that at the age of fifty-one and after thirty years' service, I would finish my career in such a deplorable way."[62] During his few remaining days Constantine stayed with his ailing wife and then on June 27 died obscurely at Vitebsk. His last words are said to have been an appeal to Nicholas: "Tell the Tsar, I am dying, I beg him to forgive the Poles."[63]

According to most sources, Constantine died of cholera which was raging in the vicinity. Still, some insist that Constantine's death was the result of other causes, poison, or suicide.[64] After his death he was buried at Tsarskoe Selo where, soon after, his wife also died.

Because the circumstances of Constantine's death were never openly explained and the St. Petersburg newspapers failed to note his demise, something customary with members of the imperial family, rumors began to spring up that Constantine was alive and either imprisoned in the Peter and Paul Fortress or wandering about under a foreign name.[65]

Constantine's death was not marked by any great mourning; rather a sense of relief seemed to be the dominant reaction in the capital. Probably reflecting Nicholas' view, Benckendorff wrote with regard to his death in the *Third Section Survey* for 1831 that "although his passing had saddened many, in another sense the public had judged that this circumstance will remove much of the opposition to the government's orders relating to affairs with Poland."[66]

In this way, then, a man who held the destiny of one country in his hands for years, and might have controlled the fate of a still larger one, died as he himself anticipated, no differently than "a small official in retirement."[67] The loss was perhaps not so much in his humble death; rather, in the fact that his aspirations and work had ended in total frustration.

CONCLUSION

Although originating in the period following the partitions of 1772, 1793 and 1795, the Polish Question emerged as a truly perennial issue of European politics during the Napoleonic wars. An important concern at the Congress of Vienna in 1815 following the fall of Napoleon, Poland's fate at that international conclave took on a new shape, however, that of a problem of Russo-Polish relations. Initially, at least, a partial resolution to this problem seemed to emerge from Vienna in the form of a Polish "Congress Kingdom," an autonomous territorial unit wedded to Russia but possessing a number of distinguishing governmental forms which could not help but preserve the memory of the old independent Poland to its citizens. Yet, by 1830, the atmosphere of cautious good will about the Kingdom's relationship with St. Petersburg had become transformed into one marked by suspicion and hostility.

This study with its focus upon the person of Grand Duke Constantine has been directed toward determining more fully the causes of the breakdown in Polish- Russian relations in 1830, a development which led to an ultimately disastrous insurrection, followed by massive tsarist repression and the termination of the Congress Kingdom's special status in the Empire. Up to the present, there has been relatively little emphasis placed upon assessing the role of Grand Duke Constantine in affecting the course of Russo-Polish relations during his fifteen year long tenure as *de facto* ruler of the country. Students of the period who have given him some attention have generally maintained two perspectives, although they share common negative overall evaluations of his career. Only one major exception to these negative opinions exists and this is to be found in the work of the Russian historian E.P. Karnovich, who assessed Constantine more positively. However, his late nineteenth century biography of Constantine is not

115

without its own flaws, particularly in terms of its lack of adequate documentation.

Historians seeing Constantine's role as being of only minor significance such as, Handelsman, Kukiel and Kieniewicz, for example, tend to ignore Constantine in their analyses of the Congress Kingdom, at best noting his appointment as commander in chief of the Polish Army or his somewhat nebulous and informal status as "Viceroy" in the Kingdom. Ironically, other writers including Askenazy, Kraushar and Lojek, although also ignoring Constantine's overall importance, individually point to the Grand Duke's crucial role in one or another area such as the Army, the police and cultural life. In any case, both groups of scholars fail to integrate into their studies an appreciation of Constantine's involvement in shaping Russo-Polish relations.

In my judgment, from the time of his first contacts with the Kingdom as Acting Head of the Polish Army in 1814 Constantine not only defined the political and social character of the Kingdom in ways that affected its development both positively and negatively; he also established a unique arrangement between Warsaw and St. Petersburg that clearly bore his imprint.

By 1815, having been confirmed by Alexander as commander in chief of the Army, Constantine directed its formation and stamped its subsequent evolution with the mark of his personality, habits and attitudes. He imposed alien and oppressive military procedures upon his troops, while severely restricting the promotion of Polish officers in the Army of the Congress Kingdom. His actions, when considered in light of the revolutionary and nationalist aspirations that influenced a segment of the Polish population by the late 1820's contributed to the Army's eventual involvement in the November, 1830 Revolution. Later with special grants of power received from Alexander in the Kingdom and the old Polish "Eastern Provinces" already absorbed directly into the Empire, Constantine was able to assume the position of *de facto* ruler in both territories. Not only was all governmental authority in the Kingdom as defined by the constitution under Constantine's control, he also formed a kind of personal "government" outside the constitution headed by Mohrenheim, Novosiltsev and Drucki-Lubecki in which everyone carried out his wishes. Through his manipulation of both of these "governments" and thanks to his penchant for detail and great capacity for work, Constantine personally directed domestic and foreign affairs pertaining to the Kingdom and the Eastern Provinces, whether these concerned significant issues or the seemingly most trivial.

Constantine from the beginning was the overseer of the country's political, moral and cultural life. In support of the conservative land-owners and higher clergy he led the drive against liberal, anti-feudal and anti-clerical attacks. Under his direct supervision parliamentary opposition was crushed, liberal orientations in cultural and political life were suppressed, and the press, theater and mails were thoroughly censored. Because of his scrupulous insistence that nothing escape his attention, not one but several police systems reported directly to him. Consequently, in view of his great governmental powers as well as his intimate involvement in all aspects of the Kingdom operation, Constantine's role in the Kingdom can be assessed as having become all-pervasive. Hence, no study of the period can be considered adequate or accurate without taking him into account as the leading political actor in the Kingdom and in its relations with the Empire.

Sharing this view of Constantine are two of his own contemporaries, Harring and Moriolles. However, their evaluations leave much to be desired in that they failed to note the major change that took place in Constantine's relationships with the Poles over the years which gradually led him to develop more positive feelings and policies toward his subjects. In their interpretation, they assert that since he was an all-powerful tyrant and inhumane martinet, he drove the freedom-loving Poles to revolution.

Nevertheless, as devoted as Constantine was to the merits of the oppressive Prussian military system, he also displayed a concern for his troops' welfare on numerous occasions; as the years rolled on he seemed increasingly reluctant to use them in military combat situations as well. Under the impetus of long years of living among the Poles and following his marriage to Grudzinska, Constantine openly began to identify himself with the Poles, albeit the most conservative variety. It is true that Constantine did not represent the views of the increasingly vocal liberal elements in the Kingdom and subjected them to repressive measures. Yet, in so far as their views reflected genuine Polish nationalist aspirations, such as in the matter of the reunion of the Eastern Provinces, Constantine represented them too as their spokesman *vis-a-vis* Tsar Nicholas. In other areas, also, Constantine frequently tried to defend the Polish point of view, for example in his efforts to minimize the Polish repercussions of the Decembrist Revolt and to insist upon adherence to constitutional procedures for the investigation and the trial of accused Poles.

In his political conservativism Constantine found support for his actions and views among like-minded Poles. His repression of radicals had their unequivocal support and while his repressive measures drove some toward a more revolutionary frame of mind, they also strengthened the loyalty other Poles felt to his regime. To them, Constantine's stance represented the preservation of the social conditions of the *status quo* while allowing for a modicum of patriotic Polish feeling justifying the existence of the separate and autonomous Polish Kingdom.

The evolution of Constantine's policy of autonomy for the Kingdom, one that differed noticeably from what many liberal Poles, or for that matter Alexander, or Nicholas sought, first developed under the influence of his gradual polonization and the succession difficulties in Russia, which deprived him of any claims he might have made to the throne. Not unreasonably he began to see the advantages of a special and permanent position for himself in the Kingdom as a compensation for his renunciation of his claims to succeed Alexander. Constantine's policy, which pressed for the Kingdom's autonomy under his personal rule, clearly did not satisfy Polish demands for total independence or Russian aspirations aimed at the complete absorption of the Kingdom into the Empire. Yet it did find support among those in both Poland and Russia who favored a solid and peaceful relationship between the two states. But such a policy depended largely upon two factors, the Tsar's own support and that of influential Poles in the Kingdom. This Constantine succeeded in maintaining until 1825 because both Alexander and the conservative Polish establishment backed his rule for various reasons — the need to resolve the matter of imperial succession, personal advantage, conservative supremacy, political realism. Thus, his policy might well have continued indefinitely had it not been for Alexander's death and his replacement by Nicholas in the confusion and mutual recriminations of December, 1825. The rise of a revolutionary political climate in the Kingdom due partly to adverse economic conditions in the years that followed in turn undercut his position there. These developments, then compounded by Constantine's own failings and indecision caused the eventual failure of his policy in 1830.

Given his more authoritarian and nationalistic outlook and the strange circumstances of his own assumption of power, Nicholas was unsympathetic to both his brother and the Poles. He had long disdained the autonomous existence of a Polish Kingdom, even under Constantine's conservative rule. In addition, he was unfavorable to the Grand Duke's recommendations in support of the unification of the Eastern Provinces with the Congress Kingdom. Nicholas overruled Constantine during the Russo-Turkish War and he expressed growing alarm in response to the news of rising liberal and revolutionary activity among the Poles, blaming Constantine for this development. While the Polish arrangement desired by Constantine had been sanctioned by Alexander, for Nicholas other possibilities were more to his liking, such as the Kingdom's absorption into the Empire. All that was required was a provocation justifying Russian action to dissolve the Kingdom, something that radical, disgruntled Poles unwittingly provided by their Revolution of November, 1830 and their decision to formally depose Nicholas as King in January of 1831, a move that gave the Tsar ample excuse to nullify the entire arrangement. The Russian conquest of Poland thus not only ended the autonomous existence of the Kingdom but also coincided with the death of the troublesome Constantine.

A question of particular interest is whether Constantine could have done anything to prevent the failure of his policy after 1825. In the light of Nicholas' own resolve, and his basic antipathy to his older brother, the Poles and the autonomous Polish Kingdom, it seems doubtful that Constantine could have changed the Tsar's attitude. Similarly, it is difficult to determine whether Constantine could have done much more than he actually did to repress the growth of revolutionary ideas in Poland, or to find ways of improving the country's economic conditions. Still, at the moment of the actual outbreak it is clear that Constantine could and might have taken direct action. If he had put down the revolt at its inception, as he claimed he could have, and had not left the matter up to conservatives like Czartoryski, Chlopicki and Drucki-Lubecki (who soon found themselves dominated by radical elements and acting as leaders of the very rebellion they regarded as the height of folly), it is quite probable that the revolt could have been suppressed and the *status quo* maintained, at least for a time. Indeed, much of the Army initially supported Constantine, and not the revolutionaries. But instead of taking decisive action, Constantine wavered and thus permitted the revolt to spread. His failure at the critical movement meant not only the end of the Congress Kingdom and the triumph of Nicholas' reactionary solution to the Polish Question, but devastation for the Polish lands followed by thirty years of martial law.[1]

Clearly an individual with enormous talents as a political strategist, diplomat and military leader could have contributed much to the preservation of the delicate balance established by Alexander and Czartoryski. That Constantine was not qualified for so complex a task is evident. Yet this fact does not lessen the extent of the complicated role, both positive and negative, that he played in shaping relations between Poland and Russia which after him have been marked by continuing antagonism, punctuated by repression and violence under tsars and commisars alike. This despite the hopes of generations desirous of a more harmonious state of affairs in Poland and Russia alike.

NOTES

CHAPTER I
GRAND DUKE CONSTANTINE PAVLOVICH IN RUSSIA, 1779-1813

1. Count Gregory Orlov, (1734-1783), as an influential officer in the guards, aided Catherine in her rise to power and was her lover until 1772. Although afterwards always her personal friend, he lost his political influence with her at the end of their *liaison*.

2. Prince Gregory Potemkin, (1739-1791), was Catherine's official favorite only from 1774 to 1776; however, his political influence lasted much longer, until the time of his death in 1791. In addition, the politically ambitious Potemkin also worked for the establishment of a Kingdom of Dacia which was to be an adjunct to a revived Byzantine Empire under Constantine.

3. E. P. Karnovich, *Tsesarevich Konstantin Pavlovich* (St. Petersburg: A. S. Suvorin, 1899), pp. 5, 9.

4. "Imperatritsa Ekaterina II i Kn. Potemkin," *Russkaia Starina*, XVI (August, 1876), p. 586.

5. *Ibid.* The city of Constantinople was often called Tsargrad in Russia.

6. The Treaty of Iasi, January 9, 1792, transferred to Russia Ockakov, the territory between the Dniester and the Bug rivers, recognized the annexation of the Crimea and confirmed the earlier Treaty of Kuchuk-Kainarji.

7. Stanislas August Poniatowski, (1732-1798), another of Catherine's lovers, was placed on the Polish throne by Catherine in 1764 and reigned as Poland's last king until 1795. Although unable to check Russian interference in Poland and prevent the Partitions, Poniatowski gave great inspiration and encouragement to the revival of Polish cultural and political activity in the second half of the eighteenth century.

8. Szymon Askenazy, "Bracia," *Kurier Warszawski*, CXXXXIII (May, 1933), 6; also Wladyslaw Bortnowski, *Wielki Ksiaze Konstanty podczas Powstania Listopadowego*, (Warsaw: Ministerstwo Obrony Narodowy, 1965), p. 196.

9. N. K. Schilder, *Imperator Aleksandr Pervyi* (St. Petersburg: A. S. Suvorin, 1904), 1, 49.

10. N. Chechulin, "Konstantine Pavlovich," *Russkii Biograficheskii Slovar*, ed. A. A. Polovtsov, IX (1903), 157.

11. *Rys Zycia Jego Cesarzewiczewskiego Mosci Wielkiego Xiecia Konstantego Pawlowicza*, (Warsaw, 1837), p. 5.

12. Karnovich, p. 11.

13. Cechulin, pp. 157-158.

14. Karnovich, pp. 13-15. One of Saltykov's collaborators in the education of the grand dukes, A. P. Masson, has a differing opinion on the merits of Saltykov. To him, Saltykov's only real contribution toward the development of his young charges was that he protected them from drafts and indigestion. For that matter, in his opinion, all of the individuals entrusted with the boys' education, with the exception of LaHarpe, were "ignorant, bigots and buffoons." However, Masson had great regard for Catherine's educational plan; he believed that if it has been followed, Alexander and Constantine would have been the "best educated princes in Europe." A. P. Masson, *Memoires secrets sur la Russie*, (Paris: Librairie de Firmin Didot Freres, Fils et Cie, 1859), pp. 213, 215.

15. LaHarpe (1754-1838), it appears, even in his own time, was not universally admired. Despite Masson's approval, other colleagues, such as the Count de Moriolles, viewed LaHarpe less favorably. According to Moriolles, LaHarpe was "a lively spirit, a hot head with confidence and finesse in intrigue, a heart full of hatred and vindictiveness, a great attachment to modern ideas and a very deep ambition covered over by philosophical disinterestedness,..." Alexander de Moriolles, *Memoires* (Paris: Societe d'Editions Litteraires et Artistiques, 1902), p. 138.

16. "Otchety Lagarpa grafu Mikolago Ivanovichu Saltykovu o vospitanii Velikich Kniazei Aleksandra i Konstantina Pavlovichei," *Russkaia Starina*, I (1870), 33-44; 103-132; 407-419.

17. Chechulin, p. 157.

18. Karnovich, p. 21.

19. "Pisma Velikago Kniazia Konstantina Pavlovicha k Lagarpu 1796-1829," *Sbornik Russkago Istoricheskago Obshchestva* V (1870), 56. One may wonder some about the accuracy of this pessimistic self appraisal. In any event, Constantine's formal education ended when he married, at age sixteen.

20. "Pisma germanskoi printsessy o russkom dvore 1795 god," *Russkii Arkhiv*, VII (1869), 1091.

21. "Pisma Velikago Kniazia Konstantina Pavlovicha...," p. 60.

22. Edward A. Hogetts, *The Court of Russia in the Nineteenth Century*, (New York: Charles Scribner's Sons, 1908), I, 56.

23. Chechulin, p. 160.

24. Adam Czartoryski, *Memoires du Prince Adam Czartoryski et Correspondence avec l'Empereur Alexandre Ier*, (Paris: Librairie Plon, 1887), p. 109.

25. The Czartoryskis were descendants of a noble Lithuanian family which had become polonized at the time of the Polish-Lithuanian union of 1386.

During the centuries of greatness of the Polish-Lithuanian Commonwealth, the Czartoryskis played an important part. But it was not until the middle of the eighteenth century that they reached their pre-eminent position as the most powerful family group in Poland and became known simply as "the Family."

26. Czartoryski, p. 102.

27. *Ibid.*, p. 111.

28. General Sablionkoff, "Reminiscences of the Court and Times of the Emperor, Paul I of Russia Up to the Period of his Death — From the papers of a deceased Russian General Officer," *Fraser's Magazine for Town and Country*, LXXII (August, 1865), 225, 230.

29. *Ibid.*, p. 228.

30. *Ibid.*, pp. 230-231, 237.

31. General Saltykov, "Le Mort de Paul Ier," *Revue Moderne*, XXXV (1865), 537.

32. D. Miliutin, *Istoriia voiny 1799 goda mezhdu Rossiei i Frantsiei v tsarstvovanie Imperatora Pavla I.* Vol. I (St. Petersburg, 1857), pp. 379- 380.

33. Checulin, p. 170.

34. *Rys zycia...*, p. 29; General de Vaudoncourt, "Memoires pour servir a l'histoire de la guerre entre la France et la Russie en 1812" in Adrien Ergon, *Vie d'Alexandre Ier, Empereur de Russie - suivi de notice sur les Grand-Ducs Constantin, Nicholas et Michel,* (Paris: Chez F. Denn, Libraire 1826), p. 196. There are even accounts of how Constantine later in the war of 1812 was willing to kill personally wounded prisoners of war who were unable to travel in order to terminate their suffering during the retreat of the Napoleonic army from Russia. General Sir Robert Wilson, *Narrative of Events During the Invasion of Russia by Napoleon Bonaparte and the Retreat of the French Army 1812,* (London: John Murray, 1860), p. 257.

35. *Rys zycia...*, pp. 32-33.

36. *Ibid.*, p. 171.

37. Chechulin, p. 172.

38. *Rys zycia...*, p. 33.

39. Chechulin, p. 173.

40. "Iz zapisok N. A. Sablukova," *Ruskii Arkhiv*, VII (1869), 1896.

41. "Iz zapisok Generala-Adiutanta E. F. Komarovskago," *Russkii Arkhiv*, V (1867), 244-246. Komarovskii was a colonel in Constantine's Ismailovsky Guards. Also "Iz zapisok N. A. Sablukova," p. 1897.

42. Chechulin, p. 173; "Iz zapisok N. A. Sablukova," p. 1936.

43. Chechulin, p. 174.

44. J. N. Jawaski, *Essai historique et politique sur la Royaume de Pologne, 1815-1830,* (Paris: Au Cabinet de lecture Polonais, 1846), p. 49.

45. Chechulin, p. 175.

46. Szymon Askenazy, *W. Ksiaze Konstanty i Ksieznicka Helena Lubomirska,* (Warsaw, 1913), pp. 415-416, 430, 436.

47. Chechulin, p. 176.

48. Karnovich, p. 90; Chechulin, 178.

49. Moriolles, p. 152; Karnovich, p. 102.
50. Moriolles, p. 153; Chechulin, p. 178.
51. Saltykov, p. 117; Karnovich, p. 97.
52. "Dnevnik Shtats Sekretaria Grigoriia Ivanovicha Villamova 1775-1842," *Russkaia Starina*, I (1912), 32.
53. Chechulin, p. 179; Karnovich, p. 102.
54. Chuchulin, p. 179.
55. *Ibid.*
56. *Ibid.*, "Zapiski Ivan Stepanovicha Zhirkevicha," *Russkaia Starina*, X (1874), 651.
57. Chechulin, pp. 179-180.
58. Karnovich, pp. 110-111.
59. Chechulin, p. 180; Karnovich, p. 111.
60. "Konstanty Pawlowicz," *Wielka Encyklopedya Powszechna Ilustrowane*, (Warsaw: W Drukarni Gazety Handlowy, 1904), XXXVII, 703.

CHAPTER II
CONSTANTINE AND THE FORMING OF THE POLISH CONGRESS
KINGDOM, 1813 — 1815

1. The *szlachta* was the Polish gentry class. It was made up of approximately ten percent of the Polish population, many of whom were nearly landless and impoverished, yet prided themselves in their noble origins.
2. The King of Saxony was Napoleon's puppet ruler in the short-lived Duchy of Warsaw.
3. Gryzelda Missalowa, "Ziemie polskie w dobie autonomicznej Krolestwa Polskiego (1813-1830)," *Historia Polski*, ed. Stefan Kieniewicz and Witold Kula (Warsaw: Panstwowe Wydawnictwo Naukowe, 1958), II, 189, 190.
4. Adam Czartoryski shared many of Alexander's liberal views, among them constitutional rule and national self-determination, and became one of his closest friends and political collaborators. In 1804, as a member of Alexander's Secret Committee and Acting Head of the Russian Ministry of Foreign Affairs, Czartoryski had proposed to Alexander that he take the title of King of Poland and rule over a kingdom made up of all the Polish provinces included in pre-partition Poland. Adam Czartoryski, *Memoires du Prince Adam Czartoryski et correspondence avec l'Empereur Alexandre Ier*, ed. by Charles de Mazade (Paris: Librairie Plon, 1887), II, 63. Further information about Czartoryski's proposals for Alexander with regard to Poland in later years is to be found in "Papiery tyczace sie projektu ogloszenia Alexander I krolem Polski z lat 1806-1810." The Czartoryski Library, Krakow, 5231 V and in Marian Kukiel, *Czartoryski and European Unity 1770-1861*, (Princeton: Princeton University Press, 1955), especially Chapters 4-8. See also M. K. Dziewanowski, "Czartoryski and his 'Essai sur la

diplomatie,' " *Slavic Review*, 30, Number 3 (1971), 589-605; and Charles Morley, "Czartoryski as a Polish Statesmen," *Slavic Review*, 30, Number 3 (1971), 606-614.

5. As a result of the Napoleonic Code, many reforms affecting the situation of the peasantry in the Duchy were passed; whereas, in the Polish territories earlier annexed to Russia the peasantry was still subject to feudal controls. Union of the two sections of former Poland would eventually have required uniformity in peasant status and hence strong opposition to Polish unification on the part of liberals in the Duchy, who feared loss of newly won peasant rights and on the part of conservatives in the Empire, who refused even to consider emancipation.

6. Michel Oginski, *Memoires de Michel Oginski*, (Paris: Chez Ponthieu, Librairie, 1827), III, 236-237 in Barbara Grochulska, *Ksiestwo Warszawskie*, (Warsaw: Wiedza Powszechna, 1966), p. 207.

7. Oginski, p. 237.

8. Alexander I to Adam Czartoryski, January 23, 1813, (Copy), The Polish Library, Paris, 340, p. 9.

9. Already at this time Russian opposition to Alexander's pro-Polish activities was manifested. When Colonel Falkowski was sent to Russia to bring back Polish prisoners he was met with hostility and a refusal to cooperate on the part of Russian officers. He was then forced to appeal to Dabrowski and Constantine. Constantine to Falkowski, Jagiellonian Library, Krakow, 6284 IV (5), pp. 95-98. Also see Waclaw Tokarz, *Armja Krolestwa Polskiego (1815- 1830)*, (Piotrkow: Nakladem departamentu Wojskowego Naczelnego Komitetu Narodowego, 1917), p. 13.

10. Harold Nicolson, *The Congress of Vienna*, (London: Constable and Co., Ltd., 1917), p. 148.

11. See Nicolson *supra*; also C. K. Webster, *The Congress of Vienna 1814-1815* (London: G. Bell and Sons, Ltd., 1945); H. Montegomery Hyde, "The Congress of Vienna," *The Cambridge History of Poland*, ed. W. F. Reddaway *et al*. (Cambridge: At the University Press, 1951), pp. 257-274.

12. Constantine Pavlovich, "Rozkaz dzienny do Narodowego Wojska Polskiego," The Jagiellonian Library, Krakow, 6025 III. (3), p. 89; also Constantine Pavlovich, "Orde du jour du grand-duc de Russie Constantin, Varsovie, decembre 11, 1814," The Ossolineum, Wroclaw, II, 327, pp. 139-39'; in Polish, pp. 139- 40.

13. T. Ostrowski, *Zywot T. Ostrowskiego*, (Paris, 1840), II, 657, in Kazimierz Bartoszewicz, *Utworzenie Krolestwa Kongresowego*, (Krakow: Nakladem Centralnego Wydawnictw, N.K.N., 1916), p. 120. The curious and contrary behavior on the part of Alexander is explained by Nicolson as being a product of Alexander's schizophrenic mentality. According to Nicholson, Alexander acted under the impulse of two different sets of theories, hence at the Congress he was moody, secretive and uncertain and could at one moment send "Constantine to Warsaw to raise and equip a Polish army to fight on his side against the Western powers which stood in the way of an enlarged kingdom completely subservient to him and at another moment

he would write to Jeremy Bentham asking the philosopher to draft for him a model constitution for Poland on the most advanced lines." Nicholson, *The Congress of Vienna*, pp. 149-150.

14. *Le Grand-Duc Constantin a Varsovie pendant le Congres de Vienne*, (Paris: Librairie Slave, 1847), pp. 59-60.

15. Alexander undoubtedly took into account Russian public opinion which "after so great an ordeal and so vast a victory, would not have tolerated the cession (even to a satellite or protectorate) of territory which had been Russian territory, however illgotten..." Nicholson, *The Congress of Vienna*, p. 28.

16. "Acte final du Congres de Vienne, signe le 9 juin 1815," in Comte D'Angeberg (Leonard Chodzko), *Recueils des traites, conventions et actes diplomatiques concernant la Pologne 1762-1862*, (Paris: Amyot, Editeur des Archives Diplomatiques, 1862), pp. 696-699.

17. By way of comparison, Russia's population was forty-five million and its total area was eighteen million square kilometers. Stefan Kieniewicz, *Przemiany spoleczne i gospodarcze w Krolestwie Polskim 1815-1830*, (Warsaw: Ksiazka i Wiedza, 1951), p. 7.

18. Comte D'Angeberg, *loc. cit.*, pp. 696-699.

19. "Rozkaz dzienny do Wojska Polskiego 30/12 kwietnia-maj, 1830," The University of Warsaw Library, Warsaw.

20. Nicolson, pp. 26-27.

21. Missalowa, p. 198.

22. Tokarz, *Armja Krolestwa Polskiego...*, p. 17; also Bortnowski, *Wielki Ksiaze Konstanty...*, p. 197.

23. Pozzo di Borgo, *Memoire sur la Pologne, 1814*, The Czartoryski Library, Krakow, 5220 IV, pp. 29-41.

24. F. Marten, *Recueil des traites et conventions conclus par la Russie avec les puissances etrangers*, (St. Petersburg, 1874-1909), III, 214; VII, 63 in Bartoszewicz, p. 33.

25. Nicolson, p. 28.

26. Szymon Askenazy, *Lukasinski*, (Warsaw: Nakladem Drukarni Wl. Lazarskiego, 1929), I, 52, 74, 347, in Henryk Moscicki, *Projekty polaczenia Litwy z Krolestwem Polskim w okresie 1813-1830*, (Warsaw: Wydawnictwo Towarzystwa Strazy Kresowej, 1921), p. 9; Bartoszewicz, p. 291; Schilder, III, 551.

27. "Konstanty Pavlovich," *Encyklopedia Wojskowa*, ed. Otton-Laskowski (Warsaw, 1934), p. 467; Tokarz, p. 11.

28. Askenazy, p. 53.

29. Letter to Lubecki in Stanislaw Smolka, *Korespondencja Lubeckiego z ministrami sekretarzami stanu Ignacym Sobolewskim i Stefanem Grabowskim* (Krakow: Nakladem Akademi Umiejetnosci, 1909), I, 234, in Bartoszewicz, p. 57.

30. "Konstanty Pawlowicz," *Wielka Encyklopedya...*, p. 703.

31. Julian Orsyn Niemcewicz (1757-1841), was a Polish writer, statesman and at one time was Adam Czartoryski's adjutant.

32. Prince Joseph Poniatowski (1763-1813) was a Polish soldier, statesman and scion of the old and famous Poniatowski family. Dedicated to the restoration of Poland, he joined Napoleon and lost his life at the Battle of Leipzig in 1813.

33. Bartoszewicz, p. 62; A. M. Skalkowski (ed.),*Archiwum Wybickiego*, (Gdansk: Nakladem Towarzystwa Przyjaciol Nauki i Sztuki w Gdansku, 1950), II, 485, 487; Marcin Molski, *Do Jego Ces. Mci. Konstantego Pawlowicza na przyjazd* do Warszawy 14/26 wrzesnia, 1814, The University of Warsaw Library, Warsaw.

34. "Konstanty Pawlowicz," *Wielka Encyklopedia...*, p. 703; Szymon Askenazy, "Ministerium Wielhorskiego," *Dwa Stulecia*, (Warsaw: Naklad Gebethnera i Wolffa, 1910), p. 127.

35. "Konstanty Pawlowicz," *Wielka Encyklopedia...*, p. 703.

36. Comte D'Angeberg, pp. 627-631; Wladyslaw Kozlowski, *Autonomia Krolestwa Polskiego 1815-31*, (Warsaw: Glowny Sklad w ksiegarni E. Wende i Ska., 1907), p. 73. The term confederation refers to a traditional extra-governmental organization, usually a union of nobles, organized on an *ad hoc* basis to achieve a specific goal, such as the maintenance of order during an *interregnum*.

37. Comte D'Angeberg, pp. 631-633; Jozef Bojasinski, *Rzady Tymczasowe w Krolestwie Polskim*, (Warsaw, 1902), p. 16.

38. Tokarz, p. 21.

39. Comte D'Angeberg, pp. 633-634.

40. Bojasinski, p. 16.

41. Bojasinski, pp. 26, 40-42.

42. Bartoszewicz, p. 171.

43. Bojasinski, p. 43.

44. Chlopicki (1771-1854) became a leader in the Revolution of November, 1830, which deprived Constantine of his position in the kingdom.

45. *Ibid.*, p. 44.

46. See Kieniewicz, *Przymiany spoleczne i gospodarcze...*, pp. 56-84. The full text of the constitution and the text of the "Organic Statute" of 1832, which replaced it following the collapse of the Revolution of 1830, are to be found as appendices to this study.

47. Missalowa, p. 201.

48. Missalowa, pp. 199-202; M. Handelsman, "The Polish Kingdom, 1815-1830," *The Cambridge History*, ed. by W. F. Reddaway, J. H. Penson *et al.*, (Cambridge; At the University Press, 1951), II, 276.

49. Bojasinski, p. 137.

50. Bortnowski, *Wielki Ksiaze Konstanty...*, p. 197.

51. Kukiel, pp. 133-134.

52. Missalowa, p. 254.

53. Kukiel, pp. 134, 36-37; Bartoszewicz, pp. 205-207.

54. Askenazy, "Ministerium Wielhorskiego," pp. 157-158.

55. *Protokoly Rady Administracyjnej Krolestwa Polskiego*, 455, pp. 118-119, Archiwum Glowne Akt Dawnych, Warsaw.

56. The article to which Wielhorski referred stated: "ministers, heads of departments and members of governmental ministries must answer to and are responsible to the High National Court for each infraction of constitutional acts, laws and decrees of the king of which they are judged culpable.

57. Wielhorski to Constantine, January 16, 1816, in Askenazy, "Ministerium Wielhorskiego," pp. 158-161, 522-524.

58. *Ibid.*, p. 160.

59. *Ibid.*, p. 161.

60. Askenazy, "Ministerium Wielhorskiego," pp. 160-161.

61. Wielhorski to Alexander, in Askenazy, "Ministerium Wielhorskiego," pp. 162-163, 524-525.

62. *Ibid.*, pp. 167-168.

63. Together with his letter of resignation, Wielhorski sent a letter to Sobolewski in which he described Constantine's harsh treatment of officers and Constantine's conception of imperial pardon, which was an increase of the punishment. Wielhorski to Sobolewski, April 28, 1816, *Ibid.*, pp. 167-169, 526-529.

64. "Rozkazy dzienne Konstantego z lat 1816-17," Vol. I, *Druki autoryzowane podpisem Szefa Sztabu Glownego Gen. Jozefa Tobinskiego, 3/15 June, 1816.* 585, No. 6, Manuscript Section, University of Warsaw Library, Warsaw.

65. Tokarz, pp. 49-50; *Protokoly Rady Administracyjnej...*, AGAD.

66. One authority, however, tends to vindicate Hauke, contending that not only did he perform his duties well, he also used his high office and influence to moderate Constantine. See Alexander Rembowski, *Spadek pismenniczy po Generala Maurycy Hr. Hauke,* (Warsaw: Nakladem Ksiegarni E. Wende i S-ka, 1905), p. XLVI.

CHAPTER III
THE GRAND DUKE AND THE POLISH ARMY, 1815 — 1820

1. Tokarz, *Armja Krolestwo Polskiego...*, p. 19.

2. Constantine to Nicholas, December 22, 1825 in "Perepiska Imperatora Nikolaia Pavlovicha s Velikim Kniazem Tsarevichem Konstantinom Pavlovichem," *Sbornik Russkago Istoricheskago Obshchestva*, I, 16 in Tokarz, p. 42.

Alexander, however, was somewhat naive in his belief that stationing Russian troops in the kingdom would have only beneficial results. First, aside from the fact that they were for many a clear sign of foreign occupation, they also represented a tremendous financial burden on the kingdom. Paradoxically, during the early years of the kingdom, the Polish Army was being supported by the Russian treasury through a loan, while the Russian Army in the kingdom was being maintained by the kingdom. Secondly, both Alexander and Constantine were mistaken in believing that the Russian troops would provide only good example for the Polish Army. Within a short period of time, the Russian Army proved as troublesome for Constantine as the Polish Army. Particularly offensive was the spread of liberal ideas in the ranks of the Russian Army, a phenomenon which Constantine felt at first was only common to the Poles. Tokarz, pp. 19, 365.

3. Constantine to Nicholas, December 22, 1825 in *Perepiska*, I, 16, in Tokarz, p. 42.

4. Tokarz, p. 43. Although Tokarz described this policy and indicated in detail how Constantine implemented it, he cited no specific document or more precise source. Waclaw Tokarz, an outstanding Polish historian particularly expert in matters relating to the Congress Kingdom and its army, writing shortly before World War I, had access to many documents and studies no longer available today. Consequently, in the matter of the above mentioned policy, as well as in several other instances in this chapter, I follow Tokarz despite the absence of scrupulous documentation.

5. *Ibid.*, p. 54.

6. *Ibid.*, pp. 68-69, 71.

7. Bronislaw Gembarzewski, *Wojsko Polskie 1815-1830*, (Warsaw: Konstanty Treptc, 1903), p. 47.

8. Tokarz, pp. 56, 58, 61.

9. According to Tokarz, in the kingdom there were 216,000 eligible men between the ages of twenty and thirty; yet never more than twenty-nine thousand served at one time. Tokarz, pp. 73, 74, 76.

10. Gembarzewski, p. 35.

11. Szymon Askenazy, *Lukasinski*, (Warsaw: Nakladem Drukarni Wl. Lazarskiego, 1929), I, 71. Constantine's hostility extended also to Russian soldiers who expressed, in his opinion, the wrong views. Leonard Chodzko, *"Equisses polonaises ou fragments et traits detaches,"* (Paris: Hector Bossange, Librairie, 1831), p. 32.

12. Constantine to General Rautenstrauch, June 28/July 10, 1830, *Zespol Akt Archiwum Komisji Rzadowej Wojny i Militarii Krolestwa Polskiego z lat 1814- 1846*, 529, pp. 23-24, AGAD.

13. Ignacy Komorowski, *Wspomnienia Podchorazego z czasow W.X. Konstantego*, (Lwow: Nakladem Redakcye "Gonca," 1863), p. 8.

14. Stanislaw Skadkowski, *Higiena w wojsku Wielkego Ksiecia Konstantego*, (Warsaw: Zaklad Graficzne "Drukarnia Bankowa," 1925), p. 21.

15. Tokarz, p. 80.

16. *Protokoly Rady Administracyjnej...*, 478, 15/415, 476, 15/222.

17. Komorowski, p. 8.

18. Skadkowski, pp. 1-2.

19. See *Zespol Akt Archiwum Komisji Rzadowej Wojny...*

20. Stanislaw Smolka, *Polityka Lubeckiego przed Powstaniem Listopadowem*, (Krakow: Nakladem Akademii Umiejetnosci, 1907), p. 105; Tokarz, pp. 125-126; *Protokoly Rady Administracyjnej...*

21. Tokarz, p. 114; Szymon Askenazy, *Rosya-Polska, 1815-1830* (Lwow: Nakladem H. Attenberga, 1907), p. 83; Letter of Constantine to General

Rautenstrauch, October 22/November 3, 1817, *Archiwum Komisji Rzadowej Wojny...* 511, p. 66; *Protokoly Rady Administracyjnej...*
22. Tokarz, pp. 116-119, 376.
23. "Decyzje J. C. M. Wielkiego Ksiecia Naczelnego Wodza," *Archiwum Komisji Rzadowej Wojny...*, 1822, 76; 1828, 82, p. 38.
24. Komorowski, p. 6: Tokarz, pp. 263-287.
25. Tokarz, p. 92.
26. Tokarz, p. 99.
27. Komorowski, p. 7; Tokarz, pp. 98-100.
28. Tokarz, pp. 147-155; 98.
29. Skadkowski, p. 3.
30. Komorowski, p. 28; *Archiwum Komisji Rzadowej Wojny...*, 518, p. 246, 1824; 523, p. 10, 1827; Askenazy, *Lukasinski*, 1, 227; Skadkowski, p. 7; Tokarz, p. 146.
31. *Archiwum Rzadowej Wojny...*, 311, p. 20, 1817; 297, p. 78, 1820; 305, p. 102, 1824, 502, p. 1, 1828; 503, p. 2, 1830.
32. Askenazy, *Lukasinski*, 1, 13; *Archiwum Komisji Rzadowej Wojny...*, 499, pp. 126-127, 1825.
33. Tokarz, p. 96.

CHAPTER IV
CONSTANTINE, ALEXANDER I AND THE CONGRESS KINGDOM, 1820 — 1822

1. Marceli Handelsman, "Kryzys w r. 1821 w Krolestwie Polskim," *Kwartalnik Historyczny*, (1939), p. 20.
2. Some signs of Alexander's intentions included the following. In May, 1815, at the time of the signing of the Treaty of Vienna, Alexander generally suggested union. *Ibid.*, p. 19. Soon after, he named Polish governors and not Russian ones to be heads of those Polish provinces incorporated into Russia and ordered that all soldiers from those provinces be dressed in uniforms similar to Polish ones, rather than Russian. Askenazy, *Lukasinski*, I, 81. Many Poles were optimistic about Alexander's promises of union; hence rumors were frequent in the kingdom that the Eastern Provinces were on the verge of being joined to the kingdom. *Policja Tajna W. Ks. Konstantego*, 40b, p. 339, AGAD, Warsaw.
3. In an attempt to pacify the Poles, Alexander gave a rather weak explanation for his appointment of Constantine, despite Constantine's obvious unpopularity. At the time of his appearance at the meetings of the first *Sejm* in 1818, Alexander said; "I know it all — but what am I to do? Am I to call Constantine back to St. Petersburg so that he would hate you even more, so that he would spoil everything for you there...Is it not better that he remains here? He will come around. For the time being, try to pacify him and have patience." Askenazy, "Bracia," p. 12.

4. Constantine, supposedly greatly surprised at the wide grant of power, is said to have asked Alexander, "What about the constitution?" In reply, Alexander answered: "I will take the constitution upon myself, you act freely and do not worry about the rest." Szymon Askenazy, "Dwie rozmowy w Belwederze," *Bibliotecka Warszawska*, II (1906), pp. 5-19. Gregoire Pissarevsky, "Istorii Kongresowego Tsarstva Polskogo (1818-1830) pri Aleksandre I," III *Nauchnye Izvestiia*, (1926), p. 303. Because of the verbal nature of this grant of power, no documents exist to prove its authenticity. That the statement was made, however, is well accepted among important Polish and Russian historians.

5. Handelsman, "The Polish Kingdom, 1815-1830" in *Cambridge History of Poland*, p. 277. For a useful recent analysis of Novosiltsev's career, see Frank Thackerey, "N.N. Novosiltsev: The Polish Years," *Polish Review*, 28, Number 1 (1983), 32-46.

6. See *Tajna Kancelaria Nowosilcowa*, AGAD; "Mikolaj Nowosilcow," *Wielka Encyklopedia Powszechna* Vol. VIII (Warsaw: Panstwowe Wydawnictwo Naukowe, 1966), p. 55.

7. Bortnowski, p. 198.

8. Handelsman, "The Polish Kingdom 1815-1830," in the *Cambridge History of Poland*, p. 277.

9. Askenazy, *Lukasinski*, I, 81.

10. Missalowa, "Ziemje polskie...," in *Historia Polski*, 11, 260-261; Maurycy Mochnacki, *Powstanie Narodu Polskiego w r, 1830-31*, (Paris: W. Drukarni P. Baudouin, 1834), p. 202; Comte D'Angeberg, "Discours pronounce par S.M. l'empereur et roi Alexandre Ier a l'ouverture de la premier diete du royaume de Pologne, le 15/27 mars 1818 a Varsovie," pp. 734-737; "Discours prononce par l'empereur et roi Alexandre Ier a la cloture de la premiere diete du royaume de Pologne, le 15/27 avril, 1818," pp. 737-739.

11. Handelsman, "The Polish Kingdom 1818-1830," in *Cambridge History of Poland*, p. 10.

12. *Ibid.*, p. 13.

13. Missalowa "Ziemie polskie," in *Historia Polski*, 11 279.

14. For a thorough study of the *Sejm* of 1825, see Ryszard Przelaskowski, *Sejm Warszawski*, (Warsaw: Nakladem Towarzystwa Naukowego Warszawskiego, 1929).

15. Missalowa, "Ziemie polskie...," in *Historia Polski*, 11, 277- 281. A less complimentary view of the Niemojowski brothers and the Kalisz Party is presented in Gajewski's *Memoirs*. In his opinion, they were only frustrated "big mouths" who did more harm than good for the Polish cause by antagonizing Alexander. Franciszek Gajewski, *Pamietniki*, (2 vols.; Poznan: Zdislaw Rzepecki i S-ka, n.d.), II, 10. Constantine evidently shared this opinion, saying that "their enemies among the Russians could not be grateful enough for their behavior." Stanislaw Szpotanski, "Z rozmow w Belwederze," *Biblioteka Warszawska*, (1913), Vol. II, Section 1, p. 102.

16. Schilder, IV, p. 469.

17. Helena Wieckowska, *Opozycja liberalna w Krolestwie Kongresowym 1815-1830*, (Warsaw: Sklad w kasie im. Mianowskiego, 1925), pp. 97-98. In his assessment of the situation, Constantine was probably correct. At that time, 1821-1822, although the country was greatly dissatisfied with the government and its unkept promises, there was no thought of revolution, and public opinion was not hostile to Alexander personally. Przelaskowski, pp. 60-61.

18. Missalowa, "Ziemie polskie...," in *Historia Polski*, II 285-86.

19. Gryzelda Missalowa, *Poczatki mysli liberalnej i demokratycznej w Krolestwie Polskim, tajne zwiazki 1815-1830*, (Warsaw: Panstwowe Zaklady Wydawnictwo Szkolnych, 1962), p. 11. The *Dekada Polska* was not the only example of political journalism of that period. There was also the *Gazeta Codzienna Narodowa i Obca*, 1818, the *Kronika*, 1819, and the *Orzel Bialy*, 1819-20. According to one authority, it was because their public journalism was suppressed that these various secret organizations turned to conspiracy. Handelsman, "The Polish Kingdom 1815-1830," in the *Cambridge History of Poland*, p. 12.

20. Missalowa, "Ziemie polskie...," in *Historia Polski*, II, 290-291.

21. Adam Mickiewicz (1798-1855) is remembered as the great national poet of Poland, one of nineteenth century Europe's greatest "romantic" writers, and the author of two epic Polish poems, *Pan Tadeusz* and *Dziady*.

22. Thomas Zan (1796-1855) was the poet-friend of Mickiewicz who is best known for his political activity on behalf of Polish independence.

23. Missalowa, "Ziemie polskie...," in *Historia Polski*, II, 294.

24. *Ibid.*, pp. 294-299.

25. Walerian Lukasinski, *Pamietnik*, (Warsaw: Panstwowe Wydawnictwo Naukowe, 1960), pp. 18, 84-85.

26. Jerzy Lojek, *Studia nad prasa i opinia publiczna w Krolestwie Polskim 1815-1830*, (Warsaw: Panstwowe Wydawnictwo Naukowe, 1966), p. 322.

27. Handelsman, "The Polish Congress Kingdom 1815-1830," in the *Cambridge History of Poland*, p. 18; Pissarevsky, p. 303.

28. The unstable and very poor economic conditions also provoked in turn a social crisis of sorts. As early as 1817, numerous peasant revolts took place. *Ibid.*, p. 13; Andrzej Sienkiewicz, "Materialy do zagadnienia ucisku i walki spolecznej w aktach policji tajnej w. ks. Konstantego 1821-30," *Teki Archiwalne*, III-IV, (1954), pp. 8-37.

29. Missalowa, "Ziemie polskie...," in *Historia Polski*, II, p. 261.

30. Stanislaw Smolka, *Polityka Lubeckiego*, (Krakow: Nakladem Akademii Umiejetnosci, 1907), p. 101. For an insightful look at his thought and politics see Rett Ludwikowski, "Ks. Drucki-Lubecki," *Studia Historyczne*, 24, Number 4 (1981), 557-564.

31. For an excellent and detailed study of Drucki-Lubecki's economic policies and their significance, see: Mieczyslaw Ajzen, *Polityka gospodarcza Lubeckiego 1821-1830*, (Warsaw: Nakladem Towarzystwa Naukowego Warszawskiego, 1932).

32. Smolka, pp. 400-401.

33. Handelsman, "The Polish Kingdom, 1815-1830," in the *Cambridge History of Poland*, p. 18.

34. Gajewski, II, 11; Jozef Krasinski, "W pierwszych latach Krolestwie Kongresowego," *Biblioteka Warszawska*, (April, 1913), Vol. II, Section 1, p. 67.

35. Gajewski, II, 19; Edmund Jezierwski, *W. Ks. Konstanty i Ksiezna Lowicka* (Warsaw: Nakladem Ksiegarni W. Jakowickego, 1916), pp. 29-30; Waclaw Gasiorowski, *Ksiezna Lowicka*, (Warsaw: Ludowa Spoldzielnia Wydawnicza, 1960), p. 9.

36. Chechulin, p. 192.

37. "Razkazy Kniazia Sergiia Mikhailovicha Golitsyna," *Russkii Arkhiv*, VII (1869), p. 632.

38. The one exception to all the favorable comments about Grudzinska is to be found in Moriolles' *Memoirs*. According to him, Grudzinska was suffering from bad health and consequently tended towards day-dreaming and mysticism. Further, despite many Polish and Russian contemporary accounts of her great tact and high character, Moriolles painted her as an ambitious, tactless, insincere and cold woman. He was forced, however, to admit that she was attached to her husband. Moriolles, pp. 7, 81, 96-97.

39. Gajewski, 11, 19; *Policja Tajna Konstantego*, 73, p. 96.

40. Gasiorowski, p. 8.

41. Napoleon Sierawski, *Pamietnik Napoleona Sierawskiego oficera konnego pulku gwardyi z czasow W. Ks. Konstantego*, (Lwow: Naklad Gubrynowicza i Schmidta, 1907), p. 56.

42. Jezierski, p. 32; *Posluchanie prezez W. Ksiecia Konstantego poslom i deputowanym wdtwa. Kaliskiego udzielona dnia 15 czerwca 1830*, (Warsaw, 1831), p. 5.

43. Chechulin, p. 193.

44. Mieczyslaw Offmanski, *Krolestwo Polskie*, (Warsaw: Wydawnictwo M. Arcta, 1907), p. 27.

45. Schilder, IV, 12, 15, 16-17, 45.

46. Mochnacki, p. 235.

47. Askenazy, *Lukasinski*, I, 163.

48. On two occasions at least the brothers discussed the matter. The first when they were traveling to Opawa (October, 1820), and the second when they were returning from Lublana (May, 1821). Handelsman, "The Polish Kingdom 1815- 1830," in the *Cambridge History of Poland*, p. 20.

49. Constantine to Alexander, January 24, 1822 in Adrian Ergon, *Vie d'Alexandre Ier Empereur de Russie*, (Paris: Chez F. Denn, 1826), p. 217.

50. Alexander to Constantine, February 2, 1822 in *Ibid.*, pp. 216- 218.

51. Missalowa, "Ziemie polskie...," in *Historia Polski*, II, 259; Szymon Askenazy, *Rosja-Polska 1815-1830*, p. 168.

52. Handelsman, "The Polish Kingdom 1815-1830," in the *Cambridge History of Poland*, pp. 19, 21.

53. Of course their reasons differed; Constantine saw it purely as a matter of an increase in his personal power, while the Poles expected it to lead to reunion and eventual independence.

54. Henryk Moscicki, *Projekty polaczenia Litwy...*, pp. 12-13.

55. According to Askenazy, Constantine was delegated full power in these territories as the result of two decrees from the St. Petersburg Senate as of July 11, 1822. They stated that Constantine was given in the districts of Wilno, Grodno, Minsk, Wolynia, Podolia and Bialystok, the power of Head of the Active Army on the strength of the provisions promulgated on February 8, 1812. The Head of the Active Army had full jurisdiction, including full civil jurisdiction in the designated area. Askenazy, *Lukasinski*, I, 166-67.

56. *Ibid.*, p. 167.

57. Moscicki, p. 20; Offmanski, p. 28.

CHAPTER V
GRAND DUKE CONSTANTINE PAVLOVICH: "VICEROY" OF THE POLISH KINGDOM, 1822-1825

1. Stanislaw Smolka, *Polityka Lubeckiego...*, p. 133.

2. To recapitulate, these were Constantine's appointment as Commander in Chief of the Polish Army in 1815, the granting of *carte blanche* in 1819, and finally, the privileges flowing from the succession agreements of 1819 and 1822.

3. Handelsman, *Kryzys w r. 1821...*, p. 40.

4. Missalowa, "Ziemie polskie...," in *Historia Polski*, 11, 254.

5. For further information about Mostowski, see: Marion Kukiel, *Dzieje Polski porozbiorowe, 1795-1921*, (London: B. Swiderski, 1963), pp. 177-179.

6. Evidently there was no question too mundane for Constantine's interest; for example, Constantine decided *in lieu* of Mostowski whether to build a certain quay along the Vistula and whether to build a canal near Warsaw. *Archiwum W. Ks. Konstantego*, 340, pp. 357, 369, The Polish Library, Paris.

7. Within a very short time Potocki accomplished a great deal. In 1816 the University of Warsaw was established. Soon after the Warsaw Polytechnic was founded along with new schools of forestry, teachers' colleges and seminaries for both priests and rabbis. In all, twenty-nine high schools were established and the number of elementary schools increased from 720 to 1,222. Kukiel, *Dzieje...*, p. 176.

8. During his term of office there was a drastic reduction in the number of elementary and secondary schools, a ban was placed upon foreign study for Polish students, and in cooperation with Constantine and Novosiltsev, a police and spy system was incorporated within the educational system. "Stanislaw Grabowski," *Wielka Encyklopedia Powszechna*, (Warsaw: Panstwowe Wydawnictwo Naukowe, 1964), p. 370.

9. "Ze wspomnien Jana Bartkowskiego" in *Zbior pamietnikow do historyi powstania polskiego z r. 1830-31*, (Lwow: Nakladem Dra. Tomasza Rayskiego, 1822), p. 230.

10. Believing it to be to their advantage to have the tsar's brother as their representative in the *Sejm*, the citizens of Praga elected Constantine to this position. Moscicki, *Projekty polaczenia Litwy...*, p. 15.

11. Schilder, *Alexander I*, IV, p. 90 in Smolka, *Polityka Lubeckiego*, p. 262.

12. S. B. Gnorowski, *Insurrection of Poland in 1830-31; and the Russian Rule Preceding It Since 1815*, (London: James Ridgeway, Piccadilly, 1839), pp. 20-21.

13. Przelaskowski, p. 190.

14. "Ze wspomnien Jana Bartkowskiego," in *Zbior...*, p. 234.

15. Missalowa, "Ziemie polskie...," in *Historia Polski*, 11, 260; Handelsman, "The Polish Kingdom 1815-1830," in the *Cambridge History of Poland*, p. 6.

16. Moscicki pp. 19-20; *Rozmowy: 1823-1827-1828-1829 roku Xiecia z Wielkiem Xieciem Konstantynym, E.W. 3207, The Jagiellonian Library, Krakow*.

17. Kukiel, *Dzieje...*, p. 191.

18. Lojek, *Studia...*, pp. 324-325.

19. *Ibid.*, p. 326; Missalowa, "Ziemie polskie...," in *Historia Polski*, 11, 281-84.

20. *Zespol Akt Archiwum Komisje Rzadowy Wojny...*, 519, p. 92; Sienkiewicz, pp. 9-37.

21. Missalowa, "Ziemie polskie...," in *Historia Polski*, 11, 272- 73.

22. *Ibid.*, pp. 272-276; for a fuller treatment of Szaniawski see: Maria Manteufflowa, *J.K. Szaniawski, ideologia i dzialnosc 1815-1830*, (Warsaw: Nakladem Towarzystwa Warszawskiego, 1936).

23. "Ze Wspomnien Jana Bartkowskiego," in *Zbior...*, p. 229.

24. Various documents refer to these bureaus as "sections," others openly called them "ministries." Smolka, *Polityka Lubeckiego...*, pp. 279, 511.

25. Harro Harring, a contemporary, claimed that an actual "Secret Chancellery" existed and that "it exercised control over everything connected with literature, education etc..." Harro Harring, *Poland under the Domination of Russia*, (London: James Cochrane and Co., 1831), p. 83.

26. The fact that Constantine had formed a Bureau of Internal Affairs was noted by two diplomatic representatives in Warsaw: by Duchet in his letter to Metternich of October 22, 1822, and by Julius Schmidt in his letter to Bernstorff of October 26, 1822, in Smolka, *Polityka Lubeckiego...*, pp. 279-80.

27. Already in operation and reporting to Constantine were Rozniecki's secret military police and Mostowski's and Matthew Lubowidzki's (Lubowidzki was vice-president of the City of Warsaw) secret police.

28. Askenazy, *Lukasinski*, I, p. 346.

29. H. Eile, "Tajna Policja Wielkiego Ksiecia Konstantego," *Gazeta Administracji i Policji Panstowej*, 11 (January, 1931), p. 60.

30. According to Karolina Beylin, *Tajemnice Warszawy* (Warsaw: Panstwowy Instytut Wydawniczy, 1956), there are ninety-eight volumes; according to Lojek, sixty volumes; my count, 113.

31. *Policja Tajna W. Ks. Konstantego*. Constantine's most famous and diligent employee in the secret police seems to have been the Pole Henry Mackrott. It appears that Mackrott fell into the job of spying quite naturally; his father Tobias, a hairdresser, was also a spy and one of the best known agents of the Russian secret police which organized in Warsaw immediately after the Kosciuszko Insurrection in 1794. Henry first began spying on his fellow students in high school and then at the University of Warsaw where he was a medical student. He made himself out to be a radical patriot, attended secret student meetings and soon had a great deal of information to pass on to Constantine about secret organizations among students. Mackrott was also interested in the activities of the Masons and since his father had been a high-ranking Mason, he also gained easy entry into this ever-more suspect organization.

32. Lojek, "Szpiegowskie kariery," p. 23; "Ze wspomnien Jana Bartkowskiego," in *Zbior...*, pp. 237-238. With regard to Constantine's surveillance of mail it was noted that "all clerks of the post-office wear the Russian uniform of the Grand Duke's office, which is green with dark-red facings, whereas the other Polish civil officers wear the blue uniform of the country.

In conformity with the Russian law it is the practice ... that no letter be delivered or forwarded to its address unless it has been opened and read ... suspected letters are transmitted by the readers to the different sections of the secret police ... they send those on Russia and Russians to Novosiltsev, on foreign affairs to General Fenshaw, or military persons or militiary affairs to Baron Sass, who reports either to General Rozniecki or to the Grand Duke through Kouruta." Harring, pp. 202-204.

33. "Ze wspomnien Jana Bartkowskiego," in *Zbior...*, pp. 237-238.

34. Bortnowski, p. 198; Lojek, *Studia...*, p. 322.

35. This too was noted by Duchet in his October 22, 1822 letter to Metternich and by J. Schmidt in his October 26, 1822 letter to Bernstorff in Smolka, *Polityka Lubeckiego...*, pp. 279-280, 511; Askenazy, *Dwa stulecia*, p. 342.

36. Harring, p. 79.

37. "Ze wspomnien Jana Bartkowskiego," in *Zbior...*; *Archiwum W. Ks. Konstantego*, 339-43.

38. *Ibid*, 341, Pt. 1; 342, 4; 341, 10b; 343, 1, p. 1489; 343, 6, p. 719; 343, 7, pp. 1041-1042; *Akta Misji Polskiej w Paryzu*, 350, 3, pp. 111b, The Polish Library, Paris.

39. *Archiwum W. Ks. Konstantego*, 339, 14a, pp. 261-262, 14-d, pp. 325-327.

40. *Protokoly Rady Administracii...*, 140, pp. 296-297; 119, p. 209.

41. See *Tajna Kancelaria Nowosilcowa*; also Alexander Kraushar, *Senator Nowosilcow i censura za Krolestwa Kongresowego (1819-1829)*, (Krakow: G. Gebethner i S-ka, 1913).

42. Lojek, *Studia...*, pp. 79-85.

43. Kraushar, p. 9.

44. Among others, particularly disturbing to Constantine were uncomplimentary statements about the army in the Polish press. It seems that Constantine, who was growing tired of demanding retractions from recalcitrant editors, simply preferred to demand stricter censorship. Natalia Gasiorowska, "Ustanowienie cenzury w Krolestwie Kongresowem," *Biblioteka Warszawska*, (July, 1912), Vol. III, Section 1, pp. 249-250; Constantine to Novosiltsev, January 29/February 10, 1820, *Kancelaria Nowosilcowa*, 481, p. 3; Kraushar, pp. 11-15.

45. Novosiltsev to Constantine, January 26/February 7, 1820, *Kancelaria Nowosilcowa* 481, pp. 1-2.

46. Lojek, *Studia...*, pp. 326-327.

47. Kraushar, p. 40

48. *Ibid.*, pp. 38-40.

49. Nemezy Kozuchowski, "W. X. Konstanty, Pozzo di Borgo i Monitor," VI, *Kronika Emigracji Polskiej* (1837), pp. 392-397.

50. Lojek, *Studia...*, p. 327.

51. Harring, p. 201.

52. "Ze wspomnien Jana Bartkowskiego," in *Zbior...*, pp. 239-240; *Policja Tajna Konstantego*, 40b, p. 353; Kraushar, pp. 6-7; Zbior "Rekopisow Willanowskich," p. 213; Franciszek S. Dmochowski, *Wspomnienia od 1806 do 1830 roku*, Warsaw: Panstwowy Instytut Wydawniczy, 1959), p. 341.

53. Missalowa, "Ziemie polskie..." in *Historia Polski*, 11, 272-76; Kraushar, p. 119.

54. Alexander Kraushar, *Sprzysiezenie Studenckie*, (Warsaw, 1910), pp. 1-41.

55. Staszic (1755-1826) was a priest, scholar, writer and patriot. Included among his major accomplishments was the founding of the University of Warsaw.

56. Joachim Lelewel, Vol. I *Dziela*, ed. Helena Wieckowska (Warsaw: Panstwowy Instytut Wydawniczy, 1957), p. 73; Alexander Krauschar, *Towarzystwo Krolewskie Przyjaciol*, Bk, 111, Sec. 3., p. 279 in Lelewel.

57. Anatol Lewicki, *Zarys historii polskiej* (Warsaw: n.d.), p. 404 in Dmochowski, p. 355; Harring, p. 83.

CHAPTER VI

NICHOLAS I AND THE EROSION OF CONSTANTINE'S POSITION, 1825-1830

1. In the autumn of 1819, Alexander visited Warsaw and indicated at that time that he was considering abdicating. In reply, Constantine said, "in this event I shall ask for myself the position of your second valet. I will serve you and I will, if necessary, clean your boots..." Leonid I. Strakhovsky,

Alexander I of Russia, (New York: W. W. Norton and Company, 1947), pp. 206-207. According to Almedingen, Alexander reacted to this flippant comment by answering: "When that moment comes, I will let you know so that you can write to my mother about your plans," E. M. Almedingen, *The Emperor Alexander* (London: The Bodley Head, 1964), p. 187.

2. Nicholas V. Riasanovsky, *Nicholas I and Official Nationality in Russia, 1825-1855*, (Berkeley: University of California Press, 1959), p. 38.

3. Askenazy, *Lukasinski*, p. 365.

4. Riasanovsky, *Nicholas I...*, p. 28.

5. Askenazy, *Lukasinski*, p. 365.

6. Nicholas' first governess was a Scottish nurse, Miss Jane Lyon. She was in Warsaw during the Kosciuszko Insurrection of 1794, and because of some painful experiences, came to harbor bitter feelings against the Poles. These views she may have communicated to the young and impressionable Nicholas. Riasanovsky, Nicholas I ..., p. 23.

7. Constantin de Grunwald, *Tsar Nicholas I*, (New York: The Macmillan Company, 1955), p. 99.

8. According to de Grunwald, Nicholas bitterly complained to his Prussian brothers-in-law that he was not informed of affairs of state nor included in the Council of Ministers as they were in their country. Nicholas said, "I wish very much that they would do the same with me; it would make my entry into the affairs of state infinitely easier, if I could be accustomed to them beforehand." De Grunwald, p. 36.

9. De Grunwald suggests several interesting possiblilities in explanation of Alexander's behavior. For example, perhaps "Alexander wanted, before renouncing his power and proclaiming to the nation the name of his successor, to complete some vast governmental enterprises he was planning in his mind: to settle accounts with Turkey, to unite Lithuania with the Kingdom of Poland, to endow Russia with a constitutional regime (Schiemann). Alexander wanted, when the moment came, to initiate the enthronement of Nicholas himself; a sudden death would have prevented the execution of this plan. Or Alexander was simply jealous of his younger brother: he feared the rivalry of an heir who would outshine him in the eyes of his people. (Manuscript Memoirs of N. Gretch)." De Grunwald, p. 37.

10. According to Riasanovsky, it was Nicholas' and not Constantine's behavior that required explanation. However, in defense of Nicholas, Riasanovsky suggests several reasons which might have prompted Nicholas to refuse the throne until the time that Constantine reaffirmed his resolve to decline. First, he suggests that in Nicholas' mind the legal issue was very confused; could Alexander's manifesto bypassing Constantine and proclaiming him tsar indeed supersede Paul's law of succession which specifically aimed at abolishing personal decisions with regard to dynastic matters? Also, was it not questionable that a dead monarch's unpublished manifesto be valid in the reign of another autocrat? Secondly, Riasanovsky suggests that Nicholas was unpopular and that a number of prominent individuals, including the Governor General of St. Petersburg Count Nicholas Miloradovich, prevailed

upon Nicholas to step aside in favor of Constantine, who at least at that moment appeared to be more popular and the legitimate heir. Finally, Nicholas' attitude, according to Riasanovsky, "was a factor. It seems that he was not only reluctant to ascend the throne, but also tried to avoid and forget the entire issue, just as he had earlier, apparently, failed to profit by the emperor's warnings about his future and as later he would invariably depict himself as an outsider suddenly thrust into imperial office..." Further, "Nicholas' behavior in regard to the imperial succession had...deeper psychological roots that those recognized by the historians who suggest that he was sullen and uncooperative in December, 1825, because he was offended at not having been consulted earlier about the matter." Riasanovsky, *Nicholas I...*, p. 32.

As for Riasanovsky's second point, Florinsky goes further by saying that the major factor which determined Nicholas' conduct was the attitude of the guards who clearly preferred Constantine. Florinsky, II, pp. 746-747.

Another criticism is presented by de Grunwald who implies that Nicholas should have accepted the throne from the beginning as Alexander wished, instead of waiting for Constantine's resignation. According to him, both Constantine and Grand Duke Michael believed Nicholas' duty was "to conform, like everyone else, to the will of the late Tsar. If not, his conduct assumes a 'revolutionary aspect'." Consequently, Constantine was clearly in the right by insisting that

> I can never abdicate, for I never was Emperor and never will be...Were I to come to St. Petersburg now I would seem to be coming to dethrone my brother and I have no right to do that. Your invitaiton to arrive as soon as possible cannot be accepted.

De Grunwald, p. 40. Reflecting a view critical of Constantine is Yarmolinsky, who contends that "Constantine failed to act promptly and unequivocally. He refused to make a formal statement of his abdication or come to the capital. This coupled with delay due to slow communications, resulted in uncertainty and confusion. For over three weeks the country was in a strange predicament, as the *London Times* puts it, "of having two self-denying Emperors and no active ruler..." Avrahm Yarmolinsky, *Road to Revolution*. (New York: The Macmillan Company, 1959), p. 36.

11. Constantine to the Empress Mother, 25 November/7 December, 1825, Constantine to Nicholas; 25 November/7 December, 1825, in Warren B. Walsh (ed.), *Readings in Russian History*, Vol. II (Syracuse: Syracuse University Press, 1963), pp. 305-307.

12. Strakhovsky, p. 233.

13. Szymon Askenazy, *Rosya-Polska, 1815-1830*, (Lwow: Nakladem H. Attenberga, 1907), p. 33; Askenazy, *Lukasinski*, p. 330.

14. *Tajna Policia Konstantego*, 103, p. 1069, AGAD, Warsaw.

15. Askenazy, *Rosya-Polska*, p. 33.

16. *Ibid.*
17. De Grunwald, p. 38.
18. Strakhovsky, p. 233.
19. Levin, pp. 88 in Bortnowski, *Wielki Ksiaze Konstanty...*, p. 200.
20. Constantine to Alexander, 14/26 January, 1822, in Walsh, p. 303.
21. Askenazy, *Lukasinski*, p. 330.
22. De Grunwald, p. 40.
23. Later in a letter to Nicholas, Constantine explained why he did not wish to come to St. Petersburg. According to Constantine, it was because he feared his presence would provoke disorders. Constantine to Nicholas, December 30, 1825, "Perepiska Imperatora Nikolaia Pavlovicha s Velikim Kniazem Tsesarevichem Konstantinom Pavlovichem," *Russkaia Starina* I (1910), p. 18.
24. Constantine to Nicholas, 6/18 December, 1825 in Walsh, p. 307.
25. "Pisma Tsesarevicha Velikago Kniazia Konstantina Pavlovicha k Markiz Dekluber," *Russkaia Starina*, VIII, No. 7 (1871), p. 409.
26. This edict included among other documents Constantine's self-abasing letter of resignation to Alexander. "Edict of Nicholas," in Ergon, pp. 214-216.
27. De Grunwald, p. 40.
28. For studies of the Decembrists in English see: Anatole G. Mazour, *The First Russian Revolution 1825*, (Stanford: Stanford University Press, 1961). Mikhail Zetlin, *The Decembrists* (New York: International Universities Press, 1958), Marc Raeff, *The Decembrist Movement* (Englewood Cliffs, New Jersey: Prentice Hall, Inc., 1966).
29. The membership of this early organization was small and its aims were rather vague: to establish a representative government of some sort, preferably a constitutional monarchy.
30. At first this association was reform-minded and not at all revolutionary, looking to the Emperor to head a reform movement. In time, however, serious dissension appeared as the movement became more revolutionary.
31. From the beginning the Northern Society and Southern Society were plagued with the problem of how to establish effective cooperation between themselves. Despite their mutual desire to establish a representative government and to emancipate the serfs, both groups were hopelessly at odds concerning all practical aspects of the proposed reform and the methods by which it was to be achieved.

The Northern Society, under the leadership of Prince Serge Trubetskoii, Prince Eugene Obolenskii and the poet Conrad Ryleev, was based in St. Petersburg. Basing its stance on the views expressed by Nikita Muravev in his unfinished "Constitution," the Northern Society made a commitment to work for the establishment of a federated Russian state under a constitutional monarch. Equality of citizens before the law was to be guaranteed as well as freedom of press and religion; however, the right to vote and the right to be elected to parliament or public office was to be restricted by high property qualifications. Emancipation of the serfs was demanded, but the interests of the landed aristocracy were to be protected. Influenced by the aristocratic and rich guardsmen of St. Petersburg, this constitution not only followed a more conservative line, but also shied away from the use of violence as a means of achieving its political and social ideals. Tensions among the members were rather great; consequently the Northern Society lacked decisive leadership and accomplished little.

32. The Southern Society under the dynamic leadership of Paul Pestel, Serge Muravev-Apostol and Michael Bestuzhev-Riumin, in contrast, grew in numbers and discovered and incorporated into its organization other secret groups. Based in Tulchin, headquarters of the Russian Second Army, the Southern Society took its program from Paul Pestel's *Russkaia Pravda*. Written between 1821 and 1825, Pestel's *Pravda* embodied a political program which called for a centralized democratic republic where serfdom was nonexistent and every citizen was to be entitled to enough land to support himself and his family. Together with a program of political, social, and economic radicalism, Pestel advocated a very aggressive nationalism. Ruthless russification was called for in all lands held by Russia with the exception of Poland. Pestel's following generally was from among the lesser nobility and particularly from 1823 on favored a more radical line.

33. Wereszycki, "The Kingdom of Poland and the November Insurrection (1815-1831), in *History of Poland*, Alexander Gieysztor and Stefan Kieniewicz et. al. (eds.), (Warsaw: Polish Scientific Publishers, 1968), p. 445; according to Mazour, it was the Poles who took the initiative in seeking an alliance with the Russians. Mazour, p. 139.

34. Later, while Pestel was testifying before the Committee of Investigation, he reported the negotiations somewhat differently. See Mazour, p. 141.

35. Pestel was said to have expressed the fear that the Poles might betray the Russians by reaching some sort of understanding with Constantine. I. Bekker, "Dekabrysci, a sprawa Polska," in *Powstaniu Listopadowym*, Wladyslaw Bortnowski (ed.), (Warsaw: Wydawnictwo "Prasa Wojskowa," 1950), p. 24.

36. Wereszycki, p. 445.

37. Actually the Northern Society greatly overestimated what Nicholas actually knew about their conspiracy, *Mazour*, p. 163.

38. *Ibid.*, p. 158.

39. *Ibid.*

40. According to popular lore, some soldiers were so ignorant of the Decembrists' political ideas that they believed the "Constitution" was Constantine's wife. Ivan Spector, *An Introduction to Russian History and Culture*, (Princeton, New Jersey: D. Van Nostrand Company, Inc., 1969), p. 93.

41. Mazour, p. 159.

42. Tatishchev, *Imperator Nikolai i inostrannye dvory*, p. 49 in Mazour, pp. 160-161.

43. Florinsky, II, p. 751.

44. *Lettres et papiers du Chancellor Comte de Nesselrode, 1760-1850*, VI, pp. 266-268 in Mazour, p. 179.

142

NOTES

45. "Decyzje Wielkiego Ksiecia Naczelnego Wodza," *Archiwum Krolestwa...*, 46, p. 1, 520, p. 1, AGAD.
46. Missalowa, p. 303.
47. De Grunwald, p. 59.
48. Bekker, p. 25.
49. Constantine to Nicholas, December 20/January 2, 1825-1826, in *Perepiska*, p. 14; "Rozkaz dzienny Wielkiego Ksiecia Konstantego, January 14/26, 1826," Ossolineum, Wroclaw; "Rozkaz dzienny Wielkiego Ksiecia Konstantego, January 20/February 1, 1826," Ossolineum.
50. *Ibid.*
51. Nicholas to Constantine, January 4/16, 1826, in *Perepiska*, pp. 24-25.
52. Askenazy, *Lukasinski*, p. 334.
53. Schilder, p. 278 in Bortnowski, *Wielki Ksiaze Konstanty...*, p. 200.
54. Nicholas to Constantine, January 28-29-30/February 10-11-12, 1826, in *Perepiska*, pp. 44-48.
55. Askenazy, *Lukasinski*, p. 334.
56. *Ibid.*, p. 335.
57. Missalowa, p. 303.
58. Constantine to Nicholas, February 15, 1826, in *Perepiska*, p. 52.
59. Constantine to Opochinin, February 17, 1826, Schilder, *Nicholas I*, I, p. 531 in Smolka, p. 418.
60. Missalowa, p. 303.
61. Wereszycki, p. 445.
62. Bekker, p. 26.
63. Constantine to Rautenstrauch, 11/23 May, 1823, *Archiwum Krolestwa Rzadowej Wojny*, 308, p. 127, AGAD.
64. Bekker, p. 26.
65. *Ibid.*
66. Kukiel, *Dzieje Polski...*, p. 198; Bortnowski, *Wielki Ksiaze Konstanty...*, p. 201.
67. Missalowa, p. 303.
68. Bekker, p. 26. According to Kukiel, it was Nicholas who supported the calling of the Sejm Tribunal in opposition to Constantine, so that it would be highly placed Poles themselves who would pass sentence on the offenders thereby giving the punishments the highest possible political and moral sanction. Kukiel, *Dzieje Polski...*, p. 198.
69. Bekker, p. 26.
70. *Ibid.*, p. 27; Constantine to Nicholas, 10/22 May, 1828, in *Perepiska*, pp. 227-229.
71. Constantine to Nicholas, 21 May/2 June, 1828, in *Perepiska*, p. 238; Constantine to Nicholas, 21 May/2 June, 1828, in *Perepiska*, p. 238; Kukiel, *Dzieje Polski*, p. 199.
72. Tadeusz Bieczynski (ed.), *Sad Sejmowy 1827-1829 na przestepcow stanu Urzedowe Akta*, (Poznan: Drukiem J. I. Kraszewskiego, 1873), pp. v, vi, vii.
73. Missalowa, p. 304.

74. Nicholas to Constantine, 16/28 May, 1828, in *Perepiska*, p. 231; Bekker, p. 27.
75. Nicholas to Constantine, 11/23 August, 1828, in *Perepiska*, pp. 252-253; Constantine to Nicholas 24 August/5 September, 1828, in *Perepiska*, pp. 256-257.
76. Missalowa, p. 304.
77. Nicholas to Constantine, December 23/January 4, 1825-26, in *Perepiska*, p. 13.
78. Constantine to Nicholas, May 7/19, 1826, in *Perepiska*, p. 70.
79. Bortnowski, *Wielke Ksiaze Konstanty...*, p. 201. Michael Lunin (1787-1845), despite the harshness and injustice of his sentence, later proved to be one of the most steadfast and committed of the sentenced radicals.
80. "Perepiska Velikago Kniazia Konstantina Pavlovicha s Grafom Benkendorfom, 1826-1828," *Russkii Arkhiv*, No. 6 (1855), 274 in Sidney Monas, *The Third Section, Police and Society in Russia under Nicholas I* (Cambridge: Harvard University Press, 1961), p. 97; Peter Stansfield Squire, *The Third Department*, (Cambridge: Harvard University Press, 1968), p. 205.
81. Handelsman, p. 293; Missalowa, p. 304.
82. Nicholas to Constantine, February 20/March 4, 1826, in *Perepiska*, pp. 54-57.
83. *Constantine to Nicholas, March 4/16, 1826, in Perepiska*, pp. 57-60.
84. Constantine to Nicholas, March 27/April 9, 1826, in *Perepiska*, p. 64.
85. Kukiel, *Dzieje Polski...*, p. 200.
86. Constantine to General Hauke, 25 May/6 June, 1828, "Akta decyzi Jego Ces. Msci. W. Ks. Cesarzewicza Naczelnego Wodza," *Archiwum Krolestwa...*, AGAD.
87. Smolka, *Polityka Lubeckiego*, p. 382.
88. Schilder, *Nicholas II*, p. 4 in Smolka, *Polityka Lubeckiego*, p. 382.
89. S. Smolka, "w drodze do Petersburga" *Przeglad Historyczny*," (1906), p. 94.
90. Schmidt to Bernstorff, 4 August, 1826 in Smolka, *Polityka Lubeckiego*, p. 536.
91. *Ibid.*
92. Nicholas to Constantine, April 7/19, 1829, in *Perepiska*, p. 332; De Grunwald, p. 100.
93. Kukiel, *Dzieje Polski...*, p. 200.
94. Constantine to Nicholas, 9/21 April, 1829, M. 9, pp. 77-81; Manuscript Section, University of Warsaw Library, Warsaw.
95. Bortnowski, *Wielki Ksiaze Konstanty..., p. 203; Jozef Patelski, Wspomnienia wojskowe z lat 1823-1831*, (Wilno: Ksiegarnia Stowarzyszenia Nauczycielstwa Polskiego, 1921), p. 76.
96. Bortnowski, *Wielki Ksiaze Konstanty...*, p. 203, Patelski, p. 76.
97. "Mikolaj I Pawlowicz," Wielka Encyklopedia Powszechna, VII (1967), p. 308.
98. De Grunwald, p. 99.

144 NOTES

99. "Suppressed Passage of the Speech of the Emperor Nicholas at Warsaw; with observations on the Practical Results of that Speech. October 16, 1835," in *The Portfolio*, Vol. 1 (London: James Ridgeway and Sons, 1836), p. 39.
100. Constantine to Nicholas in Moscicki, p. 20.
101. Nicholas to Constantine, 26 March/November 5, November 24, 1827 in De Grunwald, p. 102; Nicholas to Constantine 12/24 November, 1827 in *Perepiska*, p. 187.
102. Nicholas to Constantine, 24 October/5 November, 1827, in *Perepiska*, p. 184; Bortnowski, *Wielki Ksiaze Konstanty...*, p. 202; Kukiel, *Czartoryski...*, p. 42; Schilder, *Imperator Nikolai I i Polsha*, pp. 295-296 in Bortnowski, *Wielki Ksiaze Konstanty...*, p. 202.
103. Constantine to Nicholas, 27 November/8 October, 1827, in *Perepiska*, p. 187.
104. Karnovich, "Cesarevich Konstantin Pavlovich," *Russkaia Starina* XXI (1878), 8 - 11 in Bortnowski, *Wielki Ksiaze Konstanty...*, p. 202.
105. R. F. Leslie, *Polish Politics and the Revolution of November 1830*, (The University of London: The Athlone Press, 1956), p. 102.
106. Lojek, *Studia...*, p. 329.
107. *Ibid.*, p. 210.
108. *Policja Tajna Konstantego*, 73, pp. 1311, 1325, in Lojek, *Studia...*, p. 211.
109. Lojek, pp. 207, 329.
110. Leslie, p. 114.
111. *Ibid.*
112. *Ibid.*, pp. 252-253.
113. Constantine to Nicholas, 1/13 June, 1828, in *Perepiska*, p. 238.
114. Constantine to Nicholas, 12/21 July, 1828 in *Perepiska*, p. 248.
115. Lojek, *Studia...*, pp. 329-330.
116. *Policia Tajna Konstantego*, 16, 18 March, 1828 in Lojek, *Studia...*, p. 230.
117. *Ibid.*, pp. 230-231.
118. *Ibid.*, pp. 330.
119. *Ibid.*, p. 236.
120. Constantine to Nicholas in Lojek, *Studia...*, p. 237.
121. *Policja Tajna Konstantego*, 82, 86, 90 in Lojek, *Studia...*, pp. 236-238.
122. *Ibid.*, pp. 239-240.
123. *Policja Tajna Konstantego*, 95, 96 in Lojek, *Studia...*, p. 268.

CHAPTER VII
THE COMING OF THE NOVEMBER REVOLUTION:
THE END OF ASPIRATIONS, 1830 — 1831

1. Leslie, p. 116.
2. Drucki-Lubecki to Grabowski, 28 October, 1830 in *Wybor tekstow zrodlowych z historii Polski w latach 1795-1864*, Stefan Kieniewicz, Tadeusz

Mencel and Wladyslaw Rostocki (eds.,), (Warsaw: Panstwowe Wydawnictwo Naukowe, 1956), p. 395; Memorial Lubeckiego do Sekretarza Stanu S. Grabowskiego, 6 listopada, 1830, *Korespondencya Lubeckiego*, F. Smolka (ed.) in Jozef Dutkiewicz, *Wybor zrodel do Powstania Listopadowego*, (Wroclaw: Zaklad Narodowy im. Ossolinskich, 1957), p. 6.

3. Leslie, p. 122; *Policja Tajna Konstantego*, 99, pp. 1099, 1228; Missalowa, p. 306.

4. Constantine to Nicholas, 13/25 July 1830, in *Perepiska*, Vol. II, pp. 30-31.

5. *Papiery gen. J. Krukowieckiego*, M. 6 pp. 32-35, Library of Warsaw in Lojek, *Studia...*, p. 278.

6. *Ibid*; Constantine to Nicholas, 25 July, 1830 in *Perepiska*, Vol. II, pp. 30-31.

7. Constantine to Nicholas, 2/14 August, 1830 in *Perepiska*, Vol. II, p. 34.

8. Constantine to Nicholas, 11 September, 1830 in *Perepiska*, Vol II, p. 48.

9. Lojek, *Studia...*, p. 332.

10. Constantine to Nicholas, 12/21 August, 1830 in Perepiska, Vol II, pp. 39-40.

11. *Ibid.*, Bortnowski, *Wielki Ksiaze Konstanty...*, pp. 204-205.

12. Bortnowski, p. 205.

13. Smolka, *Korespondencya Lubeckiego, III*, 364; *Perepiska* September and October in Bortnowski, *Wielke Ksiaze Konstanty...*, p. 204.

14. Lojek, *Studia...*, p. 286.

15. *Policja Tajna Konstantego* 99, p. 1122; Bortnowski, *Wielki Ksiaze Konstanty...*, p. 205.

16. Lojek, *Studia...*, pp. 295, 331.

17. Handelsman, p. 295.

18. Lojek, *Studia...*, p. 331, T. Lepkowski, in *Historia Polski*, p. 425. According to Leslie, however, there is little to indicate that the Poles rose to prevent the Polish army from being used to suppress foreign revolution, rather it was used as justification to claim French sympathy, Leslie, p. 120.

19. Tokarz, *Sprzysiezenie Wysockiego i Noc Listopadowa*, (Warsaw, 1925), p. 97 in Bortnowski, *Wielki Ksiaze Konstanty...*, p. 207.

20. *Ibid.*, p. 97 in Bortnowski, p. 207.

21. *Ibid.*

22. *Ibid.*

23. Pissarevsky, *Historii polskoi revolucii*, (Baku, 1930), in Bortnowski, *Wielki Ksiaze Konstanty...*, p. 205.

24. Bortnowski, *Walka o cele powstania listopadowego*, (Lodz, 1960), pp. 41-43; Bortnowski, p. 205.

25. *Ibid.*, p. 207.

26. *Ibid.*, p. 208.

27. Bronislaw Pawlowski, *Szkola Podchorazych Piechoty a wybuch rewolucji 29 listopada, 1830*, (Lwow: Nakladem Wydawnictwo "Kurjera Lwowskiego," 1906), p. 21.

146 NOTES

28. L. Chodzko, *Esquisses polonaises ou fragmens et traits detaches*, (Paris: H. Bossange Librarie, 1831), pp. 40-41.

29. Lepkowski, p. 427.

30. Dembowski, *Moje Wspomnienia*, (St. Petersburg, 1898), II, 28, in Leslie, p. 124.

31. Leslie, p. 127; Bronislaw Pawlowski, *Zrodla do dziejow wojny Polsko-Rosyjskiej 1830-31 r.* (Warsaw: Wojskowe Biuro Historyczne, 1931), pp. II, 14; Tokarz, *Armja Krolestwa Polskiego*, p. 337.

32. Leslie, p. 127.

33. Joachim Lelewel, *Delegowani w Wierzbnie dnia 8 grudnia 1830 roku*, (Avignon, 1832), pp. 1-16.

34. Pawlowski, p. 23.

35. Leslie, p. 130.

36. Riasanovsky, *Nicholas I...*; Bortnowski, *Wielki Ksiaze Konstanty...*, p. 206.

37. Pawlowski, p. 26; Chodzko, p. 40.

38. J. Lojek, *Szanse Powstania Listopadowego*, (Warsaw: Pax, 1966), p. 18.

39. Tokarz, *Wojna Polsko-Rosyjska 1830-1830*, pp. 56-58, T. Morawski, *Dzieje narodu polskiego*, VI, 308-309, Zamoyski, I, 376- 378, in Kukiel, *Czartoryski...*, p. 171; Handelsman, p. 296; *Pamietniki generala Jozefa Dwernickiego*, (Lwow: L. Plagowski, 1870), p. 7.

40. Handelsman, p. 297.

41. *Lettres et papiers du Chancelier Comte de Nesselrode, 1760-1850*, VII, 161, in Leslie, p. 123.

42. Puzyrevski, *Polsko-Russkaia Voina 1831 goda*, pp. 3-7, in John Shelton Curtiss, *The Russian Army Under Nicholas I 1825-1855*, (Durham, North Carolina: Duke University Press, 1965), p. 75.

43. "Relation d'une entrevue qui a eu lieu entre S.A.I. le Grand Duc Cesarewitch et Wolicki, le 5 et 6 decembre, 1830," 7274, Library of the Polish Army, Warsaw.

44. Chodzko, pp. 40, 55; V. Oeshsner, "Relacje Konsula Generala Austriackiego w Warszawie Barona V. Oeshnera o Powstaniu Listopadowym," *Rozprawy i Szkice* Wladyslaw Tokarz (ed.), Vol. 1 (Warsaw: Panstwowe Wydawnictwo Naukowe, 1959), p. 392.

45. Jezierski, pp. 47-48.

46. Constantine to Nicholas, 25 January/6 February 1830 in *Perepiska*, Vol. 11, p. 4; Constantine to Nicholas 4/16 February, 1830 in *Perepiska*, Vol. 11, p. 6; Constantine to Nicholas, 22 October/3 November, 1830, in *Perepiska*, Vol. 11, p. 60.

47. *Pamietniki Generala Pradzynskiego*, Bronislaw Gembarzewski (ed.), Vol. 1 (Krakow, 1909), pp. 211-212.

48. "Papiery odnoszace sie eskortowania wojsk rosyjskich odchodzacych z Krolewstwa za Bug," 2B; Ossolineum, Wroclaw.

49. Alexander Kraushar, *Miscellanea historyczne XII — Wielki Ksiaze Konstanty i obywatele lubelscy*, (Krakow: W drukarni "Czasu," 1907), pp. 21-22.

50. De Grunwald, p. 116.

51. *Ibid.*, p. 118.

52. Nicholas to Constantine, November 26/8 December, 1850, in *Perepiska*, Vol. II, p. 69.

53. Constantine to Nicholas, 3/15 December, 1830 in *Perepiska*, Vol. II, p. 69.

54. Constantine to Nicholas, 8/20 December, 1830 in *Perepiska*, Vol. II, p. 77.

55. Constantine to Nicholas, 8/20 December, 1830 in *Perepiska*, Vol. II, p. 77.

56. Jezierski, p. 54.

57. Constantine to Nicholas, February 22/March 6, 1831 in *Perepiska*, Vol. II, pp. 121 in Kukiel, *Czartoryski...*, p. 186.

58. *Ibid.*, p. 247; De Grunwald, p. 118.

59. Nicholas to Constantine, 25 February/March 9, 1831 in *Perepiska*, Vol, II, p. 132.

60. Constantine to Nicholas, 6/18 April, 1831, in *Perepiska*, Vol. II, p. 160.

61. Constantine to Nicholas, 7/19 June, 1831 in *Perepiska*, Vol. 11, p. 230, Constantine to Nicholas 9/21 June, 1831 in *Perepiska*, Vol. II, pp. 232; Constantine to Nicholas, 13/25 June in *Perepiska*, Vol. 11, p. 239.

62. De Grunwald, p. 120.

63. Jezierski, p. 53.

64. *Rys zycia*, p. 147; also noted in copy dated 1835 by Bayer in Ossolineum, Wroclaw; "Konstantin Pavlovich," *Bolshaia Sovetskaia Entseklopediia*, Vol. 22 (1953), p. 419; Schilder quoted in Kukiel, *Czartoryski...*, p. 247; Jezierski, p. 54; De Grunwald, p. 120.

65. Jezierski, p. 54; *Krestianskoe dvizhenie, 1827-1869*, E. A. Morokhovets (eds.), Moscow, 1931), p. 87 in Monas, p. 276.

66. *Ibid.*, p. 89.

67. De Grunwald, p. 120.

CONCLUSION

1. An interesting if neglected perspective on the revolution of 1830 is presented by Aleksander Bochenski in *Dzieje glupoty w Polsce; pamflety dziejopisarskie* (Warsaw: Panteon, 1947), pp. 271, 315. This author argues that the revolution itself was catastrophic and a folly, unthought through by the revolutionists, "simply a battle cry rather than a political idea."

BIBLIOGRAPHY

DOCUMENTS

The major documentary sources of this work are the following libraries and archives in Poland and France: the Archiwum Glowne Akt Dawnych (AGAD), The University of Warsaw Library, the Army Library in Warsaw, the Jagiellonian Library and the Czartoryski Library in Krakow, the Ossolineum Library in Wroclaw, and the Polish Library in Paris.

Akta Misji Polskiej w Paryzu z 1831. The Polish Library, Paris.

Alexander I to Adam Czartoryski, January 1/13, 1813 (Copy). The Polish Library Paris.

Archiwum Wielkiego Ksiecia Konstantego. The Polish Library, Paris.

Constantine Pavlovich. *Ordre du jour du Grand-Duc de Russie Constantin, Varsovie, decembre 11, 1814,* Vol. II, Sec. 327, pp. 139-139'. The Ossolineum, Wroclaw.

_____,*Rozkaz dzienny do narodowego wojska Polskiego,* Vol. III, Sec. 3, p. 89. The Jagiellonian Library, Krakow.

Constantine to Nicholas, 9/21 April, 1829. M 9, pp. 77-81. Manuscript Section, The University of Warsaw Library, Warsaw.

Papiery odnoszace sie eskortowania Wojsk Rosyjskich odchodzacych z krolestwa za Bug. The Ossolineum, Wroclaw.

Papiery tyczace sie projektu ogloszenia Alexander I krolem Polski z lat 1806-1810. Vol. 5231 V. The Czartoryski Library, Krakow.

Policja Tajna Konstantego. AGAD, Warsaw.

Pozzo di Borgo. *Memoire sur la Pologne, 1814.* Vol 5220 IV, pp. 29-41. The Czartoryski Library, Krakow.

Rozkaz dzienne do Wojska Polskiego, 1817, 1830. The Army Library, Warsaw.

Rozkaz dzienny Wielkiego Ksiecia Konstantego, January 14/26, 1826. The Ossolineum, Wroclaw.

Rozkaz dzienny Wielkiego Ksiecia Konstantego, January 20/February 1, 1826. The Ossolineum, Wroclaw.

149

Rozkaz dzienny do Wojska Polskiego, April 30/May 12, 1830. The University of Warsaw Library, Warsaw.

Rozmowy: 1823-1827-1828-1829 roku Xiecja z Wielkim Xieciem Konstantym. Vol. E. W. 3207. The Jagiellonian Library, Krakow.

Tajna Kancelaria Nowosilcowa. AGAD, Warsaw.

Trzy konstytucje: 1791- 1807, 1815. M. Handelsman, ed. Warsaw-Lwow: E. Wende, 1915. Second Revised edition.

Zbior "Rekopisow Wilanowskich." AGAD Warsaw.

Zespol Akt Archiwum Komisji Rzadowy Wojny i Militarii Krolestwa Polskiego z lat 1814 — 1846, AGAD, Warsaw.

Memoirs

Czartoryski, Adam. *Memoires du Prince Adam Czartoryski et correspondence avec l'empereur Alexandre Ier.* Edited by Charles de Mazade. 2 Vols. Paris: Librairie Plon, 1887.

Dmochowski, Franciszek. *Wspomnienia od 1806 do 1830 roku.* Warsaw: Panstwowe Wydawnictwo Naukowe, 1959.

Gajewski, Franciszek. *Pamietniki.* 2 Vols. Poznan: Zdzislaw Rzepecki i S-ka, n.d.

Gembarzewski, Bronislaw (ed.). *Pamietniki Generala Pradzynskiego.* Krakow, 1909.

Harring, Harro. *Poland under the Domination of Russia.* London: James Cochrane and Company, 1831.

Komorowski, Ignacy A. *Wspomnienia podchorazego z czasow W. X. Konstantego.* Lwow: E. Winiarz, 1863.

Lukasinski, Walerian. *Pamietnik.* Warsaw: Panstwowe Wydawnictwo Naukowe, 1960.

Masson, A. P. *Memoires secrets sur la Russie.* Paris: Librairie de Firme Didot Freres Fils et Cie., 1859.

Moriolles, Alexandre. *Memoire de Comte du Moriolles sur l'emigration, la Pologne et la cour du Grand-Duc Constantin(1789-1833).* Paris: Society d'Editions Litteraires et Artistiques, 1902.

Oginski, Michel. Vol. III of *Memoire de Michel Oginski.* Paris: Chez Ponthieu, Librairie, 1827.

Ostrowski, T. Vol. II of *Zywot Ostrowskiego.* Paris: 1840.

Patelski, Jozef. *Wspomnienia wojskowe z lat 1823-1831.* Wilno: Ksiegarnia Stowarzyszenia Nauczycielstwa Polskiego, 1921.

Pamietniki Generala Jozefa Dwernickiego. Lwow: L. Plagowski, 1870.

Posluchanie przez W. Ksiecia Konstantego poslom i deputowanym wdtwa. Kaliskiego udzielona dnia 15 czerwca 1830, Warsaw, 1831.

Sierawski, Napoleon. *Pamietnik Napoleona Sierawskiego oficera konnego pulku gwardyii z czasow W. Ks. Konstantego.* Lwow: Gubrynowicz i Schmidt, 1907.

Skadkowski, Stanislaw. *Higiena w wojsku Wielkiego Ksiecia Konstantego*. Warsaw: Zaklad Graficzne "Drukarnia Bankowa," 1920.
Wilson, Robert. *Narrative of Events during the Invasion of Russia by Napoleon Bonaparte and the Retreat of the French Army in 1812*. London: John Murray, 1860.
Zamoyski, Andrzej. *Moje Przeprawy: Pamietnik o czasach powstania listopadowego, 1830-1831*. Krakow: G. Gebethner, 1911. Second edition.

Histories

Gnorowski, S.B. *Insurrection of Poland in 1830-1831 and the Russian Rule Preceding It Since 1815*. London: John Ridgeway, 1839.
Jaworski, J. N. *Essai historique et politique sur la royaume de Pologne, 1815-1830*. Paris: Au Cabinet de Lecture Polonais, 1846.
Millutin, D. Vol. I of *Istoriia voiny 1799 goda mezhdu Rossii i Frantsii v tsarstvovania Imperatora Pavla I*. St. Petersburg: Tipografiia Imperatorskoi Akademii Nauk, 1857.
Mochnacki, Maurycy. *Powstanie narodu polskiego*. Paris: P. Baudoin, 1834.

Contemporary Literature

Bieczynski, Tadeusz (ed.). *Sad sejmowy 1829 na przestepcow stanu Urzedowe Akta*. Poznan: J.I. Kraszewski, 1873.
Chodzko, Leonard. *Esquisses polonaises ou fragmens et traits detaches*. Paris: Hector Bossange Librairie, 1831.
Ergon, Adrien. *Vie d'Alexandre Ier, empereur de Russie, suivi de notices sur les Grand-Ducs Constantin, Nicholas et Michel*. Paris: Chez F. Denn, Librairie, 1826.
Lelewel, Joachim. *Delegowani w Wierzbnie dnia 2 grudnia 1830 roku*. Avignon, 1832.
_____. *Dziela*. 2 Vols. Warsaw: Panstwowe Wydawnictwo Naukowe, 1957.
(Nakwaski, _____). *Le Grand-Duc Constantin a Varsovie pendant le Congres de Vienne*. Paris: Librairie Slave., 1847.
Rys zycia Jego Cesarzewiczowskiej Mosci Wielkiego Xiecia Konstantego Pawlowicza. Warsaw, 1833.

Other Printed Primary Sources

D'Angeberg, Comte (Leonard Chodzko). *Receuil des traites, conventions et actes diplomatiques concernant la Pologne, 1762-1862*. Paris: Amyot, Editeur des Archives Diplomatiques, 1862.

"Dnevnik Shtats Sekretaria Grigoriia Ivanovicha Villamova 1775-1842," *Russkaia Starina*, I (1912).

Dutkiewicz, Jozef. *Wybor zrodel do powstania listopadowego*. Warsaw: Zaklad Narodowy im. Ossolinskich, 1957.

"Iz zapisok Generala-adiutanta Grafa E. F. Komarovskago," *Russkii Arkhiv*, V (1867).

"Iz zapisok N. A. Sablukova," *Russkii Arkhiv*, VII (1869).

Kieniewicz, Stefan, *et. al.* (eds.)... *Wybor tekstow zrodlowych z historii Polski w latach 1795 — 1864*. Warsaw: Panstwowe Wydawnictwo Naukowe, 1856.

Kozuchowski, Nemezy. "W. X. Konstanty, Pozzo de Borgo i Monitor," *Kronika Emigracji Polskiej*, VI (1837).

Molski, Marcin. *Do Jego Ces. Mci. Konstantego Pawlowicza na przyjazd do Warszawy 14(26) wrzesnia 1814*. The University of Warsaw Library, Warsaw.

Oeshsnera, V. "Relacje Konsula Generala Austriackiego w Warszawie Barona V. Oeshsnera o Powstaniu Listopadowym," in Vol. I of *Rozprawy i Szkice*. Edited by Wladyslaw Tokarz. Warsaw: Panstwowe Wydawnictwo Naukowe, 1959.

"Otchety Lagarpa Grafu Nikolago Ivanovicha Saltykovu o vospitanii velikich Kniazei Aleksandra i Konstantina Pavlovichei," *Russkaia Starina*, I (1870).

Pawlowski, Bronislaw. *Zrodla do dziejow wojny polsko-rosyjskiej 1830-31 r*. Warsaw: Wojskowe Biuro Historyczne, 1931.

"Perepiska Imperatora Nikolaia Pavlovicha s Velikim Kniazem Tsesarevichem Konstantinom Pavlovichem," *Sbornik Russkago Istoricheskago Obshchestva*, I, II (1910-1911).

"Perepiska Velikago Kniazia Konstantego Pavlovicha s Grafom Beckendorfom 1826-1828," *Russkkii Arkhiv*, VI (1885).

"Pisma germanskoi printseesy o russkom dvore 1795 god," *Russkii Arkhiv*, VII (1869).

"Pisma Tsesarevicha Velikago Kniazia Konstantina Pavlovicha k Markiz Dekluber," *Russkaia Starina*, VIII (1871).

"Pisma Velikago Kniazia Pavlovicha k Lagarpy 1796-1829," *Sbornik Russkago Istoricheskago Obshchestva*, V (1870).

"Razkazy Kniazia Sergiia Mikhailovicha Golitsyna," *Russkii Arkhiv*, VII (1869).

Relation d'une entrevue qui a eu lieu entre S.A.I. le Grand Duc Cesarewitch et Wolicki, le 5 et 6 decembre 1830. The Library of the Polish Army, Warsaw.

Rembowski, Alexander. *Spadek pismenniczy po Generala Maurycy Hr. Hauke*. Warsaw: Nakladem Ksiegarni E. Wende i S-ka, 1905.

Rozkazy dzienne Konstantego z lat 1816-17. Vol I of *Druki autoryzowane podpisem szefa sztabu glownego Gen Jozefa Tobinskiego. 3/15 czerwca, 1816. No. 6*. The University of Warsaw Library Warsaw.

Sablionkoff, General. "Reminiscences of the Court and Times of the Emperor Paul I of Russia, up to the Period of his Death, from the Papers of a Deceased Russian General Officer," *Fraser's Magazine for Town and Country*, LXXII (August, September, 1865).

Sienkiewicz, Andrzej. "Materialy do zagadnienia ucisku i walki spolcznej w aktach policji tajnej W. ks. Konstantego, 1821-1830," *Teki Archiwalne*, III-IV (1954).

Skalkowski, A.M. (ed.). Vol II of *Archiwum Wybickiego*. Gdansk: Nakladem Towarzystwo Przejaciol Nauki i Sztuki w Gdansku, 1950.

Smolka, Stanislaw. *Korespondencya Lubeckiego z ministrami sekretarzami stanu* Ignacym Sobolewskim i Stefanem Grabowskim. Krakow: Nakladem Akademii Umiejetnosci, 1909.

"Suppressed Passage of the Speech of the Emperor Nicholas at Warsaw; with Observations on the Practical Results of that Speech, October 16, 1935," in Vol. I of *The Portfolio*. London: James Ridgeway and Sons, 1836.

Walsh, Warren B. (ed.). Vol. II of *Readings in Russian History*. Syracuse: Syracuse University Press, 1963.

Zapiski Ivana Stepanovicha Zhirkevicha," *Russkaia Starina*, IX, X, XI (1874).

Zbior pamietnikow do historyi powstania polskiego z r. 1830-31. Lwow: Nakladem Dra. Tomasza Rayskiego, 1882.

Secondary Works
Articles and Periodicals

Askenazy, Szymon. "Bracia," *Kurier Warszawski*, CXXXXIII (May, 1933).

_____ "Dwie rozmowy w Belwederze," *Bibliotecka Warszawska*, II (1906).

Bekker, I. "Dekabrysci a sprawa Polska," *Powstania Listopadowego*, Edited by Wl. Bortnowski. Warsaw: Wydawnictwo "Prasa Wojskowa," 1950.

Chechulin, N. "Konstantin Pavlovich," *Russkii Biograficheskii Slovar*, IX (1903).

Dziewanowski, M. K., "Czartoryski and his 'Essai sur la diplomatie'" *Slavic Review*, XXX, 3 (1971).

Eile, M. "Tajna policja Wielkiego Ksiecia Konstantego," *Gazeta Administracji Policji Panstwowy*, II (January, 1931).

Gasiorowska, Natalia. "Ustanowienie cenzury w Krolestwie Kongresowym," *Biblioteka Warszawska*, III (July, 1912).

Handelsman, Marceli. "Kryzys w r. 1821 w Krolestwie Polskim," *Kwartalnik Historyczny*, (1939).

"Imperatritsa Ekaterina II i Kn. Potemkin," *Russkaia Starina*, XVI (August, 1876).

"Konstantin Pavlovich," *Bolshaia Sovetskaia Entseklopediia*, XXII (1953).

"Konstanty Pawlowicz," *Encyklopediia Wojskowa* Warsaw, 1934.

"Konstanty Pawlowicz," *Wielka Encyklopedia Powszechna Illustrowana*, XXXVII (1904).

Kukiel, Marian, "Lelewel, Mickiewicz and European Revolution, 1816-1833," *Polish Review*, V, 3 (1960).

Krasinski, Jozef, "W pierwszych latach Krolestwie Kongresowym,: *Biblioteka Warszawska*, Vol. II, Section I (April, 1913).

BIBLIOGRAPHY

Lojek, Jerzy, "Szpiegowskie kariery," *Stolica*, (April, 1965).
Ludwikowski, Rett, "Ks. Drucki-Lubecki," *Studia Historyczne*, XXIV, 4 (1981).
"Mikolaj I Pawlowicz," *Wielka Encyklopedia Powszechna*, VII (1967).
"Mikolaj Nowosilcow," *Wielka Encyklopedia Powszechna*, VIII (1966).
Morley, Charles, "Czartoryski as a Polish Statesman," *Slavic Review*, XXX, 3 (1971).
Pissarevskii, Gregorii, "Istorii kongresowego tsarstva 1818-1830 pri Alexander I," *Nauchnye Izvestia*, III (1926).
"Powstanie Listopadowe," *Wielka Encyklopedia Powszechna*, IX (1967).
Saltikov,_____. "La mort de Paul Ier," *Revue Moderne*, XXX (1865).
Smolka, Stanislaw. "W drodze do Petersburga," *Przeglad Historyczny*, II (1906).
"Stanislaw Grabowski," *Wielka Encyklopedia Powszechna*, IV (1964).
Szpotanski, Stanislaw. "Z rozmow w Belwederze," *Biblioteka Warszawska*, II (1913).
Thackerey, Frank, "N. N. Novosiltsev: The Polish Years," *Polish Review*, XXVIII, 1 (1983).
Walker, Franklin, "Constantine Pavlovich," *Slavic Review*, XXVI, 3 (1967).

BOOKS

Ajzen, Mieczyslaw. *Polityka gospodarcza Lubeckiego, 1821-1830*. Warsaw: Nakladem Towarzystwa Naukowego Warszawskiego, 1932.
Almedingen, E. M. *The Emperor Alexander*. London: The Bodley Head, 1964.
Askenazy, Szymon. *Dwa stulecia* 2 Vols. Warsaw: Nakladem Gebethnera i Wolffa, 1910.
_____*Lukasinski*. 2 Vols. Warsaw: Nakladem Drukarni Wl. Lazarskiego, 1929.
_____*Rosja-Polska, 1815-1830*. Lwow: Nakladem H. Attenberga, 1907.
_____*Wielki Ksiaze Konstanty i Ksiezniczka Helena Lubomirska*. Warsaw, 1913.
Bartoszewicz, Kazimierz. *Utworzenie Krolestwa Kongresowego*. Krakow: Nakladem Centralnego Biura Wydawnictw, 1916.
Beylin, Karolina. *Tajemnice Warszawy*. Warsaw: Panstwowy Instytut Wydawniczy, 1956.
Bojasinski, Jozef. *Rzady tymczasowe w Krolestwie Polskim*. Warsaw: 1902.
Bortnowski, Wladyslaw. *Wielki ksiaze Konstanty podczas Powstania Listopadowego*. Warsaw: Ministerstwo Obrony Narodowej, No. 8, 1965.
Curtiss, John Shelton. *The Russian Army under Nicholas I 1825-1855*. Durham, North Carolina: Duke University Press, 1965.
Czaplinski, W. and Ladogorski, T., editors, *Atlas Historyczny Polski*. Warsaw: Panstwowe Przedsiebiorstwo wydawnictw kartograficznych, 1979. Fourth edition.

Czynski, Jan. *Cesarzewicz Konstanty i Joanna Grudzinska; czyli Jakubini Polscy*, Warsaw: Czytelnik, 1956.

De Grunwald, Constantin. *Tsar Nicholas I*. New York: The Macmillan Co., 1955.

Florinsky, Michael T. *Russia — A History and an Interpretation*. 2 Vols. New York: Macmillan Company, 1961.

Gajewski, *Pamietniki*. 2 Vols. Poznan: Zdislaw Rzepecki 1 S-ka, n.d.

Gasiorowska, Natalia. *Wolnosc druku w Krolestwie Kongresowem*. Warsaw: Gebethner i Wolff, 1916.

Gasiorowska, Waclaw. *Ksiezna Lowicka*. Warsaw: Ludowa Spoldzielnia Wydawnicza, 1960.

Gembarzewski, Bronislaw. *Wojsko polskie 1815-1830*. Warsaw: Konstanty Treptc, 1903.

Grochulska, Barbara. *Ksiestwo Warszawskie*. Warsaw: Wiedza Powszechna, 1966.

Hodgetts, Edward. Vol. I. of *The Court of Russia in the Nineteenth Century*. New York: Charles Scribner's Sons, 1908.

Jezierski, Edmund. *Wielki Ksiaze Konstanty i Ksiezna Lowicka*. Warsaw: Nakladem Ksiegarni W. Jakowieckiego, 1916.

Karnovich, E. P. *Tsesarevich Konstantin Pavlovich*. St. Petersburg: A.S. Suvorin, 1899.

Kieniewicz, Stefan and Kula, Witold (eds.). Vol. II of *Historia Polski*. Warsaw: Panstwowe Wydawnictwo Naukowe, 1958.

_____. *Przemiany spoleczne i gospodarcze w Krolestwie Polskim*. Warsaw: Ksiazka i Wiedza, 1951.

Kozlowski, Wladyslaw. *Autonomia Krolestwa Polskiego 1815-1830*. Warsaw: E. Wende i S-ka, 1907.

Kraushar, Alekander. *Miscellania historyczne XXII — Wielki Ksiaze Konstanty i obywatele lubelscy*. Krakow: W Drukarni "Czasu" 1907.

_____ *Senator Nowosilcow i censura za Krolestwa Kongresowego 1819-1829*. Krakow: G. Gebethner i S-ka, 1913.

_____ *Sprzysienzenie studenckie 1810-1827*. Lwow: Nakladem Autora, 1905.

Kukiel, Marian. *Czartoryski and European Unity, 1770-1861*. Princeton: Princeton University Press, 1955.

_____ *Dziele Polski porozbiorowe, 1795-1921*. London: B. Swiderski, 1963.

Leslie, R. F. *Polish Politics and the Revolution of November, 1830*. London: The University of London, Athelone Press, 1956.

Lojek, Jerzy. *Studia nad prasa i opinia publiczna w Krolestwie Polskim 1815-1830*. Warsaw: Panstwowe Wydawnictwo Naukowe, 1966.

_____ *Szanse Powstania Listopadowego*. Warsaw: Pax, 1966.

Malachowski-Lempicki, Stanislaw. *Raporty szpiega Mackrotta o Wolnomularstwie Polskim 1819-1822*. Warsaw: Gebethner i Wolff, n.d.

Manteufflowa, Maria. *J. K. Szaniawski*. Warsaw: Nakladem Towarzystwa Warszawskiego, 1936.

Mazour, Anatole G. *The First Russian Revolution 1825*. Stanford: Stanford University Press, 1961.

156   BIBLIOGRAPHY

Pienkos, Angela. "Grand Duke Constantine Pavlovich - A Study in Early
    Nineteenth Century Russo-Polish Relations, 1815-1831" Ph. D. Diss.
    University of Wisconsin, 1971.
Przelaskowski, Ryszard. *Sejm Warszawski*. Warsaw: Nakladem Towarzystwa
    Naukowego Warszawskiego, 1929.
Raeff, Marc. *The Decembrist Movement*. Englewood Cliffs, New Jersey:
    Prentice-Hall, Inc., 1966.
Reddaway, W. F. *et al*. (eds.). Vol. II of *The Cambridge History of Poland*.
    Cambridge: At the University Press, 1951.
Riasanovsky, Nicholas. *Nicholas I and Official Nationality in Russia,
    1825-1855*. Berkeley: University of California Press, 1959.
Schilder, N. K. *Imperator Alexandr Pervyi*. St. Petersburg: A. S. Suvorin,
    1904.
Skurnowicz, Joan. *Romantic Nationalism and Liberalism: Joachim Lelewel
    and the Polish National Idea*. Boulder, Colorado and New York: Eastern
    European Monographs, 1981.
Smolka, Stanislaw, *Polityka Lubeckiego przed Powstaniem Listopadowym*.
    2 Vols. Krakow: Nakladem Akademii Umiejetnosci, 1907.
Spector, Ivan. *An Introduction to Russian History and Culture*. Princeton:
    D. Van Nostrand Co., Inc., 1969.
Squire, Peter Stansfield. *The Third Department*. Cambridge: Harvard Univer-
    sity Press, 1968.
Stanley, John. "A Political and Social History of the Duchy of Warsaw,
    1807-1813," Ph. D. diss. University of Toronto, 1979.
Strakhovsky, Leonid I. *Alexander I of Russia*. New York: W. W. Norton
    and Company, 1947.
Tokarz, Waclaw. *Armja Krolestwa Polskiego, 1815-1830*. Piotrkow:
    Nakladem departmentu Wojskowego Naczelnego Komitetu Narodowego,
    1917.
Wandycz, Piotr. *The Lands of Partitioned Poland, 1795-1918*. Seattle and
    London: University of Washington Press, 1974.
Webster, C. K. *The Congress of Vienna 1814-1815*. London: G. Bell and
    Sons, Ltd., 1945.
Wieckowska, Helena. *Opozycja liberalna w Krolestwie Kongresowym,
    1815-1820*. Warsaw Sklad w kasie Mianowskiego, 1925.
Wyspianski, Stanislaw. *Dramaty o powstaniu Listopadowym: "Warsza-
    wianka," "Lelewel," "Noc Listopadowa."* Wroclaw: Zaklad narodowy
    imienia ossolinskich, 1967.
Yarmolinsky, Avrahm. *Road to Revolution*. New York: The Macmillan
    Company, 1959.
Zetlin, Mikhail. *The Decembrists*. New York: International Universities Press,
    1958.

APPENDICES

THE POLISH CONSTITUTION OF 1815 AND THE ORGANIC STATUTE OF 1832

CONSTITUTIONAL LAW OF THE KINGDOM OF POLAND

OF THE POLITICAL RELATIONS OF THE KINGDOM

Article 1. The Kingdom of Poland is forever united to the Empire of Russia.

Article. 2. The civil and political relations in which we place it, and the bonds by which this union is to be secured, are determined by the Law which we now grant.

Article. 3. The crown of Poland is hereditary in our person and that of our descendants, heirs, and successors, according to the order of succession established for the imperial throne in Russia.

Article. 4. The Constitutional Law determines the manner, the principle, and the exercise of the sovereign authority.

Article. 5. The King, in case of absence, shall name a governor general (*namiestnik*) who is to reside in the Kingdom; which governor general shall be removed at the King's pleasure.

Article. 6. When the King does not appoint for his governor general a Prince Imperial of Russia, his choice shall fall upon a native, or upon some person to whom he has granted naturalization, in the manner prescribed by the thirty-third article.

Article. 7. The nomination of the governor general shall be made by a public act; which act shall precisely determine the nature and extent of the power entrusted to him.

Article. 8. The external political relations of our Empire shall be common to the Kingdom of Poland.

Article. 9. The sovereign alone shall have the power to determine the participation of the Kingdom of Poland in the Russian wars, as well as in the treaties of peace which that power may conclude.

Article. 10. In every instance in which Russian troops may be introduced into Poland, or Polish troops into Russia, or in the event of the passage of these troops through any province of either of these Kingdoms, the support of such troops, and the expenses attendant upon their journey, shall rest entirely with the nation to which they belong. The Polish Army shall never be employed out of Europe.

GENERAL GUARANTEES

Article. 11. The Roman Catholic religion, being professed by the majority of the inhabitants of the Kingdom of Poland, the government shall make this religion the object of special care, without in any degree, derogating thereby from the freedom of other religious sects, which shall all, without exception, have full and public liberty to carry on their respective worship, and shall all enjoy the protection of the government. The different forms of Christian worship, shall occasion no difference in the enjoyment of civil and political rights.

Article. 12. The ministers of all the different denominations shall be under the protection and under the inspection of the government.

Article. 13. The property already in the possession of the Roman Catholic Church and what may hereafter be granted by our special decree, shall be declared inalienable and common to the whole ecclesiastical hierarchy, as soon as the government shall have appointed and assigned to the said clergy, the national domains which are to constitute such gifts.

Article. 14. The Senate of the Kingdom of Poland shall admit as members as many bishops of the Roman Catholic Church as there may be provinces by law appointed. It shall admit also one bishop of the Uniate Church.

Article. 15. The clergy of the confession of Augsburg and of the Evangelical Reformed denomination shall receive such annual support as we shall be disposed to grant for their use.

Article. 16. The liberty of the press is guaranteed. The law shall determine the method of restraining its abuses.

Article. 17. The law shall protect every class of citizens alike, without regard to their rank or condition.

Article. 18. The ancient fundamental law "*neminem captivari permittemus nisi jure victum*" shall be observed with regard to all classes of the inhabitants, as below explained.

Article. 19. No man shall be arrested except with procedures and in the cases prescribed by the law.

Article. 20. Every man shall be informed immediately, and by writing, of the cause of his arrest.

Article. 21. Every individual, so arrested, shall be presented within three days, at the most, before the competent tribunal, that he may be there examined or tried. If on the first examination he be found to be innocent, he shall be forthwith discharged.

Article. 22. In such cases as the law directs, the prisoner, if he gives bail, shall be set at liberty for the time.

Article. 23. No man shall be punished except in conformity with the existing laws, and by the decree of the competent magistrate.

Article. 24. Every Pole is at liberty to remove his person, or his property, according to the procedures by law prescribed.

Article. 25. Every condemned criminal shall undergo the penalty prescribed by law, in his own country; and nobody shall be carried out of the country except in the case of banishment decreed by law.

Article. 26. All property, of whatever description or nature, whether it may be on the surface or below the earth, and to whomsoever it may belong, is hereby declared sacred and inviolable; and no authority shall infringe upon it, under any pretense whatever. Any person attempting to appropriate the property of another, shall be held to be a disturber of the public peace, and punished accordingly.

Article. 27. Government has, nevertheless, the power of exacting from any individual, the sacrifice of his property, when the public good requires it, providing for the individual a previous and equitable indemnification. The law shall determine the cases, and the manner in which this principle is to be applied.

Article. 28. All public affairs, executive, judicial, and military, without any exception, shall be transacted in the Polish language.

Article. 29. All public offices, civil and military, shall be filled by Poles only. The presidents of tribunals for the first hearing of causes, presidents of provincial commissions, of tribunals of appeals, the members of the chamber of deputies and the senators shall be, without exception, landed proprietors.

Article. 30. All public officers in the executive part of the administration, are liable to be displaced by the same authority by which they were appointed; and all, without exception, are responsible for their conduct.

Article. 31. The Polish Nation shall have forever a national representation; and this representation shall consist of the *Sejm* (legislature), composed of the King and of the two chambers; the Senate shall constitute one chamber, and the Chamber of Deputies the other.

Article. 32. Every properly registered foreigner shall enjoy the protection of the laws, and the advantages which they secure, on the same footing as the other inhabitants. He shall be able, like them, to remain in the Kingdom or to leave it (conformably to the rules therein established), to return to it, to acquire landed property, and to qualify himself for becoming a citizen.

Article. 33. Any foreigner who has become a landed proprietor and been naturalized, and who has also acquired the Polish language, is admissible to a public office, after five years of residence and of acceptable behavior.

Article. 34. The King also of his own pleasure, or on the representation of his Council of State, may appoint foreigners of talent to any offices not excepted by Article Ninety.

GOVERNMENT
CHAPTER I
The King

Article. 35. The government resides in the person of the King. He exercises in all their fullness the functions of executive power. All executive and administrative authority must emanate from him.

Article. 36. The person of the King is sacred and inviolable.

Article. 37. The public acts of all tribunals, courts, and magistracies shall be drawn up in the King's name. The impressions upon all coin and stamps shall be of his choice.

Article. 38. The disposition of the armed forces, in the time of peace, as well as in war, and the nomination of generals and officers belong exclusively to the King.

Article. 39. The King disposes of the revenues of the state, conformable to the budget, which is to be drawn up and submitted for his approbation.

Article. 40. The right of making war, and of concluding all treaties and conventions, is reserved to the King.

Article. 41. The King is to nominate the senators, the ministers, the counsellors of state, the masters of requests, the presidents of provincial commissions, the presidents and judges of the different tribunals which are reserved for his nomination, diplomatic and commercial agents, and all other functionaries; and he may do this either directly himself, or indirectly, by means of the authorities, to whom he may be pleased to delegate his power.

Article. 42. The King is to nominate the archbishops and bishops of the different denominations, the prelates, and canons.

Article. 43. The power of granting a pardon is exclusively the King's. He may remit or commute the penalty.

Article. 44. The institution, the regulation, and the power of appointment to all civil and military orders, belong to the King.

Article. 45. All our successors on the throne of Poland are hereby engaged to be crowned King of Poland in the capital, according to the form which we shall prescribe; and they shall make oath as follows: "I swear and promise before God and upon the Holy Gospels to maintain and execute, to the utmost of my power, the Constitutional Law."

Article. 46. The power of conferring nobility, of naturalizing a foreigner, and of granting titles of honor, resides in the King.

Article. 47. All orders and decrees of the King shall be counter-signed by a minister, the head of a department, who shall be responsible for anything that the said orders and decrees may contain contrary to the Constitutional Law.

CHAPTER II
Regency

Article. 48. The cases of regency which are, or may be admitted for Russia, and the powers of the Regent, shall be common to the Kingdom of Poland, and the same principles shall obtain in both realms.

Article. 49. In case of regency, the secretary of state is compelled, upon his own personal responsibility, to announce to the governor general the establishment of the regency in Russia.

Article. 50. The governor general, on receiving the communication respecting the regency in Russia, and the memorial of the secretary of state, shall convoke the Senate for the election of the members of a regency in the Kingdom of Poland.

Article. 51. The regency of the Kingdom shall be composed of the Regent of Russia, of four members elected by the Senate, and the secretary of state. It shall hold its sittings in the capital of the Russian Empire; and the Regent shall preside.

Article. 52. The authority of the regency of the Kingdom shall be equal to that of the King, except that it shall not have power to nominate senators, and that all its nominations shall be subject to the approbation of the King, who may revoke them when he takes the reins of government into his own hands. The council shall publish all its decrees in the name of the King.

Article. 53. The nomination and the power of recalling the governor general belongs to the regency during its administration.

Article. 54. When the King takes the reins of government, he shall require from the regency an account of its administration.

Article. 55. The members of the regency of the Kingdom shall be responsible in their persons and in their property for whatever they may have done contrary to the constitution or to the laws.

Article. 56. In case of the death of one of the members of the regency, the Senate, convoked by the governor general shall fill the vacancy. The regency shall appoint a secretary to the regency.

Article. 57. The members of the regency, before they set off for the capital of Russia, shall make an oath in the presence of the Senate, that they will faithfully support the constitution and the laws.

Article. 58. The Regent of Russia shall take the same oath in the presence of the members of the council of regency.

Article. 59. The secretary of state shall be required to take a similar oath.

Article. 60. Information of the Regent's act of taking the oath shall be sent to the Senate of Poland.

Article. 61. Information of the secretary of state's act of taking the oath shall be sent in like manner to the Senate of Poland.

Article. 62. Information of the oath-taking by the members of the regency shall be forwarded, by the members of the Senate of Poland, to the Regent of Russia.

CHAPTER III
OF THE GOVERNOR GENERAL AND THE COUNCIL OF STATE

Article. 63. The Council of State in which the King, or his governor general is to preside, shall be composed of the ministers, the counsellors of state, the masters of requests, and of such other persons as it shall please the King specially to appoint.

Article. 64. The governor general and the Council of State shall administer the affairs of the Kingdom in the King's name, during his absence.

Article. 65. The Council of State shall be divided into an Administrative Council and a General Assembly.

Article. 66. The Administrative Council shall be composed of the governor general, of the ministers who are the heads of the five departments of government, and of other persons specially appointed by the King.

Article. 67. The members of the Administrative Council have deliberative voices only. The opinion of the governor general is decisive. He is to take his resolutions in Council, in conformity with the constitution, with the laws, and with the powers derived from the King.

Article. 68. Every decree of the governor general in order to be obligatory must be rendered in Council and counter-signed by a secretary of one of the departments.

Article. 69. The governor general shall present to the King (in terms of a more detailed arrangement on the subject) two candidates for every vacancy of an archbishop, bishop, senator, minister, supreme judge, counsellor of state, or master of requests.

Article. 70. The governor general shall take the following oath in the presence of the Senate, holding his hands in those of the King: ''I swear to Almighty God, that I will administer the affairs of Poland in the King's name, conformably to the constitution, to the laws, and to the powers and instructions derived from the King; and that I will remit to the King, the power entrusted to me, as soon as his Majesty shall deem it expedient.'' If the King be absent from the Kingdom the act of taking the oath in the hands of the King by the governor general shall be forwarded to the Senate by the secretary of state.

Article. 71. The King being present, the authority of the governor general is suspended. It is then at the King's pleasure to consult with the ministers separately, or to call a council of administration.

Article. 72. In case of the death of a governor general, or if the King should not think proper to appoint one, he will fill his place *''ad interim''* by a president.

Article. 73. The General Assembly of the Council of State shall be composed of all the members enumerated in Article Sixty-three. The King shall preside, or his governor general, and in their absence, the first member of the Council, in the order established by Articles Sixty-three and Sixty-six.

Its functions are:

First, to discuss and revise all proposed laws and regulations for the general administration of the country.

Second, To pass judgment upon all administrative functionaries registered by the King as being accused of collusion in office, excepting such only as are judged by the High National Court.

Third, To decide in cases of contested jurisdiction.

Fourth, To examine annually the accounts of every principal member of the administration.

Fifth, To watch over all abuses, and everything tending to encroach upon the Constitutional Law, and to make a general report of them to the King, who shall determine what objects are of a nature to be referred by his order to the Senate or to the Chamber of Deputies.

Article. 74. The General Assembly of the Council of State shall deliberate, by order of the King, or of the governor general, or at the request of a head of a department, if made in conformity with established law.

Article. 75. The decrees of the Council of State are subject to the approbation of the King or his governor general. Those relating to the trial of public officers, and to contested jurisdiction, are immediately to be carried into effect.

CHAPTER IV
OF THE BRANCHES OF THE ADMINISTRATION

Article. 76. The execution of the laws shall be confided to the different branches of the public administration as follows:

1. The ministry for religious affairs and public instruction.

2. The ministry of justice, chosen from among the members of the supreme tribunal.

3. The ministry of the interior and of the police.

4. The ministry of war.

5. The ministry of finances and of the treasury.

These different ministries shall each be presided over and directed by a minister appointed for that purpose.

Article. 77. A minister of state shall be appointed, who shall constantly reside about the person of the King.

Article. 78. There shall be a court of accounts charged with the final examination of accounts, and empowered to discharge those who present them. This court shall be responsible to the King alone.

Article. 79. The construction and the powers of the ministry for public instruction, as well as of the judicial order, shall be regulated by a specific act.

Article. 80. The ministry of the interior, the ministers of war, and of finances, shall be composed of one minister and of counsellors of state, who are directors general, in pursuance of the specific statutes on the subject.

Article. 81. The secretary of state is to present to the King the documents which are delivered to him by the governor general, and to return to the governor general the King's orders. Such foreign affairs as may concern the Kingdom of Poland are to be communicated to the secretary.

Article. 82. The heads of departments, and the members of government ministries, are answerable to the high national court for every infraction of the constitution and the royal decrees, of which they may have been guilty.

CHAPTER V
OF THE ADMINISTRATION OF THE PROVINCES

Article. 83. There shall be in each province a provincial commission, composed of a president and of commissioners charged with carrying into execution the orders of the government ministries in conformity with a separate regulation.

Article. 84. There shall be municipal authorities in the towns. A bailiff in every district shall be charged with the execution of the government orders, and shall form the last link in the administrative department.

CHAPTER VI
OF THE NATIONAL REPRESENTATION

Article. 85. The national representation shall be constituted as ordained in Article Fifty-one.

Article. 86. The legislative power resides in the person of the King, and in the two chambers of the *Sejm*, in conformity with the regulations in Article Thirty-one.

Article. 87. The *Sejm* in ordinary circumstances, shall meet once every two years in Warsaw, at the time prescribed by the King in his act of convocation. The session shall last for thirty days. The King alone has power to prorogue, adjourn, or dissolve it.

Article. 88. The King has the power of convoking an extraordinary session of the *Sejm* when he may think proper.

Article. 89. No member of the *Sejm* can be arrested, or tried for a criminal offence, while the *Sejm* is sitting, unless with the consent of the chamber to which he belongs.

Article. 90. The *Sejm* shall take into consideration all proposed civil, criminal, or administrative laws, referred to it by the King, through the Council of State. It shall deliberate on all proposed modifications or alterations of the duties of public offices and constitutional powers, such as those of the *Sejm*, the Council of State, the judicial order, and the government ministries' such change or modification being referred to its consideration by the royal authority.

Article. 91. The *Sejm* shall deliberate upon the increase or diminution of taxes, contributions, customs and political expenses of all kinds, on the alterations which they may require, on the best and most equitable method of distribution, on the formation of the budget of receipts and expenditure, on the regulation of the coinage, and on the levy of recruits; the materials for such deliberation being furnished by the government. It shall deliberate also upon all other subjects which may be referred to it by the Sovereign.

Article. 92. The *Sejm* shall also deliberate upon the communications which are made to it by the King, in consequence of the general report required from the Council of State by Article Seventy-three. Lastly the *Sejm*, after having enacted its decrees on all these subjects, receives contributions, requests, representations, or complaints presented to it by the members of the Chamber of Deputies, for the benefit and advantage of their constituents. The *Sejm* will present them to the Council of State, by which they will be submitted to the Sovereign. If they are again referred to the *Sejm* by the King, through the agency of his Council of State, the *Sejm* is to deliberate upon the laws which may be proposed in consequence of these petitions.

Article. 93. In case the *Sejm* should not decree a new budget, the old one remains in force until the next session. The budget is, nevertheless, obsolete at the end of four years, if the *Sejm* is not convoked in the meantime.

Article. 94. The *Sejm* is not to deliberate upon any other business than what is specified in the act of its convocation.

Article. 95. The two chambers shall deliberate in an open house. They are at liberty, nevertheless, to resolve themselves into a closed committee, at the request of a tenth part of the members present.

Article. 96. The proposed laws which have been drawn up by the Council of State are to be carried to the *Sejm* by the members of the said Council under the King's orders.

Article. 97. It is at the King's option to have these drafts referred to the Senate, or to the Chamber of Deputies. Be it excepted, nevertheless, that the drafts of financial laws must be first referred to the Chamber of Deputies.

Article. 98. For the discussion of these drafts, each chamber appoints three commissions of examination, which are composed in the Senate of three members, and in the Chamber of Deputies of five, the

Commission of finances.

Commission of civil and criminal legislation.

Commission of administrative and executive legislation.

Each chamber shall acquaint the Council of State with the choice it has made.

The commissions shall be in communication with the Council of State.

Article. 99. The drafts presented, by order of the King, can only be modified by the Council of State upon the representations of the respective commissions of the *Sejm*.

Article. 100. The members of the State Council, in the two chambers, and the commissioners in their respective chambers, are alone allowed to read their speeches. The other members are to speak without notes.

Article. 101. The members of the State Council have a right to sit and to speak in the two chambers whenever they are deliberating upon a government proposal. They do not have a right to vote, unless they are senators or deputies.

Article. 102. The approval of a bill shall be determined by the majority of votes. These votes shall be given audibly. A bill thus sanctioned by a majority in one chamber is to be carried to the other, which will deliberate and decide in like manner. In case of a tie vote there, the bill will be considered as having been approved.

Article. 103. A law approved by one chamber cannot be modified by the other. It must be approved or rejected *in toto*.

Article. 104. A law approved by the two chambers is to be submitted for royal approval.

Article. 105. If the King gives his assent, the law is approved. The King gives orders for its promulgation in the prescribed form. If the King refuses his assent, the law is null.

Article. 106. The general report of the state of the country, which is drawn up by the State Council and forwarded by it to the Senate, shall be read in the two chambers meeting in joint session.

Article. 107. Each chamber, by its respective commissions, shall deliberate upon this report, and present its opinion to the King on the subject. This opinion may be printed.

CHAPTER VII
THE SENATE

Article. 108. The Senate is composed
Of the princes of the royal and imperial blood.
Of the bishops
The provincial governors; and
The castellans.

Article. 109. The number of senators shall not exceed one half of the number of deputies.

Article. 110. The King appoints the senators. Their office is for life. The Senate, by the intervention of the governor general, presents to the King two candidates for every Senate vacancy among provincial governors or castellans.

Article. 111. To be a candidate for the office of senator from among the provincial governors or castellans, the individual must have completed his thirty-fifth year, he must pay an annual tax of two thousand *zloty*, and he must fulfill all the other conditions that apply to eligibility for the office.

Article. 112. The princes of the royal blood, after the age of eighteen, may take their seat and vote in the Senate.

Article. 113. The first member of the Senate, according to the order prescribed in a special decree, shall be president.

Article. 114. Besides its legislative powers, the Senate has other functions, which are to be separately defined.

Article. 115. The Senate can only meet for the discharge of its legislative duties on the request of the King, and during the *Sejm*. The president has the power of convoking it for other purposes.

Article. 116. The Senate is to decide upon the propriety of putting on trial such senators, heads of departments, counsellors of state, and masters of requests, as have been specified by the King, or his governor general, or individuals accused by the Chamber of Deputies of mal-administration in office.

Article. 117. The Senate is to give definitive judgment upon the validity of the *Sejmiki* (lesser *Sejms* or provincial assemblies), and of the assemblies of the communes, and of the elections; also, on the formation of civil lists, both in the *Sejmiki* and in the communal assemblies.

CHAPTER VIII
The Chamber of Deputies

Article. 118. The Chamber of Deputies consists:

First: — Of seventy-seven representatives appointed by the lesser *Sejms* or assemblies of the nobles, in the proportion of one representative to a district.

Second: — Of fifty-one deputies of the communes.

The King nominates a marshal from among the members, who acts as president of the Chamber.

Article. 119. The whole Kingdom is divided, for the purposes of national representation and election, into seventy-seven districts. It shall also be divided into fifty-one communes; eight in the town of Warsaw, and forty-three in the rest of the country.

Article. 120. The members of the Chamber of Deputies shall remain in office for six years. One-third is to be renewed every two years; in consequence of which, and for the first time only, one-third of the Chamber of Deputies shall remain in office only two years, and another third during four years. These members shall be chosen by lot. The members are capable of being indefinitely reelected.

Article. 121. In order to be elected a member of the Chamber of Deputies, the individual must have completed his thirtieth year, he must enjoy the rights of a citizen, and pay an annual contribution of one hundred Polish *zloty*.

Article. 122. No public officer, civil or military, can be elected into the Chamber of Deputies, unless he has previously obtained the consent of the authorities on whom he depends.

Article. 123. If any representative or deputy, who had not previously exercised any employment in the pay of government, accepts such employment after his election, a new lesser *Sejm* or provincial assembly shall be called to proceed to a fresh election of such representative or deputy.

Article. 124. The King has the power of dissolving the Chamber of Deputies. When he exercises this right the Chamber shall separate, and the King, in the course of two months, will issue writs for a new election of representatives and deputies.

CHAPTER IX
Provincial Assemblies (lesser *Sejms*)

Article. 125. The nobles, who are landed proprietors, in each district shall form a Provincial Assembly, and elect a representative, and two members of the Provincial Council; they shall also draw up a list of candidates for offices in the administration.

Article. 126. The Provincial Assemblies shall meet only on the convocation of the King, who shall also appoint the day, the duration, and the subject of their deliberations.

Article. 127. No noble can be admitted to vote in a Provincial Assembly, unless his name has been enrolled in the civil list of the nobles of the district; unless he be in the enjoyment of the rights of a citizen; unless he has completed his twenty-first year; and unless he be a landed proprietor.

Article. 128. The list of nobles of each district is drawn up by the Provincial Council, and approved by the Senate.

Article. 129. The president of the Provincial Assembly is a marshal appointed by the King.

CHAPTER X
The Communal Assemblies

Article. 130. In each commune there shall be a Communal Assembly which shall send a deputy to the *Sejm* and a member to the Provincial Council, and shall also furnish a list of candidates for offices of administration.

Article. 131. The Communal Assemblies shall consist,   First: — Of every landed proprietor who is a citizen and not noble, paying any amount of contribution upon his estate.

Second: — Of every manufacturer, artisan, or shopkeeper, possessing a shop or warehouse, worth ten thousand Polish *zloty*.

Third: — Of all rectors and vicars.

Fourth: — Of professors and tutors, and other persons engaged in public instruction.

Fifth: — Of artists, distinguished by their talents and knowledge or by the services they may have rendered to the arts or to trade.

Article. 132. No person can be admitted to vote in the Communal Assemblies, unless he be registered in the civil communal list; unless he enjoy the rights of a citizen; and unless he have completed his twenty-first year.

Article. 133. The list of landed proprietors who are entitled to vote, shall be drawn up by the Provincial Council. That of manufacturers, shop-keepers, and citizens, distinguished by their talents and by the services they have rendered, by the ministry of the interior; and that of rectors, vicars, and instructors, by the ministry for religious affairs and for instruction.

Article. 134. The president of the Communal Assemblies, shall be a marshal appointed by King.

CHAPTER XI
The Provincial Council

Article. 135. In every province there shall be a Provincial Council, composed of officers nominated by the Provincial Assemblies and Communal Assemblies.

Article. 136. The president of the Provincial Council shall be the oldest of the counsellors.

Article. 137. The principal duties of the Provincial Council are as follows:

First: — To appoint judges for the first hearing, and the first appeal.

Second: — To concur in forming the list and in selecting the candidates for the offices of administration.

Third: — To watch over the concerns of the province.

The Judicial Order

Article. 138. The judicial order is constitutionally independent.

Article. 139. By the independence of the judge, is to be understood the liberty that he has of giving his opinion with all freedom, without being influenced by the supreme authority, by the ministerial authority, or by any other consideration whatsoever. Every other definition or interpretation of the independence of a judge is declared to be an abuse.

Article. 140. The tribunals are composed of judges appointed by the King, and of judges chosen conformably to the administrative statute.

Article. 141. The judges nominated by the King are for life, and cannot be removed. The judges who hold their seats by election are also incapable of being removed during the term for which they were elected.

Article. 142. No judge can be degraded from his office but by the sentence of a competent judiciary court in case of ascertained collusion, or other misdemeanor.

Article. 143. The supervision of the magistrates when named and chosen, and the redress of grievances inflicted by them in the severity of public service, belongs to the supreme tribunal.

Article. 144. There shall be judges of the peace for all classes of inhabitants, and their office shall be that of conciliation.

Article. 145. No affair can be carried before a civil tribunal for the first hearing, until it has been laid before the competent judge of the peace; such only excepted as are forbidden by law to be arranged by conciliation.

The Tribunal for the First Hearing.

Article. 146. There shall be civil tribunals, and tribunals of the police, in every commune and in every town, to take cognizance of transactions not exceeding five hundred *zloty*.

Article. 147. In every province, there shall be several tribunals for the appeal and tribunals of assize to take cognizance of transactions in which more than five hundred *zloty* are concerned.

Article. 148. There shall be also tribunals of trade.

Article. 149. For criminal causes, and affairs of correctional police, there shall be several criminal tribunals in each province.

Courts of Appeal

Article. 150. There shall be at least two courts of appeal in the Kingdom of Poland. They shall sit in judgment upon causes whether civil, criminal, or commercial, upon which sentence has been already passed by the first courts.

Supreme Tribunal.

Article. 151. There shall be at Warsaw a Supreme Tribunal for the whole Kingdom, which shall finally determine all civil and criminal causes, state crimes excepted. It shall be composed partly of senators who shall take their seats there in rotation, and partly of judges, nominated by the King, who hold their seats during their lives.

The High National Court.

Article. 152. A High National Court shall take cognizance of crimes against the state, and of offenses committed by the great officers of the Kingdom after the Senate has decreed the trial by Article 116. The high court is composed of all the members of the Senate.

The Armed Forces.

Article. 153. The armed forces shall consist of the existing army on full pay, and of militia in readiness to reinforce that army when wanted.

Article. 154. The armed forces to be maintained by the country, are to be determined by the sovereign, with due consideration of the necessity of the case, and in proportion to the revenues established by the budget.

Article. 155. The quartering of the troops shall be regulated by the convenience of the inhabitants, conformably with the military system and the plans of the administration.

Article. 156. The army shall preserve the colors of its uniform, its particular costume, and all the badges of its nationality.

General Regulations.

Article. 157. The revenues and possessions of the crown shall consist,

First: — Of the domains of the crown which shall be separately administered for the King's benefit by a chamber or by officers of his private appointment.

Second: — Of the royal palace of Warsaw and of that of Saxony.

Article. 158. The national debt is guaranteed.

Article. 159. The punishment of confiscation is abolished, and shall not be revived in any instance.

Article. 160. The civil and military orders of Poland, that of the White Eagle — that of the St. Stanislas — and that of the Military Cross shall be continued.

Article. 161. This present Constitutional Law shall be developed by more particular laws. Those laws which are not enacted immediately after the publication of the law shall be discussed in the Council of State.

Article. 162. The first budget of revenues and expenses shall be drawn up by the King with the advice of the Council of State; and this budget shall remain in force until modified or changed by the Sovereign and the two chambers.

Article. 163. Everything not determined by an administrative statute or code, and not included in the offices and powers of the *Sejm* shall be decided by the King's decree or by a government order. The statutes and codes can only be modified or changed by the Sovereign and the two chambers of the *Sejm*.

Article. 164. The laws, decrees, and ordinances of the King shall be printed in the book of the laws. The manner of their publication shall be determined by the King's decree.

Article. 165. All previous laws and institutions which may be contrary to the present law are hereby abrogated.

Believing in our conscience, that the present Constitutional Law will answer our paternal purpose, which is to maintain among all classes of our Kingdom of Poland, peace, union, and concord, which are so necessary to their well-being, and to secure the felicity which it is our desire to procure for them; we have given and do hereby give this Constitutional Law which we adopt for ourselves and our successors, inviting all public authorities to concur in its observance.

Given at our royal palace at Warsaw, the

15/27 November, 1815.

(Signed) ALEXANDER.

AN ADDITIONAL ARTICLE OF FEBRUARY 13, 1825 TO THE CONSTITUTIONAL LAW OF THE POLISH KINGDOM

By the grace of God we, Alexander I, Emperor of all the Russias, King of Poland, etc. etc. faithful to the feelings and fatherly intentions which led us to the bestowing of Constitutional Law to our subjects of the Polish Kingdom from our own inspiration, with the aim of maintaining peace, harmony and unity for all classes of inhabitants which is so necessary for their free existence, mindful of removing dangers already caused by the abuse of one of the regulations of these laws, an abuse that could reoccur;

Taking into consideration that the holding of public deliberations in both chambers of the *Sejm*, provoking people to be ruled temporarily by popularity and not by the benefits accorded by the public good, such deliberations led to empty declarations capable of destroying our much desired unity and depriving them of moderation and dignity, which ought to be present in every significant deliberation;

Desiring to eliminate the illness at its inception, to avert the need for any influence upon all elections and opinions, and at the same time to assure the subjects of our Polish Kingdom the use of all blessings which the Constitutional Law guarantees — We have established our act changing the additional article to be one with the decree on orders of the day, which experience has exposed to us as containing very serious drawbacks.

With this aim in mind we have decided to establish what follows.

ADDITIONAL ARTICLE

The meetings intended for the opening and closing of the *Sejm*, as well as those in which the royal sanction has been given for the passage of legislation, will take place as was formerly the case, with the maintenance of the usual solemnities.

At legislative votes, in ministry proceedings and in any other deliberations and discussions, the chambers will reconstitute themselves at all times into closed committees.

This article will be announced as an integral element of the Constitutional Law, one that is inseparable from it.

We direct its execution to the president of the Senate and the marshal of the Chamber of Deputies under their responsibility.

Given at Tsarskoye Selo, the day of February 1/13, 1825.

THE ORGANIC STATUTE
for the
KINGDOM OF POLAND
February 14/26, 1832.

By God's helping grace, We Nicholas I, Emperor and Supreme Ruler of all the Russias, King of Poland, etc. By Our constant and strenuous efforts for the good of the Nations entrusted to Our Scepter by the Highest Providence, We, with special attention considered the principles of the future organization of the Kingdom of Poland, and having in mind the true benefits and state of that country, also the local needs and customs of the inhabitants, with the essential need of establishing their tranquility and well-being by closer and unwavering union with the Russian State, we bequeath and convey and most generously grant the Kingdom of Poland the following basic laws.

1. GENERAL REGULATIONS.

Article. 1. The Kingdom of Poland, forever united to the Russian State, constitutes an inseparable part of that State. It (the Kingdom of Poland) will have a separate government, adapted to local needs, nonetheless its own civil and criminal codes, and all the heretofore existing local laws and acts given to cities and villages, remain in force as earlier.

Article. 2. The crown of the Kingdom of Poland is hereditary in Our Person and Our descendant's heirs and successors, according to the prescribed rule of succession to the throne of the All Russian Empire.

Article. 3. The coronation of the All Russian Tsars and Kings of Poland is contained in one and the same holy rite, which will take place in the capital city, Moscow, in the presence of deputies of the Kingdom of Poland, called to take part in such a solemnity, together with deputies of other parts of the Empire.

Article. 4. In the event a Russian regency will be established, according to existing rules or such issued in the future, the authority of the regent (male or female) of the State extends to include the Kingdom of Poland.

Article. 5. Freedom of religious belief is guaranteed in full force, to everyone. The freedom to carry out public religious rites without any obstacles remains protected by the Government, and differences held in the teachings of various Christian creeds cannot be a cause to exclude anyone from laws and privileges granted to all inhabitants of the Kingdom. Persons in holy orders of all religious beliefs remain, in equal degree, under the protection and supervision of the authorities as empowered by law. Finally, the Roman Catholic religion, being professed by the greatest number of Our subjects in the Kingdom of Poland, will be the particular object of the Government's care and protection.

Article. 6. Funds in the possession of Roman Catholic and Greek-Uniate clergy are considered to be common property, immune from control by the church hierarchies of each confession.

Article. 7. The protection of law extends uniformly to all inhabitants of the Kingdom, without any difference in class or importance. Everyone, through personal merits and talents, can attain all offices and distinctions in the country, in the manner prescribed by law.

Article. 8. Personal freedom of each person is assured and protected by the force of existing laws. No one can be arrested or brought before a court, as only in cases allowed by law, with strict adherence to maintaining the established order. Every person arrested will be notified in writing of the charge for which he is apprehended.

Article. 9. Every person arrested should appear before a court authority no more than within three days of the time he is apprehended, to question or sentence him according to established regulation. If, at such a first court appearance the person is found not guilty, he is freed immediately. Likewise, a person apprehended for a reason covered in the code of law, will be released from confinement upon depositing a sufficient bail.

Article. 10. The order of investigation and prosecution of highest officials of the Kingdom, also of persons accused of offences against the State, will be prescribed in a separate code, on a basis consistent with laws existing in other parts of Our Empire.

Article. 11. The right of individuals and associations to possessions, visible and those found in the earth, is acknowledged to be sacred and inviolable, according to existing regulation. Every subject of the Kingdom of Poland has complete freedom to change place of habitation and move his possessions to wherever he chooses, in keeping with regulation appropriate in this matter.

Article. 12. Confiscation of property constitutes a penalty for offences of the first order against the State, as it will be indicated in detail in separate regulations.

Article. 13. Announcement of opinion in print will be restricted only to that which deflects from that acknowledged as duly needed to assure respect for religion, the inviolability of the highest authorities, unimpeachable morals and highest personal honor. To that end, separate laws will be written, based upon principles which have served as a basis for regulations in other parts of Our State.

Article. 14. The Kingdom of Poland will have a proper proportion of participation in the general expenditures covering the needs of the Empire. A part of the tax and future levies for that purpose will be fixed in the strictest proportion by separate decisions.

Article. 15. All taxes and other levies which were in effect in the Kingdom of Poland to November 1830, will be collected in the future in the same manner as before, until the type and amount of those taxes and levies are revised and set up in a different way, for the purpose of equalization and relief, as much as possible, of the general obligations for the need of the country.

Article. 16. The treasury of the Kingdom of Poland, equally as the other branches of Government, should be administered separately from the governments of the other parts of the Empire.

Article. 17. The national debt of the Kingdom of Poland approved by Us, will be, as earlier, guaranteed by a warrant of the Government and paid from the income of the Kingdom.

Article. 18. The Bank of the Kingdom of Poland and existing credit regulations for real estate will remain, as earlier, under the care of the Government.

Article. 19. The course of trade relations between the Russian Empire and the Kingdom of Poland will always be established in agreement with the views commonly held by the provinces, united for the general good of the country, yet having separate administrations.

Article. 20. Our army in the Empire and the Kingdom constitutes one body, without distinguishing between Russian and Polish forces. We leave to Ourself, for the future, to determine by a separate regulation, in what proportion and on what basis the Kingdom of Poland will have a part in the general makeup of Our army. The size of the army forming the internal guard of the Kingdom, will also be determined by a separate regulation.

Article. 21. Our subjects of the Russian Empire, who have settled in the Kingdom of Poland, already or will in the future possess real estate in that country. They will exercise all of the rights due the natives in the same measure that Our subjects of the Kingdom who live and possess real estate in other provinces of the Empire. We leave to Ourselves, for the future, to grant naturalization in the Kingdom, to other persons, Russians or foreigners, even though they are not yet settled within the boundaries of the Kingdom. Our subjects of the Russian Empire who have a temporary residence in the Kingdom, no less than Our subjects of the Kingdom of Poland, with a temporary residence in other parts of the Empire, are subject to the laws of the country in which they find themselves.

II. ABOUT THE MAIN LOCAL ADMINISTRATION

Article. 22. The main administration of the Kingdom of Poland takes on the responsibility of the Administrative Council, having to rule in Our Name under the presidency of the Kingdom's governor general.

Article. 23. The Administrative Council consists of the governor general of the Kingdom, the chief directors of principal commissions, among whom the affairs of the administration are divided, the inspector general in charge of the highest accounting office, and other members, whom We will assign by Our separate orders.

Article. 24. Members of the Administrative Council will express their opinions with complete freedom, and each one has the right to demand that his opinion be entered into the minutes of the meeting. Matters are decided by a majority of votes. In the event of a tie the governor general's vote is decisive.

Article. 25. If a majority of the Council members are not in agreement with an opinion of the governor general, and he considers that their proposal has serious deficiencies, then he will withhold carrying out the decisions of the Council members. And without delay he will present the matter for Our consideration, attaching a copy of minutes of the Council meetings.

Article. 26. Complying with separate regulations that may be issued in this matter, the Administrative Council elects and presents to Us, through the governor general of the Kingdom, candidates for vacant positions: archbishops, bishops, chief directors, counsellors of state, members of the Highest Court and other officials, whose assignment concerning administrative and court matters belongs to Us. Letters of candidates will be considered and compared with other information pertaining to nominations for vacated positions presented to Us by the Administrative Council, or by other persons worthy of Our confidence, inhabitants of the Kingdom of Poland, or those of other provinces of the Empire.

Article. 27. In the event of the death, severe illness, or absence of the governor general of the Kingdom, or due to any other legitimate hindrance to carry out the duties of office, the authority of the governor general is transferred temporarily to the senior member of the Administrative Council, who will hold that (responsibility) until Our will in the matter is announced.

Article. 28. Concerning matters indicated in the following, 29th Article, in which the authorities of the Administrative Council will have no influence, We establish in the Kingdom of Poland a Council of State, also under the presidency of the governor general of the Kingdom. The following will be seated in that Council: 1) chief directors and the inspector general, as members by virtue of their office; 2)officials honored with the title Counsellor of State and others, called by Us to a permanent or temporary place in the Council of State. In the event of the governor's absence, a member of the Council, especially authorized by Us for that purpose, will preside.

Article. 29. The responsibilities of the Council of State of the Kingdom of Poland are:

1. The review and formulation of proposals of new laws and regulations, intended for the general administration of the Kingdom;

2. The resolution of disagreements and questions, arising among administrative and judicial authorities in matters of their jurisdiction;

3. The discussion of proposals and petitions from provincial assemblies of estates and provincial councils regarding the needs and good of the country, as well as to arbitrate above-mentioned proposals and petitions;

4. The review of the annual budget of income and expenses of the Kingdom drawn up by the Administrative Council, also the review of information from the inspector general concerning audits of accounts of various branches of the government;

5. The examination of reports of principal managers of various branches of government, about matters entrusted to them;

6. The undertaking of decisions whether to turn over to the court those officials who have committed offenses in office, and who may be nominated directly by us or in Our Name.

Article. 30. All of the above regulations contained in Articles 24 and 25, concerning meetings and execution of decisions of the Administrative Council, extend in full force to the activity of the Council of State of the Kingdom of Poland.

Article. 31. Matters leading to legislation and other proposals of great importance, which to Us will seem to require earlier and careful integration with existing regulations in other parts of the Empire, and affecting its general good, as well as the annual budget presented to Us by the Council of State of the Kingdom of Poland, will be submitted to the Council of State of the Russian Empire for final review and approval. To that end there will be established in said Council a department named the Department of Affairs for the Kingdom of Poland. Serving in that department will be members nominated by Us, from Our subjects of the Empire and the Kingdom.

Article. 32. Remaining at Our Person, the minister secretary of State of the Kingdom of Poland, presents to Us the business matters he will receive, through the governor general, from the Administrative Council and the Council of State. He will also convey to the governor general Our Imperial-Royal orders.

Article. 33. All laws, orders and acts sanctioned by Us, extending to the Kingdom of Poland, will be countersigned by Our minister-secretary of State of that Kingdom, and are to be posted in the daily Law Register.

Article. 34. All administrative and court matters in the Kingdom of Poland will be carried out in the Polish language.

Article. 35. Administrative affairs will be entrusted to government commissions, which will be presided over by chief directors. There will be three such commissions:

1. The commission of internal affairs and religious matters, also national education;

2. The commission of justice,

3. The commission of receipts and the treasury.

Article. 36. In addition to such commissions there will be established a Supreme Chamber of Accounting, for general review of receipts and expenditures of the Kingdom, which will be presided by the inspector general.

Article. 37. Matters, whose settlement is beyond the scope of authority of the chief directors and commissions, are transferred to the Administrative Council. Those then, whose execution is not subject to the authority of the Council and the governor general of the Kingdom, should be presented to Us by the minister secretary of State.

Article. 38. Chief directors, the inspector-general, members of the Administrative Council and of the Council of State of the Kingdom, and the government commissions are responsible for every offense against Our laws, orders (directives) and acts. As soon as such offenses are revealed in the prescribed manner and brought to the knowledge of the Council of State of the Kingdom, that Council will without delay bring the matter to Our attention, requesting Our decision to hand over the guilty ones to the court.

Article. 39. The present division of the Kingdom into provinces (*wojewodztwa*), districts, counties, city and village districts, will remain on the same basis as earlier, and each of those parts will function within its boundaries as before, until such time that changes for the general good of the Kingdom may be acknowledged as necessary.

Article. 40. In each province a provincial commission will be established. It will consist of a president and commissioners obligated to carry out the directives of the chief government commissions, according to a separately formulated statute for that purpose.

Article. 41. The administration of cities is entrusted to the authorities elected by municipal assemblies, and in village districts to the chief (*woit*) among the village officers. In cities, the mayors, and in village districts, the chiefs, are obligated to oversee the discharge of Government directives.

III. ABOUT ASSEMBLIES OF THE NOBILITY, ASSEMBLIES OF VILLAGE DISTRICTS, AND ABOUT PROVINCIAL COUNCILS

Article. 42. In all provinces there will exist, on the fabric of earlier structures, councils of the nobility, councils of municipalities and of village districts, as well as provincial councils.

Article. 43. Every county which has real estate owned by nobility will have an assembly presided over by a marshal nominated by the governor general of the Kingdom, in Our name, for the purpose of electing two members to the Provincial Council and to present a list of candidates which the Government will have to consider when announcing vacancies in the various branches of administration.

Article. 44. Assemblies of the nobility will meet only when called by the governor general, who will designate the day of the meeting, the subject for deliberation and the time necessary for that.

Article. 45. To participate in the assembly deliberations a nobleman must be registered in that county, he must exercise the rights of citizenship of the Kingdom, he must be at least twenty-one years of age, and he must possess some real property.

Article. 46. The record of the nobility in each county will be maintained by the provincial council and certified by the Administrative Council.

Article. 47. Every municipal and village district will have a district assembly, also meeting only when called by the governor general and presided by a chairman nominated by the governor general. Such assemblies will elect one member to the Provincial Council, and prepare a list of candidates which the Government will have to consider when selecting persons for various offices.

Article. 48. The following have a right to participate in meetings of district assemblies:

1. every citizen not of the nobility, though owning real estate, for which he pays any amount of tax;

2. every factory owner and manufacturer, every merchant who has a shop or warehouse with goods owned by him, and worth at least ten thousand Polish *zloty*;

3. all pastors, superiors of religious orders, and parish assistant priests;

4. professors, teachers and other persons engaged in the education of youth in educational institutions administered by the Government;

5. every artist who has become recognized through his own talent or knowledge, or applied himself toward enriching the nation's industry, commerce or the liberal arts.

Article. 49. No one may participate in district meetings whose name is not entered into the register of the municipal or village assemblies, does not exercise civil laws/rights in the Kingdom of Poland, and is not yet twenty-one years of age.

Article. 50. Owners of real property, by virtue of which, they have a right to participate in meetings of assemblies of the nobility and district assemblies, will deposit certificates of ownership with the provincial councils. And certificates of factory owners and manufacturers, merchants, citizens made famous by their talents in the liberal arts or having contributed to the general good, also credentials of pastors, superiors of religious orders, and assistant priests, no less so persons engaged in the education of youth in public educational institutions, (will be deposited) with the commission of internal affairs, religious matters and national education.

Article. 51. In every province a council will be established, consisting of counselors elected by the assemblies of noblemen and district assemblies, presided by one of the members, who will be nominated to that post by the governor general, in Our Name.

Article. 52. The principal responsibilities of the council are as follows:

1. to elect judges whose judicial jurisdiction would be of the first and second instances;

2. to participate in the selection and review of candidates which the Government will have to consider when selecting persons to various positions;

3. to watch and care for the good and the advantages of the province, turning to the Government with appropriate proposals and petitions, through the province commissions, doing all according to the regulations of the separate statute established in this matter.

IV. ABOUT THE ASSEMBLIES OF THE PROVINCIAL ESTATES

Article. 53. Assemblies of the provincial estate will be established to give counsel in matters of the general good of the entire Kingdom of Poland. The assemblies will have an advisory role in matters presented to them for consideration.

Article. 54. The makeup and the course of activity of the Provincial Assemblies will be prescribed in separate regulation.

V. ABOUT THE JUDICIAL SYSTEM

Article. 55. All judicial authority in the Kingdom of Poland is most graciously granted by Us and will be exercised in Our Name. The right of granting pardon and the reduction of punishment belongs exclusively to Us.

Article. 56. Judicial jurisdictions consist of judges nominated by Us and judges selected according to separate regulations.

Article. 57. Judges nominated by Us remain until they are relieved of that duty, when that is necessary, removed by the court for transgressions or, finally, when transferred to another office. Judges who are elected commit themselves to limited periods according to separate regulations.

Article. 58. Judges will be removed from their offices for abuse of power and for all other proven offenses (infringements) of established order, but only however as a consequence of the verdict handed by proper higher judicial authority.

Article. 59. The maintenance of order in the courts of first and second appeal, and the resolution of disputes and questions between these courts regarding the sphere of their authority rests with the institution of the highest court.

Article. 60. The law regarding justices of the peace for inhabitants of all estates reposes with the previous principle; it is their obligation to attempt to resolve matters and bring agreement among conflicting sides.

Article. 61. No matter may be brought before a civil court of the first instance unless it has been first reviewed by the appropriate justice of the peace, excluded from such rules are matters whose final settlement rest on laws that are beyond the judicial competence of the justice of the peace.

Article. 62. For matters over disputes about matters of less than five hundred Polish *zloty*, civil and police magistrates in each town and village district (commune) are appointed.

Article. 63. For matters over disputes of more than five hundred Polish *zloty*, territorial courts and conventional courts in the provinces are appointed.

Article. 64. The establishment of special courts concerned with economic (or business) matters remain as under the former system.

Article. 65. For criminal matters and those touching upon prisons, municipal courts (*grodzkie*) are to be established in each province.

Article. 66. For the rectification of sentences handed by the land, convention and municipal courts, as well as those determined in the business courts, courts of appeals are established.

Article. 67. In addition, the headquarters of the supreme court is established in Warsaw, its membership and sphere of authority will be defined in a separate law.

Article. 68. The regulations contained in the above Organic Statute, will accordingly be explained and supplemented in separate legislation.

Article. 69. All previous law standing in contradiction to the above Organic Statute is hereby nullified.

We have signed with our hand this Organic Statute and we have commanded that the seal of the Tsar be applied to this document.

Given in Saint Petersburg, on the fourteenth day of February, in the year of the birth of our Lord, 1832 and the seventh year of our reign.

Translated by Angela Pienkos and Edward Wojtkowski

Sources:
Trzy Konstytucje, ed. by Marceli Handelsman, Warsaw: E. Wende i Spolka, 1915; *Constitutional Charter of The Kingdom of Poland in the Year 1815*, Published by James Ridgeway, Piccadilly; Rowland Hunter, St. Paul's Church Yard; Effingham, Wilson, Royal Exchange; and Robert Heward, Wellington Street, London, 1831.

INDEX

LIST OF ILLUSTRATIONS

The Coat of Arms of the Polish Congress Kingdom, 1815-1830

Empress Catherine II

Emperor Paul II

Emperor Alexander I

Emperor Nicholas I

Joanna Grudzinska

Grand Duke Constantine

A Polish military review at *Plac Saski* in Warsaw before Constantine

Vincent Niemojowski

Adam Czartoryski

F. X. Drucki-Lubecki

Sentencing of Valerian Lukasinski (1824)

Peter Wysocki

Adam Mickiewicz

Joseph Chlopicki

Attack on the Belvedere Palace, November 29, 1830

The outbreak of the uprising in Warsaw;
  from a contemporary German print

The formal dethroning of Nicholas I as king of Poland
  by the Polish *Sejm* in Warsaw, January 25, 1831

Photo credits

(Unless otherwise noted, the pictures are from the photographic collection compiled by the *Epoka* Publishing House in Warsaw, 1982)

Empress Catherine II and *Emperor Paul II*, from Vincent Cronin, *Catherine Empress of All the Russias* (New York: William Morrow and Company, 1978), pp. 203, 257.

Emperor Alexander I, from Ivan Spector, *An Introduction to Russian History and Culture* (Princeton, N. J.: D. VanNostrand Co., 1969).

Emperor Nicholas I, from Sidney Harcave, *Russia, A History*, 6th ed. (Philadelphia: J. B. Lippincott Co., 1968), p. 230.

Grand Duke Constantine, from Madame la Comtesse de Choiseul-Gouffier, *Historical Memoirs of the Emperor Alexander I*, 2nd ed. (Chicago: A. C. McClurg and Co., 1981), p. 247.

Joanna Grudzinska, F. X. Drucki-Lubecki, Adam Mickiewicz, and *The Outbreak of the Uprising in Warsaw*, from Aleksander Bruckner, *Tyslac Lat Kultury Polskiej* (Paris: Ksiegarnia Polska w Paryzu, 1939), p. 694.

The Coat of Arms of the Polish Congress Kingdom, 1815-1830

Empress Catherine II

Emperor Paul II

Emperor Alexander I

Emperor Nicholas I

Joanna Grudzinska

Grand Duke Constantine

A Polish military review at *Plac Saski* in Warsaw before Constantine, at left

Vincent Niemojowski

Adam Czartoryski

F. X. Drucki-Lubecki

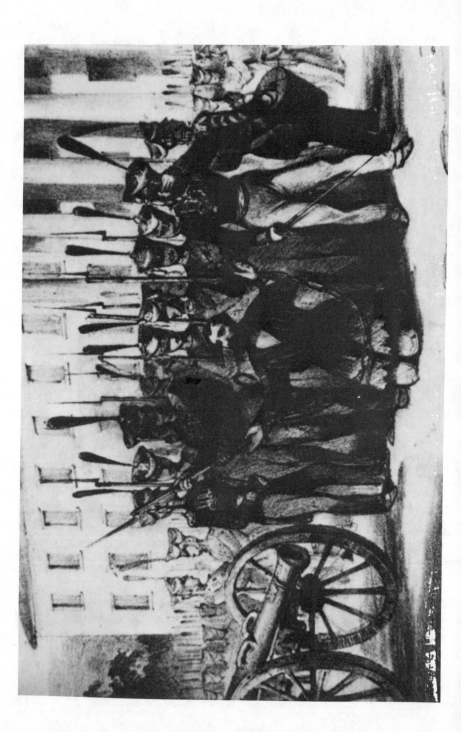

Joseph Chlopicki

Peter Wysocki

Adam Mickiewicz

Attack on the Belvedere Palace, November 29, 1830

The outbreak of the uprising in Warsaw; from a contemporary German print

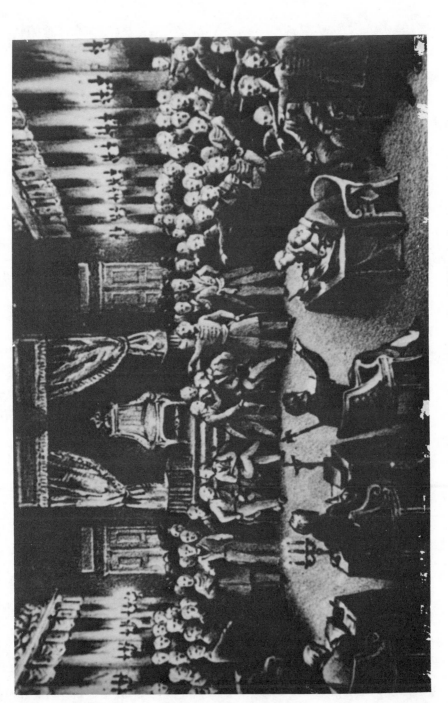

The formal dethroning of Nicholas I as king of Poland by the Polish *Sejm* in Warsaw; January 25, 1831